CHILDHOOD ONSET
ANOREXIA NERVOSA AND
RELATED EATING DISORDERS

Childhood Onset Anorexia Nervosa and Related Eating Disorders

Bryan Lask

and

Rachel Bryant-Waugh

 LAWRENCE ERLBAUM ASSOCIATES, PUBLISHERS
Hove (UK)   Hillsdale (USA)

Lawrence Erlbaum Associates Ltd., Publishers
27 Palmeira Mansions
Church Road
Hove
East Sussex, BN3 2FA
U.K.

British Library Cataloguing in Publication Data

Childhood Onset Anorexia Nervosa and
Related Eating Disorders
   I. Lask, Bryan II. Bryant-Waugh, Rachel
   616.85

ISBN 0-86377-294-3 (Hbk)

ISBN 0-86377-295-1 (Pbk)

Cover by Bridgewater Design Limited
Printed in Great Britain by Redwood Press Limited, Melksham, Wiltshire

*This book is dedicated to those children and
their families who we have tried to help,
and from whom we have learned so much.*

Acknowledgements

Many of our colleagues on the Eating Disorders Team and the Mildred Creak Unit have not contributed directly to this book. Nonetheless their ideas, creativity, support, encouragement, enthusiasm, and hard work, are reflected throughout.

The Garfield Weston Foundation has provided very generous financial support to our research programme. Without this, much of our research could not have been carried out.

Finally, we wish to express our love and gratitude to our own families who have patiently tolerated our devotion to manuscripts and word-processors. Our devotion to them prevails.

Contents

List of Contributors

All contributors to this volume have been involved in the treatment of children with eating disorders at Great Ormond Street Hospitals.

Clive Britten, Child Psychiatrist
Rose de Bruyn, Consultant Radiologist
Rachel Bryant-Waugh, Principal Clinical Psychologist
Abe Fosson, Visiting Professor in Behavioural Paediatrics
Laura Glendinning, Charge Nurse
Zyg Kaminski, Visiting Consultant Psychiatrist
Jacky Knibbs, Principal Clinical Psychologist
Bryan Lask, Consultant Psychiatrist
Maryann MacDonald, Parent
Jeanne Magagna, Principal Child Psychotherapist
Michelle Phillips, Charge Nurse
Anna Tate, Teacher-in-Charge
Shanthi Thomas, Consultant in Chemical Pathology
Marianne Tranter, Psychiatric Social Worker
Jo Trelfa, Child Care Worker
Jeremy Turk, Child Psychiatrist
Bernadette Wren, Principal Clinical Psychologist

Prologue

The prospective reader of this book may well ask: "Why yet another book on eating disorders?" Our answer is quite simply that this book is about early onset eating disorders: i.e. eating disorders occurring in people below the age of 15. It deals with children and young teenagers who suffer from anorexia nervosa and related eating disorders, and as such refers to a population distinct from that dealt with in other books. Obviously some of the issues are similar, but many are different. We believe that in many important respects, the aetiology, clinical presentation, phenomenology, and treatment all differ. Further, there is in our experience a wider range of eating disorders in this age-group.

The book is set in the context of a recent increase in dieting behaviour in children (Hill, Oliver, & Rogers, 1992). This is a cause for concern given the belief that the prevalence of diagnosable eating disorders in a specific population is likely to be directly proportional to the prevalence of dieting behaviour in the same population (Hsu, 1990). If this belief is correct then we can anticipate a further increase in the incidence of childhood onset eating disorders.

The contributors to this book are all people who have been connected with the eating disorders programme at the Hospital for Sick Children, Great Ormond Street, London. We do not claim to have produced an up-to-date state of the art review, nor the definitive textbook on this topic. We would not assert that our way is better than others, nor do we profess to have all the answers. Rather we have tried to convey our perception and understanding of these problems, and to share our clinical experience of assessment and treatment.

The book opens with a chapter written by a parent of a child with anorexia nervosa. This vividly conveys the mother's view of her child's illness and just as importantly her view of the health-care system and the treatment process. Further she has sought and incorporated the views of many other parents whose children were treated elsewhere. We have made no editorial adjustments to this chapter, for although it makes painful reading to those of us who believe we do our best, and certainly work with the worthiest of intentions, it is clear from the author's research that we, "the professionals", have a lot to learn.

The remainder of the book is divided into two sections. The first deals with the clinical presentation, both physical and psychological, of early onset eating disorders, their epidemiology, aetiology, and outcome. The second half of the book is determinedly practical and is devoted to clinical issues. Following a chapter on assessment, and an overview of treatment approaches, there are chapters on nursing, physical treatments, behaviour therapy, cognitive therapy, psychotherapy, family therapy and group therapy. The section ends with a chapter on the relationship between eating disorders and schooling.

Some, but not all of the children have been treated on our child psychiatric in-patient Unit, the Mildred Creak Unit, and this is often referred to in the case illustrations. A fuller description of the Unit is to be found in chapters 9, 15 and 16.

A few technical points:

(a) In the treatment chapters we have made frequent use of case illustrations, and many of the children are referred to in several chapters. For obvious reasons we have changed the children's names, but we have kept the pseudonyms constant throughout so that readers may cross-refer should they wish.

(b) For ease of reading, and because far more girls than boys experience eating disorders, we have referred to the children as girls, unless we are specifically discussing boys.

(c) Often in general conversation, the terms "anorexia" and "anorexia nervosa" are erroneously used as synonyms. In fact they have distinct meanings and we have tried to remain faithful to these. "Anorexia" means loss of appetite while "anorexia nervosa" refers to that disorder characterised by a determined avoidance of normal weight. The same applies to "anorectic" and "anorexic". A person with anorexia nervosa is described as "anorectic", while someone with a loss of appetite is "anorexic" (Welbourne & Purgold, 1984).

We hope that readers will find what follows of interest and value, and although we would not expect agreement with all that we say, we trust we have conveyed some of the fascination and challenge that we have experienced in working with these children and their families.

Bryan Lask and
Rachel Bryant-Waugh

REFERENCES

Hill, A., Oliver, S., & Rogers, P. (1992). Eating in the adult world: The rise of dieting in childhood and adolescence. *British Journal of Clinical Psychology, 31,* 95–105.

Hsu, G. (1990). *Eating disorders.* New York: Guilford Press.

Welbourne, G. & Purgold, J. (1984). *The eating sickness—anorexia, bulimia and the myth of suicide by slimming.* Brighton: Harvester Press.

CHAPTER ONE

Bewildered, Blamed and Broken-hearted: Parents' Views of Anorexia Nervosa

Maryann MacDonald

Editors' Note

This chapter has been written by the mother of child who had anorexia nervosa, treated in our Eating Disorders Clinic. We believe it important to include a parent's view in this volume as families' experience of living with such illnesses and treatment offered are often overlooked. We have not edited the content of this chapter in any way, as to do so would not be in keeping with our aim to give parents a free voice. The author bases her text on her own experience, but includes the views of a number of other parents whose children received treatment for an eating disorder from a wide range of different resources around the country. Together, these parents are at times highly critical of current clinical practice, yet they offer many constructive suggestions for improvement. We have found Mrs MacDonald's chapter so moving and instructive that we have decided to open our book with her words. We have benefited greatly from her contribution and we hope that in turn so will the children and families we see.

PARENTS' VIEWS OF ANOREXIA NERVOSA

What is it like to be the parent of a child with anorexia nervosa? It is to ask yourself all day and half the night what went wrong. It is to read everything you can find on anorexia nervosa to try to understand and help your child and to learn from your reading that it is your fault that your child is ill. It is to be blamed by no one more than yourself.

It is to reach out for life when you want to die, knowing that you do so to survive and help your child survive, but knowing also that for doing so you will probably be accused of being callous and uncaring. It is to have everything about you rejected by your child—your food, your body, your personality, your achievements. It is to wonder long after your child is "well" if you have caused her harm in some way that is so grievous that she will never recover.

These are some of the descriptions of the experience I have gathered from parents of anorectic children. Being the parent of an anorectic child affects one profoundly and irrevocably. My own daughter suffered from anorexia nervosa when she was twelve years old. When I was asked to write this chapter on a parent's view of the illness, I was not sure now much just one parent could contribute. After all, the book was to include sections on treatment of the illness by international experts. All I had to comment on was my own experience of living with an anorectic child for less than a year, and a half-dozen or so family-therapy sessions which had left me confused. When I asked whether I could examine our family's records to gain further insight for purposes of this chapter, I was told that this would not be possible. This made me feel that though my views were being nominally sought, as the parent of an anorectic I was not really trusted. Also, when I looked at the proposed contents of the book, I noted that "A Parent's View" was handwritten in, an afterthought, perhaps, as the last topic in the book before the conclusion.

Still, I felt that parents' views of the illness ought to be included in the book. After all, it is parents who have lived with and observed the anorectic child from birth, and who have had to deal with the anorectic child's problems first-hand, 24 hours a day. So I met with several parents of former anorectics to obtain their ideas. We decided the most useful course of action would be to gather as much reaction from other parents as possible. Together we prepared a questionnaire. It was mailed to parents who responded to an advertisement in the Eating Disorders Association newsletter, and given directly to parents of anorectics known personally. Altogether, responses were obtained from 30 families.

These responses were heartbreaking. I found myself reading them with tears rolling down my face. I feel a tremendous responsibility to speak for these varied parents, most of whom put much time and thought into their answers. It is clear that these people feel they need to be heard and have never before been asked. Many had covered every available space on the questionnaire with lengthy answers to the questions asked, striving to express every detail of their experience. Wherever possible in this chapter, I will try to quote the parents' own words, and allow them to speak for themselves.

MOTHERS AND THEIR DAUGHTERS

First of all, I think it is significant that not a single questionnaire was returned by a father. They were without exception completed by mothers. Mothers are those most intimately involved in the day-to-day difficulties of living with an anorectic child. Mothers feed children, from birth onwards, and anorexia nervosa is a refusal to be fed. The mother of an anorectic has the bitter experience of having her love and nurturing, symbolically herself, rejected. In the great majority of cases, anorexia nervosa is an illness that affects girls, often at the onset of adolescence. Why is this so? Why do these girls feel such a strong need to reject their mothers and their own female bodies?

I am convinced that the answer to this question lies in society's view of women. Women are the "second-best" sex. They are no longer respected in their traditional roles as housewives and mothers, and often find it difficult to succeed in pursuits outside the home, partly because of discrimination and partly because of the difficulties of balancing their work with their domestic responsibilities. If they do work, they are most often expected to fulfil all their traditional functions as well.

One of the most constant of a mother's responsibilities is to make sure that her family is fed. She must shop, cook and wash up every day of her life. But at the same time, she must be careful not to overeat herself. She must not get fat, for above all, society despises a fat woman. A woman can be forgiven for being "just a housewife", but she cannot be forgiven for being fat. Her obligation is to be slim and attractive to men. So she must take care of and feed everyone but herself.

This imposes a strain on a woman's life. A little girl growing up, playing with her impossibly-proportioned Barbie doll, may not see this strain. But as she moves into adolescence, she begins to look her biological destiny in the face, and what does she see? Her mother. Her mother, whom she may always have loved, she now sees with new eyes. She may, because of her love, be unable to bear the sight.

Most probably, her mother's attractiveness has begun to fade. She may, in middle age, have become somewhat overweight. She may or may not work outside the home. If she does not, her daughter, like the rest of society, cannot respect her. If she does, she no doubt experiences a greater or lesser degree of difficulty in balancing her career with her continuing need to look after her family.

This coincides with her daughter's growing awareness that she, too, will be expected to be both successful in the world and, simultaneously, feminine, sexual, and a self-denying mother. It is all too much. The daughter feels pain for her mother's life and anger that the same will be expected of her. She resolves never to be "stuck" like her mother. And the stage is set for her to begin to work compulsively to achieve in the world and to keep her body as thin and non-maternal as possible.

But what is it that makes the difference between the girl who is prepared to diet to be slim and to outstrip her mother's achievements and the girl who is prepared to starve herself to the point of emaciation and to work obsessively for success, never satisfied with her accomplishments?

Some mothers remarked on worrying characteristics in their children which pre-dated their eating disorders. My own daughter was always extremely anxious. As a baby, she never wanted to be held and cuddled. She would squirm out of my arms, seemingly restless and impatient for activity. As she was my first child, this was disappointing for me. I found myself taking her for endless walks to keep her happy and amused. She seemed always to be anxious and unsettled. Her father and I hoped that when she started school she would be busier and therefore happier, but she didn't seem to like school much at first, and often cried and did not want to go. Although she was very bright, we deliberately made a point of not making demands on her to achieve any particular grades, and in fact changed her school after several years to one that was more relaxed in the hope that she would feel less pressured. But no matter what we did, she remained nervous, constantly sucking her thumb and biting her nails. When I once discussed this with a wise and experienced teacher of hers, he remarked: "Your daughter may not be pressured by what you do or say but by who you are," implying that perhaps my child felt her parents' success in life was a hard act to follow.

Another mother, in listing factors that may have contributed to the development of anorexia nervosa in her daughter, also mentioned severe anxiety.

[She had] irrational and unexplained fears: fear of being poisoned, fear of death, fears that she was not a perfect Christian (she had become fanatical about religion although we are not religious ourselves).

Another whose "socially precocious" daughter became anorectic at the age of eight and a half remarked:

She was very highstrung and became jealous and aggressive when her sister was born. We probably didn't handle it very well, but the constant tantrums and rebellious behaviour were exhausting. Her domineering personality seemed to manipulate the entire family. By the time she was five years old, she refused to get dressed for school and said that voices told her not to do what we asked her to do. Her behaviour became disturbed and obsessional and I took her to see a child psychiatrist. Behavioural therapy was all that was offered, so I tried to reward her for good behaviour and ignore the bad ... It didn't work, and I think confirmed her darkest fears that she wasn't as good or lovable as her little sister.

Intense jealousy of siblings was a common element mentioned by parents in discussing factors that may have led to their children's illness. A mother of six said:

I realize that she was crying out for attention ... Her eldest sister was only 18 months older than her, tall, naturally slim, and has plenty of confidence in herself, she is multi-talented, and had plenty of boyfriends when they were both younger. All my anorectic daughter wanted to do was to fit into her eldest sister's clothes.

Another remarked:

My daughter is very reliant on me and always has been since she was a baby. [She] seems to want all my attention.

Mothers are likely to feel ambivalent about their anorectic daughters. They may want to nurture them, but may be worried about their lack of autonomy and feel tyrannised by their demands. Of course, an anorectic child effectively steals the limelight from her brothers and sisters for the duration of her illness. Parents repeatedly commented on this, remarking that other children had become rightfully resentful, although in certain cases brothers and sisters were exceptionally understanding of and helpful to their anorectic siblings.

THE MYTH OF THE IDEAL BODY AND OTHER CONTRIBUTING INFLUENCES

The modern emphasis on healthy eating (low fat, low sugar) was frequently referred to as a contributing factor in the development of eating disorders.

I have read hundreds of articles about diet and heart disease where we are made aware of the dangers of eating too much fat. I have never seen in one of those articles or leaflets a warning of what can happen to the body if it doesn't get any fats. A four-stone teenager is not a pretty sight.

An overweight mother wrote:

I feel extremely guilty for being overweight myself. Although I've always wanted to be a little slimmer, I've dressed smartly and worn makeup and had a happy personality. I'm not nearly so outgoing now.

Parents repeatedly report teasing and name-calling of their children, who may have been somewhat overweight, as contributing causes to their development of anorexia nervosa. The mother of a Mensa member who became anorectic at the age of ten said:

She started puberty early and was made fun of at school. She was always trying to underachieve and tended to find it difficult to fit in with the other children, which was partly due to having an IQ of 179.

My own daughter began dieting after receiving a "Fitness-o-Gram" from her school. This was a computerised evaluation of her body done at the school, in which she was compared to an "ideal" girl of her age and height. These were routinely sent home with children at my daughter's school, and were a cause of humiliation to many children because of unfavourable comparisons with the ideal and with each other. After my daughter's anorexia nervosa developed, I asked the school principal whether the results could not be mailed home to parents in sealed envelopes. He replied that this would be too costly. When I offered to pay for the mailing myself, in order to spare other children this humiliating practice, he refused, saying that he felt this precaution was unnecessary. He seemed to resent my "interfering".

Other difficulties at school such as problems with friends and the pressure of exams were mentioned as common factors preceding the onset of anorexia nervosa. Problems at home included moves, loss of grandparents, parental divorce or marital difficulties, siblings leaving home, and changes in the mother's and father's working situations, all stress-producing life changes.

WHAT HELPED AND WHAT DIDN'T

In the questionnaire, parents were provided with a listing of all the treatment techniques mentioned in this book. Few were familiar with even the names of all these treatments, although some had children who had been suffering from eating disorders for up to ten years. One mother, a doctor herself, said that she was unaware of the differences between behavioural therapy, cognitive therapy and psychotherapy.

I am a hospital consultant who qualified (in the) early 1960s when psychiatry was a tiny part of medical curriculum. I spent a year at Great Ormond Street and knew virtually nothing about this terrible wasteful illness when it hit my family.

This woman's daughter has now had anorexia nervosa for seven years, and now, at the age of twenty-one, weighs only five and a half stone, in spite of five long stays in hospital.

Parents were asked to rate the effectiveness of treatment techniques with which they were familiar. On a scale of "Very helpful", "Moderately helpful", and "Unhelpful", I am sorry to report that most techniques were rated as "Unhelpful". The only three that were conspicuously differently rated by parents were "Hospital Care", "Psychotherapy", and "Group Therapy". These three scored significantly more "Very helpful" and "Moderately helpful" ratings than all the others combined.

Parents whose children were helped by hospital treatment were most often those who had been referred to a specialist unit, not a general psychiatric ward. Nurses specially trained in the care of anorectics were again and again mentioned as being critically important in helping to overcome the anorectic's resistance to eating. Weight gain in hospital was frequently lost as soon as the child returned home, as parents stated there was little follow-up of their daughter's progress. One parent described her family's experience in an NHS hospital:

At ... the NHS professionals were secretive, and we felt patronized. Everyone seemed to feel that we were "bad parents" because our child had anorexia nervosa, and this made it all the harder for us to keep our family together during the long siege of her illness. We were not given any hopes for her recovery; on the contrary, we were told that her prospects were poor. We were never given any helpful information or advice as to how we could actively help her to recover.

This contrasts sharply with her later experience at a specialist unit:

For the first time, we were able to really share the pain and anxiety caused by our child's illness. She lived on the unit five days a week and came home weekends. This gave us a much needed rest from coping with tantrums and constant scenes in the kitchen and at the table. Most importantly, the workers on the unit showed us, by example and encouragement, how to get our daughter to eat with us again.

Parent's responses regarding the value of psychotherapy pointed up the highly variable quality of therapists. A number mentioned psychotherapy as being helpful not only for their daughters, but for themselves. Two mothers who had been discouraged from seeking psychotherapy for their daughters at low weights, but who persisted and obtained it anyway, commented on the fact that it had, after all, been beneficial. Others felt differently:

> Certainly the psychiatry/psychology was wrong for Kate. The culmination of this treatment was her being admitted to a mental hospital adolescent's unit. She emerged after three weeks' trial like a zombie ... She is a super intelligent person apart from the anorexia hang-up and did not take kindly to being put away with violent, abusive and drugged-up and guarded mental cases.

The mother of the only male anorectic in our sample writes:

> Carl went to see a psychologist at ... for seven months every week but really he was no better. I would have preferred him to see a man but it was different women every time nearly.

My daughter repeatedly requested psychotherapy, but we were told by our family therapist at first that her weight was too low for her to benefit, and later that her difficulties could be worked out within the family. Months after we finished family therapy, my husband and I again requested psychotherapy for our daughter, as we felt she was still deeply unhappy with herself. Finally, the family therapist agreed to refer her to a clinical psychologist, but by this time she then refused to go, saying it was "too late". She said that she felt that even though she had been forced to break her destructive eating habits, she still felt anxious about food, but didn't want to miss any more school or activities for doctor's visits. I am regretful about this missed opportunity to get to the bottom of what was bothering her when she might have been responsive to it, and feel that our earlier requests ought to have been respected.

It seems from our respondents as though many family therapists regard the practice as an economical form of treatment, and refuse to allow young anorectic patients private therapy apart from their families. Yet opinion on the benefits of family therapy is divided. Its usefulness no doubt depends on the family in question and the rapport they develop with the individual therapist. Many mothers dismiss it as distressing, still others swear by it and are enthusiastic about the insights gained through family therapy.

Clearly, there is family therapy that is helpful and family therapy that is destructive. Families who have been put "on camera" or watched from behind one-way mirrors without warning or permission are understandably resentful.

> Family therapy began with videotaped meetings. These were generally whodunits of family traumas and problems. Very humiliating for already highly distraught and anguished parents. The effect was to further alienate and confuse us.
>
> One day I had to bring a "picnic" for the family to eat in front of two psychiatrists, a video camera, and a one-way mirror. When my daughter violently threw food on the floor my husband and I were told we had to force it down her mouth. This was the only time actual "information" was given and it was repugnant to us all.
>
> When we told the head child psychiatrist at ... that we could not go on any more after six harrowing months of hospital admissions and discharges as our daughter went steadily downhill, she told us that we had "failed".

Parents seem to want family therapists to consider the concept of the chicken and the egg when seeing families of anorectics. By the time the family is likely to end up in therapy, they have probably undergone months or even years of almost unbearable strain which is reflected in their family interaction. I know I felt wooden and empty and afraid to speak for fear I would cry. I was criticised by the family therapist for this at the time. He said that I appeared to be "wearing a mask". Yet I really wanted to understand what was wrong and how to help my child. So I tried to be more vocal and express my thinking. Perhaps I overdid it and didn't give my daughter enough chance to speak, because after I talked too much at another session, he told me that by dominating the discussion I was contributing to my daughter's illness. I didn't know what I was supposed to say or do. At the end of the family therapy, the question I most wanted to ask was: "How is this supposed to help?"

I have been told that people in therapy are supposed to come to their own conclusions about what their problems are and how they can deal with them, but perhaps this rule should be bent somewhat in dealing with this particular problem. I think it would be more helpful to say, for example, "Families with anorectic children often have difficulty with ... Here are some ways they have learned to cope with this." This way, the family would feel neither accused or confused. Concrete advice and encouragement are probably the two things parents need most in their struggle to deal with this disorder. Some explanation of therapeutic goals would also be extremely helpful.

Many mothers report experiences of having their requests for treatment ignored or swept under the carpet by health professionals. This is especially evident in their dealings with GPs.

My doctor laughed me out of the office, told me I was an anxious mother and to leave her alone to eat the kind of food she wanted to eat. When I mentioned her periods, he said "What does she want periods for anyway? They are a nuisance."

This doctor's attitude to feminine physiology was shared by another GP consulted by one of our respondents. A mother writes:

I would like to reiterate how woefully ignorant about anorexia our GP seemed to be. When I managed after much cajoling to get my daughter along to him and explain how she had lost a substantial amount of weight and her periods had stopped, he said she didn't look too bad to him and he was sure she didn't mind not having periods. He could always start them up for her if she wished to get pregnant. When I said she wasn't eating enough he laughed it off by saying it was probably a teenage fad and she would eat again when she felt hungry.

Not only do these responses show disrespect for mothers' judgement, but they show how deep society's repugnance towards menstruation is. If even doctors feel menstruation is distasteful, how can young girls be expected to regard it positively? Mothers have a difficult task in making the idea of having periods seem attractive to an 11 or 12-year-old child. The sight of blood is regarded as disgusting or shocking in our sanitised culture. But even in our more earthy past, menstruating women were regarded as "unclean". Today, women are encouraged by advertising to regard menstruation as a kind of secret they should keep from the world. I feel the name of a popularly sold sanitary napkin says it all: "Complice".

So, having been told by their GPs that their mothers are silly and fussy and that they are fine, the anorectic has her world view confirmed and can go back to starving until her weight is so low that she is unable to function. At that point, she may or may not be lucky enough to be hospitalised in order to save her life.

When my daughter's sister took her to ... for an appointment with the resident psychiatrist and she weighed six stone (down from nine stone, eleven pounds), she was sent home with anti-depressant pills and told to eat more. When admitted to hospital two weeks later (she weighed) five stone, four pounds ...

The waiting list for a decent hospital is so long people are becoming frantic. The waiting time for admission for a patient and the family is a time of indescribable anxiety.

The need for early detection and help was mentioned again and again, both by parents whose children have recovered and by those who are still suffering. Many parents who felt specific types of treatment would be helpful for their daughters were frustrated when asking for it.

> The answer was vague but implying "no" when I asked about group therapy and yet this hospital was supposed to be well-known for its treatment of anorexia—one of the doctors had written a book on the subject but G. was not her patient. G. was in a ward with all other psychiatric patients— horrific!

WHAT MIGHT HAVE HELPED

All forms of alternative medicine seem to have been discouraged by the medical profession—acupuncture, hypnotism, homeopathy. Yet some parents experienced positive results with these methods.

> I tried to persuade her to take the homeopathic zinc, but she didn't want the sugar in the dose. After much cajoling, she finally relented. We went downstairs to watch TV, and she was calmer and pleasant. Half an hour later, she went into the kitchen and ate three muffins. She began to smile, and talk about how she guessed she could eat dinner without getting fat. Before she went to bed, she told me how happy she was and that she felt things were going to get better from that point on, and that she realized how difficult she had been and would never forget our efforts to help her. It was nothing short of a miraculous change.
>
> She was hungry again in the morning, and ate breakfast and lunch, and did not try to stop me from using oil in the cooking. She is becoming sociable and more outwardly-directed than we have seen her in months. Truly astonishing.

Parents find it difficult to understand why the medical profession is so reluctant to try alternative forms of treatment when traditional methods are often disappointing. Holistic forms of treatment would seem to be particularly appropriate for an illness which exhibits both physical and mental symptoms. Doctors who refuse to listen to mothers' suggestions make mothers feel their opinions are not respected, a feeling which is commonly reported to contribute to the development of anorexia nervosa itself.

It is already evident that many parents were disappointed with the information and support they received from medical professionals. Those most satisfied were families whose GPs had responded promptly to their concerns with adequate referrals. Even in such cases, there is often room for improvement.

Although our family GP was very helpful and arranged an appointment for us for the child and family psychiatric clinic quickly, and he admitted her to hospital, we weren't informed as to what would happen next. We didn't know the purpose of family therapy and at first thought it a waste of time. The hospital didn't tell us how her stomach would react to eating more food and we found it upsetting when she would cry in pain for lengths of time without help. We would be left to worry about things like that that could have been explained to us.

Among our respondents were some whose children became or remained ill after the age of 16. These parents complained of the difficulty of obtaining adequate information about their daughters' progress.

I have to ask for information, no one seems to think I want to know, yet I am the one who sees her 24 hours a day and has to try to see that she eats enough to stay alive.

Others expressed confusion about who has ultimate responsibility for their anorectic over-16s. They assume, probably correctly, that no-one cares about their children as much as they do, and yet feel powerless to help and are refused information because of their daughters' rights to privacy.

The psychologist tells me the health risks have been explained and that it is up to her to make the choice. Is her mind in any fit state to make a choice?

Parents seemed to do a lot of complaining about the lack of help and support from the medical profession. Given their distress, it may be impossible to do enough for some families. But here are repeated suggestions made by parents:

Nursing staff and doctors should *listen* to the parents.

A more friendly and open response to enquiries would have given a feeling of working together. When ringing the hospital for information about my daughter who was attending clinics as an outpatient, I felt a nuisance, overprotective, and was treated in an unsympathetic and patronising manner.

The psychiatrist should take the time and trouble to try and explain how and why the illness develops.

Laxatives should be sold only on prescription.

One family learned a useful technique from a psychiatrist who responded to her daughter's questions in writing:

> If (my daughter) feels desperate to have her questions answered, she now writes them down and saves them for an appropriate moment. The actual process of writing out the question seems to alleviate much of the stress. This helped the family situation a great deal, as previously, I had found myself trying to answer desperate questions at very inconvenient times.

Many praised the help obtained from the Eating Disorders Association (see address at end of chapter), for recommending appropriate medical facilities and counselling; for reviewing reading material on anorexia nervosa, self-awareness and self-assertion; for referring parents to support groups; and for simply being there on the end of the telephone line when needed. Doctors who are too busy to take telephone calls from anxious parents should refer them to the Eating Disorders Association. Anything, even advice from a stranger who is not familiar with the details of one's particular situation, is better than a brush-off.

Literature on anorexia nervosa, particularly the work of Bruch (1974) and Palazzoli (1978), seemed to me at the time of my daughter's illness to be depressing and unhelpful. However, I found consolation in a book by Bruno Bettleheim, *The good enough parent* (1987). The loving counsel of this wise man, who speaks in this book as a parent to parents, was humane and helpful. In discussing what most helped their children to recover from anorexia nervosa, many parents mentioned the love and support of their families. This book, particularly the early chapters, gives valuable guidance on how to convey that love and support. It might prove especially useful for parents who never received much love themselves.

HOPE: LOST AND FOUND

Parents speak of the terrible burden of guilt that almost overwhelms them, of the necessity of having to live with constant violent and abusive behaviour for months and even years on end, and of the unspeakable grief of watching their beloved children committing long, slow suicide before their eyes. They feel like prisoners in their own homes, afraid to go out because of what might happen while they are gone, yet feeling they must take care of themselves, if only to set an example for their children. They walk a daily tightrope, trying to know when to be firm and when to be flexible, trying to do everything they can but often feeling that their efforts are worthless.

> I feel miserable and trapped in an impossible situation. I've lost a lot weight and my hair is turning white. I saw a therapist once. She told me to go off around the world, have an affair and leave Kate to herself.

It is hard not to feel resentful especially when she uses emotional blackmail. If she feels I haven't spent long enough listening to her she will rush into the bathroom and threaten to do "something stupid" or else rush out of the house and not return for hours causing us tremendous worry. She is also violent and abusive. It is a living nightmare.

I have been changed irrevocably by her illness. I no longer have any ambitions or hope for the future of my children ... I feel I have let her down as a mother. I love her so much, as does her father, but on more than one occasion she has told us that she hates us both and the house also. I tried so hard to make her happy and nurse her through her illness, but I think she blames me, and maybe she is right.

There are times when I feel I am headed for a nervous breakdown. I have nobody to turn to for support. I live in a constant state of fear.

In the beginning I felt I hated my daughter for being so selfish, but now I think I love her more than I could ever tell her and will *never* give up on her.

Her life is a nightmare, but I see inside the obsessive, darkened child the sunny child I remember and I know we can rescue her. Tonight she told me that she knows it is difficult to be a parent to her now. I looked at her hollow eyes and thin skull and I hugged her and told her that it was alright, and that she would be getting better soon.

The refusal to give up is a factor parents often mentioned when discussing what has helped them to survive their children's illness. Also frequently mentioned is prayer and spiritual faith. Several parents mentioned renewal of religious faith and increased sensitivity to the suffering of others as the benefits of their experience. Many referred to their good marriages, which they felt helped to give them strength and courage. One mother whose daughter was anorectic for seven years spoke proudly of her daughter's recovery:

Sandra wrote a dissertation on the subject while she was at university. This helped us both to deal with her problem more effectively. I have been very proud of her efforts to help other sufferers. I think she has a better understanding of the illness than many members of the medical profession.

Sadly, a mother who has been anorectic herself cannot necessarily help her child avoid the same plight. She probably never received any treatment whatsoever, and came through her illness without any insight into her problems.

I had a very unhappy and lonely childhood. There were people around but I felt isolated, particularly from my mother. I would say that I was the scapegoat of the family and became anorectic myself at the age of 18.

This mother, with the help of a counsellor, has now:

resolved to quite a large degree the tension between myself and my own mother and have become far less anxious and guilt-ridden in general. I have changed my way of relating to other people completely. Although I feel I have still farther to go, [I] am much happier.

I suspect that I myself was somewhat anorectic for about 20 years. This is not to say that I understood this at the time. I did not think I was too thin, and I was genuinely puzzled by the fact that I seemed to have little energy, be constantly hungry, and felt consequently irritable. I explored allergies and thyroid problems as the source of these difficulties. It wasn't until my daughter became severely anorectic that I began to recognise the symptoms of the illness in myself. When I realised what I had helped bring about in my child, I felt overwhelmed with shame and guilt and could scarcely forgive myself. With the grace of God, I did, and I learned a new strength born of endurance. Without my child's breakdown, I probably would have had a hungry heart for the rest of my life. For helping to heal me, I will be grateful to her forever.

Parents of anorectics have a bad reputation. Although their daughters' responses to them are well-documented, their side of the story is seldom told.

We were not given a chance to state our case. Our daughter told some terrible lies about us and her childhood and actively got a lot of sympathy. She has told us this since ... Wouldn't a better picture emerge if parents and children were both interviewed?

It has been difficult for me within the space limitations of this chapter to try to represent the varying thoughts of so many different families. I very much appreciate their help and hope that I have spoken for them adequately. I also appreciate the help of my friend Katharine Haggiag and Dr Rachel Bryant-Waugh.

Women's lives are filled with much inescapable pain connected with their experiences of their bodies. As the mother of two daughters, I take comfort from the fact that each generation is standing on the shoulders of the last, and that, in consequence, our children will be able to see more clearly and perhaps live more wisely than we have been able to do.

REFERENCES

Bettleheim, B. (1987). *The good enough parent.* London: Thames & Hudson.

Bruch, H. (1974). *Eating disorders: Obesity, anorexia nervosa and the person within.* London: Routledge.

Palazzoli, M.S. (1978). *Self starvation.* New York: Jason Aronson.

CONTACT ADDRESS

The Eating Disorders Association
Sackville Place
44-48 Magdalen Street
Norwich
Norfolk
United Kingdom
Tel: (0603) 621414

CHAPTER TWO

Eating Disorders in Children: An Overview

Rachel Bryant-Waugh and Zyg Kaminski

INTRODUCTION

Eating disorders, in particular anorexia nervosa and bulimia nervosa, are commonly considered to afflict adolescent girls and young women. Indeed, this group includes the majority of those presenting for and receiving treatment in this context. Yet eating disorders are also known to occur in males, older females and pre-pubertal children. In general there appears to be little doubt that males and older females present with "true" eating disorders; i.e. that the clinical picture is similar to that found in the core group of eating disorder patients. The situation regarding children has been less universally accepted. Some have held the belief that eating disorders of the type occurring in adolescents and adults simply do not occur in children—for example: "Anorexia nervosa remains relatively rare. It is certainly not a problem with children before puberty." (Haslam, 1986). Where diagnostic criteria have been used that require the presence of amenorrhoea, pre-menarcheal girls have been excluded from consideration. Nevertheless, a number of recent reports have described series of young patients with anorexia nervosa aged from eight years upwards (Fosson, Knibbs, Bryant-Waugh, & Lask, 1987; Gowers, Crisp, Joughin, & Bhat, 1991; Higgs, Goodyer, & Birch, 1989; Jacobs & Isaacs, 1986). These children fulfil formal widely accepted criteria for anorexia nervosa (e.g. the DSM III R criteria of the American Psychiatric

Association 1987), and in our view present as undisputed cases of anorexia nervosa.

Is the development of eating disorders in childhood then a new phenomenon? Looking back over early publications describing cases of children presenting with disturbances in eating behaviour, we have to conclude that this is probably not the case. Two of the earliest authors presenting what are thought to be cases of anorexia nervosa in children are Collins (1894) and Marshall (1895). The former described the case of a seven-year-old girl who was emaciated and refusing food, whereas Marshall described the fatal outcome of what he called "anorexia nervosa" in an eleven-year-old girl. Since this time, sporadic reports have appeared in the literature, indicating that the young age of a patient has never entirely excluded a possible diagnosis of anorexia nervosa. Unfortunately, it is not always certain that true cases of anorexia nervosa were being presented, and in many instances food refusal, food fads or other more common childhood eating problems were probably being described (Warren, 1968).

It is only relatively recently that children have come to be regarded as a subgroup of interest within the eating disorder population. The literature on all aspects of eating disorders specifically relating to this younger age-group remains sparse. This chapter aims to summarise current understanding and knowledge, in particular of the different types of eating disorders occurring in children aged 14 and under, together with a description of behavioural and emotional features. It should be noted that in this chapter, as elsewhere in this book, the terms "early onset" or "childhood onset" are used to refer to eating disorders occurring in the 8- to 14-year-old age-group.

EATING DISTURBANCES IN CHILDHOOD: VARIATIONS ON A THEME?

The majority of children attending the Eating Disorders Out-patient Clinic at the Hospital for Sick Children have anorexia nervosa, and the greater part of this chapter will describe the features of this eating disorder in more detail. However, children may present with a number of other types of eating disorder, all of which share a common central theme of the refusal of food. The interrelationship of these disturbances of eating behaviour is not yet clear, but from the perspective of presentation, they have certain features in common. In children experiencing eating difficulties or abnormalities of eating behaviour, where no organic cause can be found, the following terms might apply:

- Anorexia nervosa.
- Food avoidance emotional disorder (FAED).
- Food refusal.
- Pervasive refusal.
- Selective eating.
- Bulimia nervosa.
- Appetite loss secondary to depression.

Food Avoidance Emotional Disorder

Food avoidance emotional disorder (FAED) is a term introduced by Higgs and colleagues (1989). They submit from their study of case records that there are a number of children who do not fully meet the criteria for anorexia nervosa and they propose that food avoidance emotional disorder may be an intermediate condition between anorexia nervosa and childhood emotional disorder (with no eating disorder). They suggest "food avoidance disorder" may be a partial syndrome of anorexia nervosa with an overall better prognosis. The characteristics of this type of eating disorder were originally described as follows:

- A disorder of the emotions in which food avoidance is a prominent symptom in the presenting complaint.
- A history of food avoidance or difficulty (e.g. food fads or restrictions).
- A failure to meet the criteria for anorexia nervosa.
- The absence of organic brain disease, psychosis, illicit drug abuse, or prescribed drug-related causes. (Higgs et al., 1989)

Food Refusal

Food refusal, fads and fetishes may take a variety of forms and represent relatively common problems in childhood, particularly in very young children. In most instances it is not difficult to distinguish between these and eating disorders, because the characteristic preoccupation of the latter with body weight and shape is absent. Food refusers are in addition usually less consistent in their avoidance of food, and will often eat favourite foods without difficulty. Alternatively, they may display relatively normal eating behaviour in certain situations, such as at a friend's house, reserving mealtime battles for home territory. Such children are not usually calorie conscious and are frequently not underweight. In most cases, this type of eating problem can be viewed as a behaviour problem which tends to resolve with time, and does not represent a serious threat to the child's general health and well-being.

Pervasive Refusal

"Pervasive refusal" is a condition described by Lask et al. (1991), manifested by profound and pervasive refusal to eat, drink, walk, talk or engage in self-care. These authors note that children with this particular combination of symptoms do not fit any existing diagnostic category, and suggest that the condition may be understood as an extreme variation of the avoidance behaviour seen in posttraumatic stress disorder. Children with pervasive refusal present as underweight, adamantly refusing food and drink, thus having some features in common with children with anorexia nervosa. However, a diagnosis of anorexia nervosa is inappropriate in such cases because not all the criteria for an eating disorder are known to be fulfilled, and the refusal exhibited extends across all areas of functioning.

Selective Eating

This term may be applied to those children who appear to exist on typically only two or three different foods. These will often be carbohydrate-based, such as biscuits, crisps or potatoes. Children with this form of extremely selective eating behaviour are often of appropriate weight and height for their age, and tend not to present as an immediate cause for concern in physical terms. Problems in social functioning often precipitate parental requests for help, as such children are usually unable to contemplate situations which might require them to eat foods outside their restricted range. In most cases selective eaters are referred for specialist help regarding social rather than physical concerns, and are clearly distinguishable from children presenting with anorexia nervosa.

Bulimia Nervosa

Bulimia nervosa is an eating disorder characterised by out-of-control behaviour regarding food. Food avoidance may alternate with over-eating, or be totally replaced by it. The exaggerated dread of fatness (found also in anorexia nervosa) persists, and episodes of overeating may be counteracted by methods of weight reduction which typically include self-induced vomiting and laxative abuse.

Of the 200 or so children attending the Eating Disorders Clinic at the Hospital for Sick Children over the past few years, only a handful have received a diagnosis of bulimia nervosa. This might be taken to suggest that this eating disorder is very rare below the age of 14. Indeed, it is certainly our experience that formal diagnostic criteria for bulimia nervosa (e.g. those of DSM III R—American Psychiatric Association

TABLE 2.1

DSM III R Diagnostic Criteria for Bulimia Nervosa

1.	Recurrent episodes of binge-eating.
2.	A feeling of lack of control over eating behaviour during the eating binges.
3.	The person regularly engages in either self-induced vomiting, use of laxatives or diuretics, strict dieting or fasting, or vigorous exercise in order to prevent weight gain.
4.	A minimum average of two binge-eating episodes a week for at least three months.
5.	Persistent overconcern with body shape and weight.

Adapted from: *Diagnostic and statistical manual of mental disorders* (1987). 3rd ed. rev. Washington, DC: The American Psychiatric Association.

1987, see Table 2.1) are only rarely applicable in our client group. In the absence of good epidemiological data specifically relating to the incidence of bulimia nervosa in those aged 14 and under, it is not possible to be certain that the small number of bulimics we see reflects prevalence rates in general. Bulimia nervosa undoubtedly occurs in individuals aged 13 and over and may well occur in children below this age. For one reason or another, such children, if they exist, have not come to the attention of our clinic.

Appetite Loss Secondary to Depression

Depressed individuals often suffer from loss of appetite, consequently children presenting with a history of non-eating should be investigated for affective disorder. It is usually not difficult to distinguish between the loss of appetite accompanying depression and anorexia nervosa as again certain core features such as determined food avoidance and preoccupation with body weight and shape will be absent. However, the picture may become somewhat less clear in the cases where anorexia nervosa is associated with depression. This appears to be not uncommon in children: Fosson et al. (1987) found that 56% of 48 children with early onset anorexia nervosa were moderately to severely depressed. The relationship between mood disorder and anorexia nervosa has long been debated in the literature (Cantwell et al. 1977), and although there are significant differentiating features, it can be argued that depression may be a secondary phenomenon of the primary eating disorder. DiNicola, Roberts, & Oke, (1989) state, however, that most studies on mood disorder and anorexia nervosa are focused on adolescents and young adults, and that in young children the relationship between eating and mood disorder is more complex and even more likely to be intertwined.

From the above it is evident that there are areas of overlap between the different types of eating disturbance that may be present in children. One feature common to all is difficulties with food intake, and to this extent they can be considered variations on a theme. Although this central problem is shared, children assigned to the various categories of eating disturbance exhibit a very wide range of psychological and physical features. The remainder of this chapter is concerned with anorexia nervosa; in particular, its diagnosis in children and its behavioural and emotional features.

THE DIAGNOSIS OF ANOREXIA NERVOSA IN CHILDREN

There remains considerable disagreement about how precisely anorexia nervosa should be defined, and some uncertainty regarding which of its many clinical features should be regarded as prerequisites for diagnosis, and which represent commonly occurring characteristics. For the purposes of research it is essential to formulate generally acceptable guidelines outlining what is—and consequently what is not—anorexia nervosa. If this is not achieved there can only be a limited amount of satisfactory interchange of ideas or comparison of results of research. For example, comparing results of outcome studies is only possible if the selection of the individuals included in different studies has been based on similar criteria for inclusion. For clinical purposes, it may be less essential to apply strict diagnostic criteria to distinguish between different forms of eating disturbance. The clinician works with presenting symptoms and difficulties in an attempt to alleviate the situation and it may be argued that in this respect it is relatively immaterial what label is attached to the child's problem.

A discussion of diagnostic criteria for anorexia nervosa in children makes the assumption, then, that this is a useful exercise. The application of diagnostic criteria in effect does no more than ascertain whether any one particular individual is displaying a pre-specified pattern of symptoms. Diagnostic labels tend to be hypothetical constructs inferred from observed patterns which actually tell you very little. In the case of such a complex disorder as anorexia nervosa, which has a wide variety of manifestations in different people, the term itself carries only a limited amount of information. It is important to remember that the behavioural and emotional aspects of the disorder are likely to differ and should be considered for each individual separately.

The most widely used diagnostic criteria for anorexia nervosa are currently those of the DSM III R (American Psychiatric Association

TABLE 2.2
DSM III R Anorexia Nervosa

1.	Refusal to maintain body weight over minimal normal weight for age and height (e.g. weight loss leading to body weight 15% below expected). or Failure to make expected weight gain during growth period leading to body weight 15% below expected.
2.	Intense fear of gaining weight or becoming fat, even though underweight.
3.	Disturbance in the experience of body weight, size or shape (e.g. claiming to feel fat when emaciated, believing that one area of body is too fat when underweight).
4.	The absence of at least three consecutive menstrual cycles when otherwise expected to occur (primary or secondary amenorrhoea).

Adapted from: *Diagnostic and statistical manual of mental disorders,* (1987). 3rd ed. rev. Washington DC: The American Psychiatric Association.

1987). These criteria (see Table 2.2) are intended primarily for use with older patients, and do not adequately address the problems of diagnosing anorexia nervosa in children. DSM III R criteria include the following: In females, the absence of at least three consecutive menstrual cycles when otherwise expected to occur. It is stated that this may be primary or secondary amenorrhoea, presumably so that girls who have not yet menstruated need not necessarily be excluded. However, it is very difficult, if not impossible, to be certain that menstruation might "otherwise" have occurred, and in the case of eight-year-olds it would certainly not be expected to occur. Similarly, the criterion relating to the refusal to maintain body weight stipulates that this should result in a maintenance of body weight 15% below the expected weight, or that there should be a failure to make the expected weight gain in individuals who should still be growing also resulting in maintenance of body weight 15% below that expected for height and age. Given that inadequate food intake may directly affect growth rates, and thus height measurements, in children this makes the calculation of expected weight difficult. Is the measured height the expected height, or should a change in the height curve also be taken into account? ICD9 (World Health Organization, 1979) does not acknowledge the existence of pre-pubertal anorexia nervosa and uses the category "unspecified eating disorder" (307.50) to identify the general population of anorexia nervosa. Both systems of classification seem to require revision to satisfactorily include pre-pubertal anorexia nervosa. For these and other reasons, we have for some years (Lask & Bryant-Waugh, 1986) made use of a diagnostic checklist specifically for anorexia nervosa in children which was adapted from criteria originally proposed by Russell (1970) for use with older individuals.

GREAT ORMOND STREET DIAGNOSTIC CHECKLIST

1. Determined food avoidance.
2. Weight loss or failure to gain weight during the period of pre-adolescent growth (10–14 years) in the absence of any physical or other mental illness.
3. Any two of more of the following:
   (a) preoccupation with body weight
   (b) preoccupation with energy intake
   (c) distorted body image
   (d) fear of fatness
   (e) self-induced vomiting
   (f) extensive exercising
   (g) purging (laxative abuse).

Determined Food Avoidance

Determined food avoidance is present in an extreme form regardless of the patient's age. It is well known that the term anorexia nervosa, in its literal meaning "nervous loss of appetite", is something of a misnomer. Many children later report having felt very hungry but being completely unable to allow themselves to eat. However, recent research suggests that patients with anorexia nervosa may experience delayed gastric emptying, and that feelings of satiety may be affected by abnormal activity in the stomach (see chapter 3). Nevertheless, there is as yet no evidence to suggest that the initial reason for refusing food is related to appetite loss, and it may transpire that the above observations are secondary features of the disorder.

Clinically, one of the central features of anorexia nervosa is the relentless pursuit of thinness achieved by reducing food intake, a pursuit which involves immense control—"malignant control". This intense striving for control may be regarded as a valiant attempt at reassurance that the individual can in fact direct her own life, but actually overlies a very profound fear of loss of control. Denial may be massive, and often centres on hunger, thinness and fatigue. To this triad can be added denial of mood changes, and at times a "pseudo-euphoria" occurs.

Children with anorexia nervosa give a variety of reasons for refusing food, the most common of which appears to be a fear of becoming obese (see "Fear of Fatness" below). Other reasons include feelings of nausea or fullness, abdominal pain, appetite loss and difficulty swallowing (Fosson et al., 1987).

Weight Loss or Failure to Gain Weight

Weight loss, or a failure to gain weight, invariably involves a change in a child's weight curve. Because children should be growing, static weight may be regarded as equivalent to weight loss in adults. In practice, all children attending our clinic with anorexia nervosa have lost significant amounts of weight. Using the Tanner-Whitehouse standards (Tanner, Whitehouse, & Takaishi, 1966), where 100% represents the desired weight for a child's sex, age and height, 80% or less is classed as "wasting". In a previous study of children attending the Hospital for Sick Children, 83% were in the wasting range at presentation (Fosson et al., 1987).

Weight loss of this degree is a real cause for concern in children, as pre-pubertal children in particular have lower total body-fat deposits and therefore do not have much fat to lose. Weight loss in these cases involves primarily the loss of muscle tissue and dehydration. Irwin (1981) has commented on the "refusal to maintain hydration" often seen in children with anorexia nervosa, and suggests that this may represent a clinical feature specific to this younger age group. It is certainly true that refusal to take fluids is not uncommon, and can rapidly lead to a state of acute dehydration. It may be that the feelings of fullness associated with drinking are experienced as "fatness" and therefore avoided.

Preoccupation with Body Weight

Children with anorexia nervosa tend to be obsessed with weight in a similar way to their adolescent and adult counterparts. They display a great resistance to gaining weight, and engage in bitterly fought battles related to target weights while in treatment. This preoccupation is mostly focused on their own body weight (or that of other anorectics) and does not usually involve the weights of family members or friends.

Preoccupation with Energy Intake

These children are often experts at calorie counting and know which foods have a high calorie content. On the whole, children with anorexia nervosa are intelligent individuals who have little difficulty grasping the concept of energy intake.

Fear of Fatness

As mentioned previously, an expressed dread of fatness is very common. Fosson et al. (1987) identified it in 56% of their series of early onset patients, and it may well have been present, though not expressed, in more. Clearly the fear of fatness is closely related to the preoccupation with body weight and shape shared by all these children. It is not uncommon for this fear to be denied early in the illness, but to emerge as treatment progresses.

Distortion of Body Image

Body image distortion in anorexia nervosa is an area of extreme complexity and continuing debate. Hsu and Sobkiewicz (1991) have suggested that it is a problematic and not particularly useful concept, and have proposed that "body disparagement" may be a more relevant term. One major problem is that distortion of body image is very difficult to assess reliably. However, when asked the question "Do you think you are fat, just right or thin?", many of the children we see will report that they consider themselves fat even when severely underweight. This is similar to the common clinical observation that older patients also state that they look and feel fat even though they may be extremely emaciated. Some preliminary work with visual analogues carried out at the Hospital for Sick Children (unpublished), suggests that anorectic children do consider themselves to be significantly fatter than they are in reality. In our view it is important not to stipulate that "distortion of body image" should be an essential diagnostic criterion, given the difficulties in ascertaining whether it is truly present, and, indeed, what it actually involves.

Self-induced Vomiting

Vomiting appears to be one of the main means of weight control, besides reduction of food intake, employed by children with anorexia nervosa. Fosson et al. (1987) reported that at least 40% of the 48 children included in their study were known to be vomiting at presentation. It is often prudent to assume that a child who is not gaining weight once treatment has been commenced must be vomiting, and to take appropriate precautions, such as supervision after mealtimes and escorting to the toilet.

Excessive Exercising

Again, excessive exercising is not uncommon in children with anorexia nervosa. Often this behaviour will have been present for some time, and perhaps initially encouraged by parents as a healthy desirable activity. Daily swimming, exercise workouts, and other sporting activities taken to excess may feature in these children's lives. Sometimes, exercising may take on a more secretive form, perhaps involving push-ups and similar exercises carried out in the privacy of bedroom or bathroom.

Laxative Abuse

Although perhaps not as common as in the older age group, abuse of laxatives does occur in children. It may be that children are less inclined to buy laxatives from the chemist, or have less access or opportunity to do so. Where it does occur, potential electrolyte imbalances and mineral deficiencies should be remedied as soon as possible.

ARE EARLY ONSET AND LATER ONSET ANOREXIA NERVOSA THE SAME?

Most people now accept that the clinical features found in children receiving a diagnosis of anorexia nervosa are similar to those occurring in older individuals, with obvious age-related differences, such as the absence of amenorrhoea in pre-pubertal girls. Opinions are, however, divided regarding the relationship between early onset and later onset anorexia nervosa in terms of severity and prognosis (see further chapter 5). The core features that include disturbances in three central areas—behavioural, psychological, and physical—appear to be largely the same. Nevertheless, there are some differences which deserve mention. Irwin (1984) stresses the difference in the distribution of adipose tissue between children and late adolescents or adults. Consequently, children tend to achieve a more severe degree of emaciation when compared to older individuals with a similar degree of weight loss. Irwin has further suggested that as children appear to deteriorate more rapidly in terms of weight, they may reach the "later stages" of anorexia nervosa more quickly: Depressive symptoms, which are generally observed to occur later in the course of the disorder, may therefore appear comparatively early in the course of early onset anorexia nervosa (Irwin, 1984). As previously mentioned, it is certainly our experience that children with anorexia nervosa are often depressed while in active treatment for their eating disorder. Finally, bingeing and laxative abuse seem to occur in a lower percentage of patients than might be expected from comparisons with older individuals.

It must be emphasised that there is no typical pattern of symptoms and complaints at presentation, and that the clinical features may vary during the course of the illness. This, together with the fact that many children present with somatic symptoms, means that the diagnosis is often missed.

SUMMARY

This chapter gives an overview of some of the types of eating disturbances occurring in children in the age range seen in our Eating Disorders Clinic (i.e. 8–14 years). The following have been mentioned in this context: Anorexia nervosa, food avoidance emotional disorder, food refusal, pervasive refusal, selective eating, bulimia nervosa, and appetite loss secondary to depression. It is suggested that anorexia nervosa can and does occur in children in a form comparable to that identified in older individuals, and that this does not appear to be a new phenomenon. The diagnosis of anorexia nervosa in children has been discussed, emphasising the importance of diagnostic criteria for research purposes, but raising the question about their relevance in a clinical context. Existing diagnostic criteria designed primarily for use with older patients have been shown to have limitations when applied to children, and alternative criteria have been proposed. The common features of the disorder have been presented, and lastly, a comparison made between early onset and later onset anorexia nervosa. It is concluded that core clinical features are similar, but that presenting symptoms show a very wide range of variation.

REFERENCES

American Psychiatric Association. (1987). *Diagnostic and statistical manual of mental disorders,* (3rd ed. rev.). Washington DC: American Psychiatric Association.

Cantwell, D., Sturzenberger, S., Burroughs, J., Salkin, B., & Green, J. (1977). Anorexia nervosa: An affective disorder? *Archives of General Psychiatry, 34,* 1087–1093.

Collins, W. (1894). Anorexia nervosa. *Lancet, i:* 202–203.

DiNicola, V., Roberts, N., & Oke, L. (1989). Eating and mood disorders in young children. *Psychiatric Clinics of North America, 12,* 873–893.

Fosson, A., Knibbs, J., Bryant-Waugh, R., & Lask, B. (1987). Early onset anorexia nervosa. *Archives of Disease in Childhood, 621,* 114–118.

Gowers, S., Crisp, A., Joughin, N., & Bhat, A. (1991). Premenarcheal anorexia nervosa. *Journal of Child Psychology and Psychiatry, 32,* 515–524.

Haslam, D. (1986). *Eat it up!* London: Macdonald and Co.

Higgs, J., Goodyer, I., & Birch, J. (1989). Anorexia nervosa and food avoidance emotional disorder. *Archives of Disease in Childhood, 64,* 346–351.

Hsu, L.K.G., & Sobkiewicz, T.A. (1991). Body image disturbance: Time to abandon the concept for eating disorders. *International Journal of Eating Disorders, 10,* 15–30.

Irwin, M. (1981). Diagnosis of anorexia nervosa in children and the validity of DSM III. *American Journal of Psychiatry, 138,* 1382–1383.

Irwin, M. (1984). Early onset anorexia nervosa. *Southern Medical Journal, 77,* 611–614.

Jacobs, B. & Isaacs, S. (1986). Pre-pubertal anorexia nervosa: A retrospective controlled study. *Journal of Child Psychology and Psychiatry, 27,* 237–250.

Lask, B., Britten, C., Kroll, L., Magagna, J., & Tranter, M. (1991). Pervasive refusal in children. *Archives of Disease in Childhood, 66,* 866–869.

Lask, B. & Bryant-Waugh, R. (1986). Childhood onset anorexia nervosa. in R. Meadow (Ed.), *Recent advances in paediatrics* (No. 8, pp. 21–31). London: Churchill Livingstone.

Marshall, C. (1895). Fatal case in a girl of 11 years. *Lancet, i,* 817.

Russell, G. (1970). Anorexia nervosa: Its identity as an illness and its treatment. In J. Price (Ed.), *Modern trends in psychological medicine.* London: Butterworth.

Tanner, J., Whitehouse, R., & Takaishi, M. (1966). Standards from birth to maturity for height, weight, height velocity and weight velocity: British children, 1965, Parts 1 and 2. *Archives of Disease in Childhood, 41,* 454–471; 613–635.

Warren, W. (1968). A study of anorexia nervosa in young girls. *Journal of Child Psychology and Psychiatry, 9,* 27–40.

World Health Organization. (1979). *Manual of the international classification of diseases, injuries and causes of death, 9th revision.* Geneva: World Health Organization.

CHAPTER THREE

Physical Aspects

Abe Fosson, Rose de Bruyn, and Shanthi Thomas

INTRODUCTION

The physical aspects of eating disorders require careful consideration for a number of reasons. First, the presenting weight loss may be due to other disorders that require exclusion. Second, there is the risk of potentially serious complications. Third, these complications can hinder psychological treatments, and their prevention, or at least early recognition and treatment, may minimize disruption. Finally, physical measures provide a useful guide to progress.

Given the severity of weight loss in anorexia nervosa—usually at least 25%—it is essential to exclude other serious and even life-threatening illnesses. Possibilities include malignancies, inflammatory bowel disease, malabsorption syndromes, mesenteric artery syndrome, diabetes, and chronic infections.

The majority of physical findings in anorexia nervosa are predominantly manifestations of the concomitant starvation and dehydration. The greater the starvation the more marked are the physical changes. Typically the findings are gradually disclosed at the initial medical consultation. During the interview the doctor observes that the patient typically hides under loose long-sleeved blouses and baggy trousers, yet her emaciated state is betrayed by pallor and the lack of buccal (cheek) fat that normally smoothes over the facial contours. Preparation for the ensuing physical examination is regularly heralded by resistance to undressing, which culminates in anger and a lack of co-operation.

On examination, patients with anorexia nervosa appear wasted with gaunt faces, thin limbs, protruding joints, poor peripheral circulation, skin discoloration and sunken abdomens. They seem not to be in distress, but vital signs are abnormal: For example, breathing is deep, sometimes with the sweet smell of acetone (due to ketosis resulting from cellular starvation), the pulse is slow and the temperature and blood pressure are low. The skin may feel cold, dry, rough, and often there is excess fine hair especially on the back, known as "lanugo". Scalp hair may appear dull while facial features are angular and eyes sunken. The teeth may be pitted, eroded and decayed from gastric acid during vomiting. The ribs protrude and there is a loss of secondary sexual characteristics such as axillary and pubic hair, and the breasts, hips and buttocks lose their contours. Though strength is diminished, reflexes and co-ordination are normal.

Although some of these findings, such as lanugo hair, are characteristic of anorexia nervosa, and the child's behaviour is often very revealing, the clinician cannot positively exclude other disorders by physical examination alone. It is wise to screen for other disorders with the use of blood and urine analysis, and diagnostic imaging. (These are discussed later in this chapter.) If the results of these tests are within normal limits or compatible with starvation, and standard diagnostic criteria for anorexia nervosa or other eating disorders are met, then it is reasonable to assume that no other disorder is present. It is important for the doctor to maintain control of the diagnostic process and ensure exclusion of organic disease but equally, unnecessary investigation should be avoided. Eliciting from the parents specific disease concerns and excluding these is helpful, especially if linked to a clear statement that this is likely to be an eating disorder. The end-point of physical investigation needs to be clearly defined.

PHYSICAL COMPLICATIONS OF ANOREXIA NERVOSA

Serious medical complications are quite common early in the course of anorexia nervosa. During the initial year of symptoms, up to 55% of patients have been found to require hospitalisation for medical complications (Palla & Litt, 1988). Cardiovascular complications are the most serious; in the early phases of the illness ventricular dysrhythmias and, during refeeding, congestive heart failure may be fatal. Bradycardia and electrocardiogram abnormalities are seen in up to 75% of patients. Among those hospitalised over 60% have postural hypotension and dizziness or occasionally syncope. Hypothermia is present in over half the patients. Feeling bloated after eating and constipation are very common and reflect gastrointestinal dysfunction. Rare but serious gastrointestinal complications such as oesophageal or gastric rupture, or pancreatitis, may be fatal. Despite their assertions to the contrary, these patients are physiologically vulnerable and need medical supervision.

Growth Impairment

The physical compensatory responses to self-starvation are:

1. The conservation of energy through the suspension of weight gain or weight loss, slowing or cessation of linear growth, and at times decreased motor activity; and
2. The mobilisation of stored nutrients through the catabolism of liver glycogen, adipose tissue lipids, and muscle tissue protein. Tissues are treated differentially when growth is suppressed by malnutrition; brain growth (head circumference) is most protected, linear growth has next priority, and weight increments the lowest priority.

The exact nature and extent of physiologic responses to self-starvation vary with patients' physical maturity as well as the severity of calorie restriction. The degree of physical insult for a given level of dietary inadequacy is inversely related to age until full physical maturity is attained. This waning vulnerability reflects decreasing growth and activity levels plus increasing physiological reserves of fluids, energy, and protein. During times of food abundance, children's ability to maintain high consumption without developing obesity is seen as an advantage by many adults. However, in the context of famine or self-starvation the underlying high nutritional requirements are exposed as one of the physiological risk factors of youth.

In most individuals, growth is predominantly governed by genetic factors. Ultimate body size, growth velocity, pubertal growth spurt, and the cessation of linear growth are genetically programmed and only occasionally or modestly influenced by disease or nutritional factors. Normal childhood growth is marked by four general features:

1. High velocities during infancy that slowly fall through the remainder of the first decade of life;
2. A brief period of accelerated growth commencing early in the second decade of life and heralding puberty;

3. An irreversible termination of linear growth towards the middle of the second decade of life when the long bones mature; and

4. A fully developed adult conformation by the end of the second decade of life through continued growth of muscular and adipose tissue.

Since the usual age of onset of anorexia nervosa is during the second decade, growth is much at risk. The usual onset of puberty is around 11 years in girls and 13 years in boys. Average pre-pubertal increases in weight and height for boys and girls are 2–3 kgs and 5–6 cms per year. A marked acceleration in weight gain and a modest acceleration in linear growth is seen in both sexes in early adolescence with average increments for girls of 4 kgs and 6–7 cms per year and for boys 6 kgs and 6–7 cms (Nelson, Behrman, & Vaughan, 1987). Starvation during these periods adversely affects ultimate adult height because long bones continue to mature, although growing at a slower pace or even not at all. Once full maturity of the long bones has been attained, further linear growth is impossible, even if nutrition becomes adequate. Thus attempts to recover "lost" height through adequate nutrition are generally futile after age 13.5 in girls and 16 years in boys. In the management of individual patients, estimates of bone age from hand and long bone X-rays provide useful guidance for growth potential. On the other hand, weight changes remain reversible throughout life as many dieting adults are painfully aware.

In clinical practice, growth can be measured by skin-fold thickness over the posterior upper arm, chest and head circumference, height and weight. Although body size and make-up are best determined by volume and density measurements, these are cumbersome and impractical. Body measurements take on much more meaning when compared to those of a peer group via anthropometric graphs (commonly called growth charts) because multiple age groups are plotted on one graph to form a smooth curve (Tanner, Whitehouse, & Takaishi, 1966). Since anthropometric graphs have been constructed by cross-sectional measurements of large groups of healthy children, an individual's dimensions can be expressed as a percentile, i.e. as larger than a percentage of healthy peers. A child whose height and weight is less than 95% of the same age population is considered "wasted". In both situations, a search for causal factors is indicated.

An alternate method for operationalising the term "wasted" is Cole's growth assessment slide rule (Cole, Donnet, & Stanfield, 1981). The slide rule is based on Tanner-Whitehouse standards for British children and can be used to calculate weight for length for ages birth to 19 years (Tanner et al., 1966). Using this approach, any child less than 80% of expected weight for height (100% being normal) is considered wasted.

Long-term outcome for body dimensions are only partially known. In large series weights at follow-up are near ideal in 54–87% of patients (Swift, 1982). Among children with early onset anorexia nervosa, 14% have been found to be over the ideal of 100% weight for height and 11% less than 80% (wasted) at follow-up (Bryant-Waugh et al., 1988). Of 19 early onset patients followed up at a mean of 9.5 years from the onset of the illness only 2 had reached average height, while 7 had failed to reach the third percentile (Russell, 1985).

Physiological Decompensation : Energy Reserves

Small reserves of energy and fat are typical of childhood except during infancy. Newborns are prepared for a three-day fast (until mother's milk comes in) and year-old infants have even higher portions of fat. However, primary-school-age children are neither chubby cheeked nor prepared for a fast. Fat stores fail to keep up with general growth during early childhood and by age six years they reach a nadir. Subsequently fat slowly reaccumulates until adult percentages are reached in mid-adolescence. Thus the early period of susceptibility to anorexia nervosa is also an age when body fat and therefore internal energy is in relatively short supply.

The status of fat stores is important during fasts because of concomitant metabolic changes (Guyton, 1986). At these times tissues of the body are broken down (catabolism) to supply the necessary energy to sustain vital functions. Most of the energy is supplied in the form of ketone bodies which are released by the breakdown of fat. All the organs of the body can use ketone bodies as substrate except the brain which must have glucose. Initially glucose is supplied from liver stores of glycogen but in a few days these are exhausted. As glycogen stores diminish, muscle cells begin to break down their protein and convert it to glucose; thus sustaining the brain and placing the body in negative nitrogen balance. The brain slowly converts to metabolism of ketone bodies over several weeks of fasting. This shift greatly enhances the conservation of muscle protein and strength. Since ketone bodies are small, volatile compounds, they are excreted through the lungs and give breath the sweet smell of acetone. Ultimately all body-energy stores are exhausted, vital functions cannot be supported, and death ensues.

Dehydration

Dehydration is present when the body contains inadequate water to sustain normal volumes of fluid compartments, e.g. blood, interstitial fluid (between cells), and intracellular fluid (within cells). Dehydration is important because it can lead to renal failure and eventually to cardiovascular shock and death. Fluids, water and salts are routinely consumed and lost during the course of a normal day. Dehydration usually results from abnormal fluid losses, i.e. vomiting, diarrhoea or diuresis, but may result from inadequate fluid intake or a combination of the two. Since children with anorexia nervosa abuse emetics, diuretics and laxatives (Fosson, Knibbs, Bryant-Waugh, & Lask, 1987), dehydration and electrolyte disturbances are likely to occur and one must be ever watchful for these complications, especially if a child's physical status deteriorates rapidly. Accordingly, familiarity with the physical signs of water imbalance and impending or overt dehydration is important. They are: crying without tears, decreased urine output, very rapid weight loss, sunken eyes (the opposite of under-eye bags), loss of skin turgor (failure of the skin to quickly recover from its former contour when the skin over the shoulder is gently pulled, firmly pressed between the thumb and forefinger, and then released), slowed capillary filling (more than two seconds for the pink colour to return to a compressed and released finger or palm), weak pulse, and low blood pressure. All of these signs of dehydration disappear within 48 hours of the institution of adequate oral or intravenous fluid therapy.

Children are much more susceptible to dehydration than adults because of their high daily turnover of fluids (Nelson et al., 1987). For example, the daily turnover of water is 25% of total body water in infancy and down to only 6% in adults. The body compensates for limited fluid intake or abnormal losses by restricting fluid losses in the urine, perspiration and bowel movements. However, persistent fluid loss eventually leads to dehydration, and this occurs two or three hours faster in children than in adults.

Delayed Sexual Maturation

Most aspects of reproduction are controlled by the hypothalamic region of the brain (Wilson & Foster, 1985). In exerting this control, the hypothalamus is responsive to diurnal cycles of light and darkness, other visual input, certain odours, psychological stress and body size. For example, psychological stress may be associated with the transient cessation of menstruation (some college women are amenorrhoeic while away from home during the academic year), and body size accounts for obese girls entering puberty younger than normal weight girls who in turn tend to enter puberty earlier than thin girls.

Hypothalamic regulation is mediated by the central endocrine gland (pituitary) and is responsive to feedback from the gonads. The complex communication patterns and relationships between the brain, the endocrine glands, and the reproductive organs are not completely understood. However, the most important communication pattern appears to be negative feedback, e.g. pituitary stimulation of the ovary causes a return signal that inhibits the pituitary. These relationships are analogous to a home furnace, hall thermostat, and room temperature; the thermostat turns off the furnace when the room temperature has risen sufficiently and turns it on when the temperature falls.

A popular theory of sexual maturation is based on changing hypothalamic sensitivity to levels of sexual hormones circulating in the blood stream (Wilson & Foster, 1985). Before sexual maturity, these levels are very low because of insignificant production by the gonads and little production by other organs. Nonetheless, these levels are sufficient to stimulate the exquisitely sensitive hypothalamus to constantly inhibit pituitary stimulation or reproductive organs—continuous negative feedback. During childhood, hypothalamic sensitivity to these chemicals seems slowly to decrease until the pituitary is released to stimulate the gonads, which in turn stimulate auxiliary sexual organs. In women, this stimulation becomes cyclic in the following way:

1. The less sensitive hypothalamus does not recognise basal levels of circulating sexual hormones.
2. Brain inhibition of the pituitary decreases.
3. The pituitary begins to release hormones into the blood stream that stimulate the growth and activity of the ovaries.
4. The ovaries increase their secretion of sexual hormones which cause development of secondary sexual characteristics and also initiate the inhibition of the pituitary via the hypothalamus.
5. Pituitary stimulation of the ovaries decreases.
6. Ovarian sexual hormones production decreases, and
7. The hypothalamus senses falling sexual hormone levels and releases the pituitary from inhibition.

In anorexia nervosa, the normal course of sexual maturation is disturbed as a result of malnutrition. Weight loss of 10–15% delays menarche, retards pubertal development in the pre-menarcheal girl, and causes secondary amenorrhoea in the post-menarcheal female. Mature breasts and pelvic contours depend heavily on adipose tissue, and these aspects of mature female conformation are lost. Auxiliary and pubic hair becomes coarse and pigmented, or depleted.

Knowledge of the outcome for fertility in children with anorexia nervosa is incomplete. However, our own long-term outcome study revealed that about 31% of the patients continued to have amenorrhoea, 14% had irregular periods, while 55% had regular menstruation (Bryant-Waugh et al., 1988).

INVESTIGATIONS

These fall broadly into two categories:
  (a) Imaging;
  (b) Laboratory findings.

The Role of Imaging

Imaging children with eating disorders may seem an unlikely pursuit, yet in recent years it has proved a valuable adjunct in the treatment of anorexia nervosa. The use of ultrasound in the investigation of disorders of puberty has developed into a reliable non-invasive method of determining gonadotrophic, ovarian and uterine maturity. It can also assist in the prediction of healthy target weight.

The value of cranial computed tomography (CT) findings requires further investigation. Preliminary results suggest that the rapidity and degree of weight loss determines the extent of abnormality on cranial CT scan.

Bone Age.   This is one parameter used in the measurement of growth and is the radiological assessment of skeletal maturity. Several methods have been devised; the most widely used method of determining bone age is the Greulich and Pyle (1959) atlas. This is based on the radiographs of the left hands of white children from Cleveland, USA. Social, racial and economic factors are known to influence the rate of skeletal maturation, and the atlas when applied to British children will result in an under-estimation of skeletal maturity. The advantage of the atlas is its acceptance throughout the world.

There have as yet been no systematic studies of bone age in early onset anorexia nervosa. Dreizen, Spirakis, and Stone (1967) compared 30 undernourished and 30 well-nourished girls from early childhood to early adulthood. Using bone age and height measurements they found that chronic malnutrition slowed the rate of skeletal maturation, delayed menarche, and prolonged the growth period. The mean difference between groups for skeletal age at menarche was 38 months, but for chronological age 14.2 months. In our own sample of 14 children with anorexia nervosa between the ages of 9 and 15, bone-age delay has varied from none to 54 months. The longer the malnutrition the greater the bone-age delay.

Ultrasound.   An important advance in recent years has been the development of high resolution ultrasound scanners and their use in the investigation of patients with menstrual disturbances (Colle, Calabet, Sanciaume, & Battin, 1984). A 5 or 3.5 MHz sector scanner with a long focus is optimal. Operator skill and familiarity with normal ovarian and uterine development and appearance is crucial for the successful use of this technique in children with eating disorders. An abdominal ultrasound examination is cheap, non-invasive, quick and simple to perform. As there is no radiation, examinations can be frequently repeated. The only requirement for a successful investigation is a full bladder. By filling the bladder, the bowel is displaced from the pelvis and the bladder is used as an acoustic window to image the uterus and ovaries. Increasingly, vaginal scanning is being used in adults to monitor ovarian morphology as it offers even better visualisation and a full bladder is not a requirement.

The value of ultrasound lies in observing the effects of past nutrition on the ovaries and uterus, thereby allowing an easy method of assessing endocrine status. Ultrasound is readily accepted by children and adolescents and the visualisation of their regressed reproductive organs on the monitor can be a powerful stimulus to weight gain.

The ovary is not quiescent in childhood. There is evidence that from foetal life there is continuous turnover and increase in the number of follicles. It is now well recognised that the ovaries pass through a number of definable stages in their maturation through puberty (Adams et al., 1985; Salardi et al., 1985; Stanhope, Adams, Jacobs, & Brook, 1985) (Fig. 3.1).

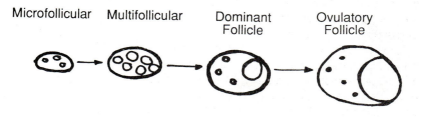

Microfollicular   Multifollicular   Dominant   Ovulatory
                                        Follicle   Follicle

FIG. 3.1. Schematic diagram of the stages of ovarian development from a small pre-pubertal amorphous appearance to the mature ovary producing ovulatory follicles.

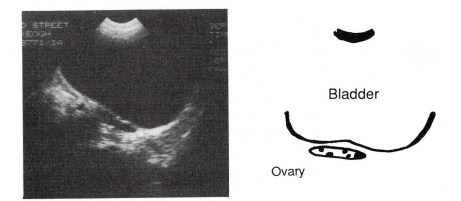

FIG. 3.2. Stage 1. Longitudinal ultrasound scan of pre-pubertal ovary. The ovary is small with only a few 2–4 mm follicles evident. The accompanying line diagram shows the orientation.

Pre-pubertal ovaries (Stage 1) are small with a number of 2–4mm diameter follicles evident (Fig. 3.2). This stage has been termed the microfollicular ovary. There is a gradual increase in size and number of follicles so that after 8.5 years (and before physical signs of puberty), the ovary has a multifollicular appearance (Stage 2). This is defined as more than 6 follicles of 4mm diameter (Fig. 3.3). Breast development

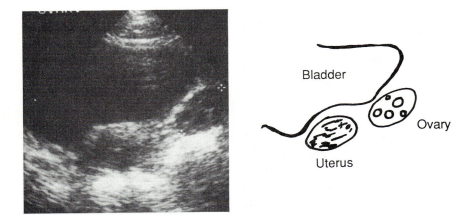

FIG. 3.3. Stage 2. The multifollicular ovary, defined as more than 6 follicles of 4mm in diameter. The accompanying line diagram shows the orientation.

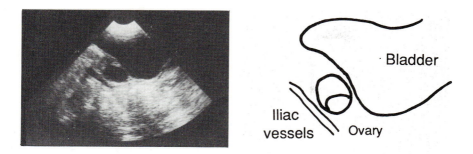

FIG. 3.4. Stage 3 or 4. This ovary shows the development of a dominant follicle. Stage 3 is the developing dominant follicle measuring up to 1.5 cm in diameter and Stage 4 is the further enlargement of the follicle to the point of ovulation.

occurs after the multi-follicular appearance. The ovarian volume of Stages 1 and 2 are between 2–4 cubic centimetres.

Stage 3 is characterised by the development of a "dominant" follicle, but less than 1.5 cms. diameter (Fig. 3.4). The follicle grows about 2mm per day and most follicles ovulate when they reach a diameter between 1.9 and 2.3 cm (Stage 4). At this point ovarian volume exceeds 4cc.

The uterus also undergoes changes in shape, size and content with maturation. The pre-pubertal uterus has a teardrop shape where the cervix-to-corpus ratio is increased and the body is long and thin (Fig. 3.5). As the uterus passes through puberty, it enlarges and changes to

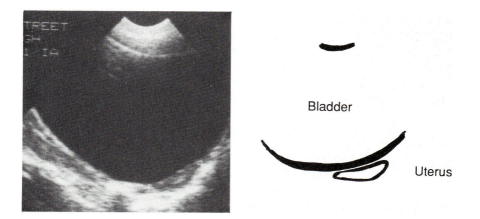

FIG. 3.5. The small pre-pubertal uterus lying behind the bladder. The cervical corpus ratio is increased giving the "typical teardrop" appearance.

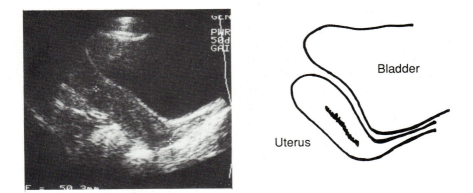

FIG. 3.6. Longitudinal scan of the uterus and bladder showing the normal adult appearance of the uterus. The corpus is developed giving the uterus the typical pear shape. When present, the endometrium can be identified as a hyperechoic (white) midline echo.

the adult pear-shaped configuration, with an increased corpus-to-cervical ratio (Fig. 3.6). The endometrium can be seen clearly on the ultrasound as a midline hyper-reflective (white) line known as an endometrial echo. The uterine volume between the ages of 2 and 14 years is usually in the range of 2–14 cubic centimetres, while the adult volume range is 15–25 cubic centimetres.

Treasure et al. (1988) have used ultrasonography to establish a target weight in adults. They have shown that weight loss results in regression of the uterus and ovaries to pre- or pubertal size and appearances. They found the changes in ovarian morphology resembled those of normal pubertal development but on a more rapid timescale. At low weight adult anorectics had ovarian volumes similar to those of 8–12-year-olds. This evidence supports neuro-endocrine findings of a regression of the hypothalamic-pituitary-gonadal axis to a pubertal pattern with weight loss.

Conversely, an increase in follicle stimulating hormone (FSH) was the first response to weight gain and was related to the change from an amorphous to a multi-follicular pattern (Tucker, Adams, Mason, & Jacobs, 1984). The later luteinising hormone (LH) rise was associated with ovarian growth and the development of a dominant follicle, whereas uterine growth was later associated with the oestradiol produced from the dominant follicle.

Ultrasound was used to establish whether weight gain was sufficient and to assist in determining healthy target weight. Despite small numbers, ultrasound appearances at discharge predicted outcome. Of those discharged with a multifollicular pattern, 41% were readmitted to hospital having relapsed compared with only 16% of those who were discharged with a dominant follicle on ultrasound. This suggests that discharge should be delayed until ultrasound reveals a Stage 3 or Stage 4 pattern of ovarian development.

In our experience, those teenagers with anorexia nervosa who develop secondary amenorrhoea show similar findings. The more prolonged the illness, the more severe the regression. One of our patients had an acute illness with rapid weight loss. She had quiescent ovaries while her uterus retained an adult configuration.

The generally younger patients with primary amenorrhoea show a delay in ovarian and uterine development with a persistence of pre-pubertal appearances. It is noteworthy that children with weight loss due to other conditions (e.g. food refusal or food avoidance emotional disorder—see chapter 2) demonstrate a similar delay in pubertal development. It may be that delayed puberty observed in developing countries is one of the costs of poor nutrition whereas the trend towards earlier puberty in Europe and the USA may be explained by improved health and nutrition.

Computerised Tomography.   There have been increasing numbers of reports over the last decade of cerebral atrophy in adults with anorexia nervosa even though abnormal neurological findings are rare (Datlof, Coleman, Forbes, & Kreipe, 1986; Dolan, Mitchell, & Wakeling, 1988; Lankenau et al., 1985; Nussbaum, Shenker, Marc, & Klein, 1980; Palazidou, Robinson, & Lishman, 1990). The use of computerised tomography (CT) imaging in this group is not routine and studies are still experimental. However, although numbers are small, we have detected cerebral atrophy in some children with considerable weight loss.

The abnormalities found include enlargement of the lateral and/or third ventricles and widening of the superficial cortical sulci. About half of the anorectics studied by Nussbaum and colleagues revealed ventricular enlargement. In their study, those with ventricular enlargement had superficial cortical sulci widening. However, other studies by Kohlmeyer, Lehmkuhl, and Poutska (1983) and Enzmen and Lane (1977) did not correlate. The latter investigators found enlargement of the cortical sulci in nearly all of their patients studied. Figure 3.7 demonstrates the superficial cortical widening (image on right) and dilation of the cerebral ventricles (image on left) as seen in cerebral atrophy. Figure 3.8 shows a normal scan for comparison purposes.

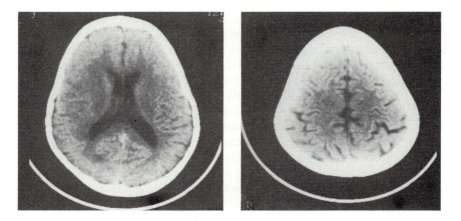

FIG. 3.7. Cranial CT in anorexia nervosa. The image on the left demonstrates the ventricular dilation, and the image on the right cortical atrophy with widening of the sulci.

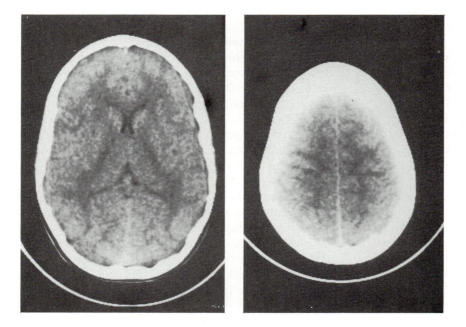

FIG. 3.8. A cranial CT on a normal patient showing similar coronal sections for comparison.

In the comparison between those patients with more rapid weight loss and a greater absolute or relative weight loss and those without, studies have shown an increase in the abnormal findings on computed tomographic scanning (Lankenau et al., 1985). On the other hand, the duration of weight loss did not correlate with CT abnormality. Clinical features such as bradycardia, hypotension, leucopenia or amenorrhoea did not predict CT changes. Similarly, age at presentation, diuretic and laxative abuse, excessive exercise and bulimia failed to show significant associations with CT abnormalities. Only hypothermia correlated significantly with cerebral atrophy. IQ scores were not significantly different in those anorectic patients with lateral ventricular enlargement compared to those with normal CT scans (Lankenau et al., 1985).

Partial or total remission of the CT findings in eating disordered patients has been described following weight gain. The mechanism of this sometimes reversible dilation of cerebral spaces is poorly understood. Postulates include decrease in serum protein due to malnutrition and shift of fluids from the intravascular to the subarachnoid spaces. However, total serum proteins are often found to be in the normal range in this group of patients (Heinz, Martinez, & Haenggeli, 1977). Increased glucocorticoids and catabolism of proteins has also been suggested. Similar atrophic changes have been described in Cushings Disease, steroid therapy and alcoholism. Documented increase in glucocorticoids also occurs in anorexia nervosa. Other hypotheses include alteration in cerebro-spinal-fluid pressure dynamics, or regeneration of neural cells. The clinical value of diagnosing these abnormalities on CT remains debatable. Certainly further investigation into the pathological mechanisms and their clinical significance is required.

Possibly the most exciting prospects for the future lie in positron emission tomography (PET) in the investigation of cerebral metabolism and relating this to abnormal findings currently found on CT. Several papers have been published on a small sample of adults with anorexia nervosa and bulimia describing the changes in metabolism before and after weight gain (Emrich et al., 1984; Herholz et al., 1987; Krieg et al., 1986; Wu et al., 1990). Significant hypermetabolism of the caudate bilaterally, as well as significant cortical hypermetabolism, was found. These normalised with weight gain.

Laboratory Findings

A wide range of biochemical changes have been described in eating disorders, although there is little information specifically relating to early onset subjects.

Urea, Creatinine and Electrolytes.   Raised, normal and low values of urea have all been reported in anorexia nervosa (Umeki, 1988; Mira, Stewart, Vizzard, & Abraham, 1987), and are determined by levels of hydration and protein intake. The low levels of potassium and chloride and the alkalosis seen in anorexia nervosa are normally related to low fluid intake, vomiting, and diuretic and purgative abuse. Raised plasma creatinine, low creatinine and creatinine clearance seen in anorexia nervosa are partly due to decrease in muscle mass and partly due to renal micro-vascular changes (Boag et al., 1985).

Liver Function Tests.   Liver enzymes such as alanine transaminase (ALT), aspartate transaminase (AST), and alkaline phosphatase (ALP) are usually raised (Mira et al., 1987; Halmi & Falk, 1981) and less frequently gamma-glutamyl transpeptidase (GGT) levels are raised (Umeki, 1988). Total bilirubin does not usually rise. These changes probably reflect the fatty degeneration of the liver associated with malnutrition. Plasma albumin levels may be low or normal.

Biochemical Indices of Bone Metabolism.   Hypocalcaemia is not a frequent finding in anorexia nervosa, with mean calcium levels significantly higher than (Mira et al., 1987) or the same as control subjects (Fonseca et al., 1988). Phosphate levels may be normal (Fonseca et al., 1988) or low (Mira et al., 1987), and life-threatening hypophosphatemia has been reported in some patients (Sheridan, & Collins, 1983). There is evidence of hypovitaminosis D especially in countries where there is a deficiency of ultra-violet light (Fonseca et al., 1988), but parathyroid hormone levels are not abnormal. Low plasma levels of magnesium may be seen in some patients with anorexia nervosa (Fonseca & Havard, 1985), causing hypocalcaemia and hypokalaemia. In these cases magnesium replacement may prevent cardiac arrhythmias or failure.

Zinc.   Anecdotal reports of zinc deficiency in children with anorexia nervosa have been substantiated by Lask, Fosson, Thomas, and Rolfe (in press), but this seems to be due purely to malnutrition, and is readily reversed on refeeding.

Plasma Lipids.   Some increases in cholesterol levels have been reported, and the changes may be resistant to therapy and contribute in the long-term to increased risk of cardiovascular disease. The risk is aggravated by the increased platelet aggregation and A2 thromboxane release (Mikhailidis et al., 1986) seen in anorexia nervosa.

Hypothalamic–Pituitary–Ovarian Function. Gonadotrophin (luteinising hormone and follicle-stimulating hormone) levels in plasma are usually low in anorexia nervosa. The 24-hour pulsatile pattern in adult anorectics regresses to a pre-pubertal pattern (i.e. pulses more in sleep), but reverts to the adult pattern with weight restoration (Newman & Halmi, 1988). Indirect evidence also exists of increased dopamine secretion and disturbances in neuro-transmitters which can account for the changes in gonadotrophins.

Hypothalamic–Pituitary–Adrenal Function. Hypercortisolism is seen in anorexia nervosa. Both 24-hour mean plasma levels and 24-hour free urinary cortisol excretion are increased, and the cortisol production rate corrected for body surface area or body weight is also increased in anorexia nervosa. This is in contrast to hypercortisolism associated with other forms of malnutrition where the cortisol production rate is decreased. Plasma ACTH levels have been reported as low (Bliss & Migeon, 1957) or normal (Takahara et al., 1976). However, the ACTH and cortisol response to corticotrophin-releasing factor (CRF) is blunted, and is restored to normal only after long-term weight restoration (Gold, Gwirtsman, & Avgerinos, 1986; Hotta, Shibash, & Masuda, 1986). These studies therefore suggest a central hypothalamic defect with intact negative feed-back control at the level of the pituitary. Several workers have reported hypersecretion of CRF and postulated that this contributes to the behavioural disturbances seen in anorexia nervosa (Hotta et al., 1986; Gold et al., 1986; Kaye, Gwirtsman, & George, 1987).

Growth Hormone. Basal plasma levels of growth hormone are elevated in about a half of emaciated anorectics. There is also evidence that somatomedin-C levels are decreased and thus there is a diminished negative feed-back control of growth hormone secretion. Growth hormone response to dopamine and insulin-induced hypoglycaemia is attenuated (Aro, Lamberger, & Pelkonen, 1977; Blickle et al., 1984; Casper, Davis, & Pandy, 1977; Naka et al., 1987; Sherman & Halmi, 1977), and there is a paradoxical increase in growth hormone levels in response to glucose load. Some workers have reported disturbances in dopamine receptor impairment (Halmi & Sherman, 1977). Thus there is some evidence of disturbances of central neurotransmitter function in anorexia nervosa that may account for some of the disturbances in growth hormone secretion.

Hypothalamic–Pituitary–Thyroid Function. Total thyroxine (T4) levels are within the normal range although anorectic population means may be lower than the control population. Triodothyronine (T3) levels are usually low with increased levels of reverse triodothyronine (T3) (Burman et al., 1977; Leslie et al., 1978; Miyai et al., 1975; Moore & Mills, 1979). In spite of the low T3 levels the thyrotropin (TH) levels are not elevated, simulating the pattern seen in chronically ill patients. The TSH response to thyroid releasing hormone is delayed as seen in hypothalamic dysfunction. The disturbances in thyroid function seen in anorectics are primarily a consequence of malnutrition. However, a hypothalamic component cannot be ruled out.

Argine Vasopressin. Anorectic patients usually demonstrate an inability to concentrate urine and the vasopressin response to hypertonic saline infusion is subnormal (Vigersky, Loriaux, & Anderson, 1976; Gold, Kaye, & Robertson, 1983).

Haematological Findings   Anaemia usually of mild degree is not an unusual finding in anorexia nervosa (Mant & Faragher, 1972). Folate levels are low in some. Iron stores in the bone marrow are depleted with low serum iron concentrations. Leucopenia has been found in about half of patients, some showing pancytopaenia and hypoplastic anaemia (Warren & Vande Weile, 1973).

Conclusion

Although the changes in biochemical parameters are not specific for anorexia nervosa, future research into the neurochemical aspects of anorexia should help in the understanding of the clinical changes associated with the disorder.

PHYSICAL PARAMETERS AS OUTCOME MEASURES DURING TREATMENT

Serial biomedical appraisals of the child with anorexia nervosa are useful outcome measures in spite of their limited scope. For example, ingestion of calories can be quantified by 24-hour calorie counts. These can be compared with the individual patient's needs for maintenance and growth and the percentage used to monitor improvement in intake. This monitoring system is subject, of course, to manipulation by the patient through food hiding and self-induced emesis.

Changes in physical dimensions provide more useful serial data that are easily obtained and less subject to patient manipulation. Weight is the only external dimension that changes rapidly enough to be useful.

Data from serial weights can be used directly or compared with normal peers' weights or weight for height. It is often useful to establish target weights and to plot interval changes on a graph.

Other physical measures to plot progress include serum protein and albumin levels. These reflect the state of nutrition and are useful for acute and chronic monitoring of general nutritional status, since metabolic complications disappear with improvement (and reappear with relapses). Monitoring the state of hydration by serial physical examination, and infrequent serum electrolytes determinations, may also be helpful. Similarly, sequential urinalysis can document the presence of fasting-induced ketonuria.

In the longer term ultrasound imaging of the uterus shows changes in size toward adult status in the recovering female and may provide a useful long-term monitoring strategy, while blood levels of pituitary and gonadal-producing hormones fluctuate with remissions and exacerbations and can be useful as long-term monitoring data.

SUMMARY

The physical aspects of the early onset of eating disorders are summarised in Tables 3.1 to 3.3.

TABLE 3.1
Key physical changes

Weight loss
Dehydration
Slow pulse
Low blood pressure
Poor peripheral circulation
Cold extremities
Skin ulceration
Pallor
Lanugo hair
Amenorrhoea
Failure to develop, or loss of secondary sexual characteristics
Growth delay

TABLE 3.2
Imaging

Pelvic ultrasound scan shows immaturity or regression of uterine and ovarian development.

Computerised tomography (CT) shows cortical atrophy and ventricular enlargement.

TABLE 3.3
Laboratory investigations

Often raised	—	Liver enzymes
		Plasma growth hormone
Often lowered	—	Haemoglobin
		White blood cells
		Serum potassium
		Plasma proteins
		Plasma gonadotrophins
		Plasma zinc
		Serum iron
Variable	—	Blood urea

REFERENCES

Adams, J., Franks, S., Polson, D.W., Mason, H.D., Abdulwahid, N., Tucker, M., Morris, D.V., Price, J., & Jacobs, H.S. (1985). Multifollicular ovaries; clinical and endocrine features and response to pulsatile gonadotrophin releasing hormone. *Lancet, ii,* 1375–1379.

Aro, A., Lamberger, B.A., & Pelkonen, R. (1977). Hypothalamic endocrine dysfunction in anorexia nervosa. *Acta Endocrinology, 85,* 673.

Blickle, J.F., Reville, P., Stephan, F., Meyer, P., Demangeat, C., & Sapin, R. (1984). The role of insulin, glucagon and growth hormone in the regulation of plasma glucose and free fatty acid levels in anorexia nervosa. *Hormonal Metabolism Research, 16,* 336.

Bliss, E. & Migeon, C.J. (1957). Endocrinology in anorexia nervosa. *Journal of Clinical Endocrinology and Metabolism, 17,* 766.

Boag, F., Weerakoon, J., Ginsburgh, J., Havard, C.W.H., & Dandona, P. (1985). Diminished creatinine clearance in anorexia nervosa: Reversal with weight gain. *Journal of Clinical Pathology, 60,* 63.

Bryant-Waugh, R., Knibbs, J., Fosson, A., Kaminski, Z., & Lask, B. (1988). Long-term follow-up of patients with early onset anorexia nervosa. *Archives of Disease in Childhood, 63,* 5–9.

Burman, K.D., Vigersky, B.A., Loriaux, D.L., Strum, D., Djuh, Y.Y., Wright, F.D., & Wartofsky, L. (1977). Investigations concerning thyroxine deiodinative pathways in patients with anorexia nervosa. In R. Vigersky (Ed.), *Anorexia nervosa* (p. 255). New York: Raven Press.

Casper, R.C., David, J.M., & Pandy, G.N. (1977). The effect of nutritional status and weight change on hypothalamic function tests in anorexia nervosa. In R. Vigersky (Ed.), *Anorexia nervosa* (p. 137). New York: Raven Press.

Cole, R., Donnet, M., & Stanfield, J., (1981). Weight-for-height indices to assess nutritional status—a new index on a slide-rule. *American Journal of Clinical Nutrition, 34,* 1935.

Colle, M., Calabet, A., Sanciaume, C., & Battin, J., (1984). Contribution of pelvic ultrasonography (PUS) to endocrine investigation in girls. *Paediatric Research, 18,* 113.

Datlof, S., Coleman, P.D., Forbes, G.B., & Kreipe, R.E. (1986). Ventricular dilation of CAT scans of patients with anorexia nervosa. *American Journal of Psychiatry, 143,* 96–97.

Dolan, R.J., Mitchell, J., & Wakeling, A. (1988). Structural brain changes in patients with anorexia nervosa. *Psychological Medicine, 18,* 349–353.

Dreizen, S., Spirakis, C., & Stone, R. (1967). A comparison of skeletal growth and maturation in undernourished and well nourished girls before and after menarche. *The Journal of Paediatrics, 70,* 256–263.

Emrich, H.M., Pahl, J.H., Herholz, K., et al. (1984). PET investigation in anorexia nervosa: Normal glucose metabolism during pseudoatrophy of the brain. In K.M. Pirke & D. Ploog (Eds.), *The psychology of anorexia nervosa* (pp. 172–178). Berlin: Springer-Verlag.

Enzman, D.R. & Lane, B. (1977). Cranial computed tomography findings in anorexia nervosa. *Journal of Computerised Tomography, 1,* 410–414.

Fonseca, V. & Havard, C.W.H. (1985). Electrolyte disturbance and cardiac failure with hypomagnesaemia in anorexia nervosa. *British Medical Journal, 291,* 1680–1682.

Fonseca, V.A., D'Souza, V., Houlder, S., Thomas, M., Wakeling, A., & Dandona, P. (1988). Vitamin D deficiency and low osteocalcin concentrations in anorexia nervosa. *Journal of Clinical Pathology, 41*(2), 195–197.

Fosson, A., Knibbs, J., Bryant-Waugh, R., & Lask, B. (1987). Early onset anorexia nervosa. *Archives of Disease in Childhood, 62,* 114–118.

Gold, P.W., Kaye, W., Robertson, G.L., & Ebert, M. (1983). Abnormalities in plasma and cerebro-spinal fluid arginine vasopressin in patients with anorexia nervosa. *New England Journal of Medicine, 308,* 1117.

Gold, P.W., Gwirtsman, H., Avgerinos, P.C., Nieman, L.K., Galluci, W.T., Kaye, W., Jimerson, D., Ebert, M., Rittmaster, R., & Loriaux, D.L.,. (1986). Abnormal hypothalamic-pituitary-adrenal function in anorexia nervosa. Pathophysiologic mechanisms in underweight and weight-corrected patients. *New England Journal of Medicine, 314,* 1335.

Greulich, W.W. & Pyle, S.I. (1959). *Radiographic atlas of skeletal development of the hand and the wrist* (2nd ed.). Stanford University.

Guyton, A.C. (1986). *Textbook of medical physiology* (7th ed.). Philadelphia: Saunders.

Halmi, K.A. & Sherman, B.S. (1977). Dopaminergic and serotonergic regulation of growth hormone secretion in anorexia nervosa. *Psychopharmacological Bulletin, 13,* 63.

Halmi, K.A. & Falk, J.R. (1981). Common psychological changes in anorexia nervosa. *International Journal of Eating Disorders, 1,* 16–27.

Heinz, E.R., Martinez, J., & Haenggeli, A. (1977). Reversibility of cerebral atrophy in anorexia and Cushings syndrome. *Journal of Computerised Tomography, 1,* 415–418.

Herholz, K., Krieg, J.C., Emrich, H.M., Pawlik, G., Beil, C., Pirke, K.M., Pahl, J.J., Wagner, R., Weinhard, K., & Ploog, D. (1987). Regional cerebral glucose metabolism in anorexia nervosa measured by positron emission tomography. *Biological Psychiatry, 22,* 43–51.

Hotta, M., Shibash, T., Masuda, A., Imaki, T., Demura, H., Ling, N., & Shizume, K. (1986). The responses of plasma adrenocorticotropin and cortisol to corticotropin-releasing hormone (CRH) and cerebrospinal fluid immunoreactive CRH in AN patients. *Journal of Clinical Endocrinology and Metabolism, 62,* 319–324.

Kaye, W.H., Gwirtsman, H.E., & George, D.T. (1987). Elevated cerebrospinal fluid levels of immuno-reactive corticotropin-releasing hormone in anorexia nervosa: Relation to state of nutrition, adrenal function, and intensity of depression. *Journal of Clinical Endocrinology and Metabolism, 64,* 203.

Kohlemeyer, K., Lehmkuhl, G., & Poutska, F. (1983). Computed tomography of anorexia nervosa. *American Journal of Nuclear Imaging, 4,* 437–438.

Krieg, J.C., Emrich, H.M., Backmund, H., et al. (1986). Brain morphology (CT) and cerebral metabolism (PET) in anorexia nervosa. In E. Ferrari & F. Brambilla (Eds.), *Disorders of eating behaviour: A psychoneuroendocrine approach.* New York: Pergamon Press.

Lankenau, H., Swigar, M.E., Bhimani, S., Luchins, D., & Quinlau, D.M. (1985). Cranial CT scans in eating disorder patients and controls. *Comprehensive Psychiatry, 26,* 136–147.

Lask, B., Fosson, A., Thomas, S., & Rolfe, U. (In press). *Zinc deficiency and anorexia nervosa in children.*

Leslie, R.D.G., Isaacs, A.J., Gomez, J., et al. (1978). Hypothalamo-pituitary-thyroid function in anorexia nervosa: Influence of weight gain. *British Medical Journal, 2,* 256.

Mant, M.J. & Faragher, B.S. (1972). The haematology of anorexia nervosa. *British Journal of Haematology, 23,* 737.

Mikhailidis, D.P., Barradas, M.A., De Souza, V., Jeremy, J.Y., Wakeling, A., & Dandona, P. (1986). Adrenaline-induced hyperaggregability of platelets and enhanced thromboxane release in anorexia nervosa. *Postaglandin Leukotrophin Medicina, 24,* 27–34.

Mira, M., Stewart, P.M., Vizzard, J., & Abraham, S. (1987). Biochemical abnormalities in anorexia nervosa and bulimia. *Annals Clinical Biochemistry, 24,* 29–35.

Miyai, K., Yamamoto, T., Azukizawa, M., Ishibashi, K., & Kumahara, Y. (1975). Serum thyroid hormones and thyrotropin in anorexia nervosa. *Journal of Clinical Endocrinology and Metabolism, 40,* 334.

Moore, R. & Mills, I.H. (1979). Serum T3 and T4 levels in patients with anorexia nervosa showing transient hyperthyroidism during weight gain. *Clinical Endocrinology, 10,* 443.

Naka, Y., Koh, T., Konoshita, F., et al. (1987). The prolactin, growth hormone and cortisol responses to insulin induced hypoglycaemia in anorexia nervosa. *International Journal of Eating Disorders, 6,* 357.

Nelson, W., Behrman, R., & Vaughan, V., (1987). *Nelson textbook of paediatrics* (13th Ed.). Philadelphia: Saunders.

Newman, M.M. & Halmi, K.A. (1988). The endocrinology of anorexia nervosa and bulimia nervosa. *Neurologic Clinics, 6,* 195–212.

Nussbaum, M., Shenker, I.R., Marc, J., & Klein, M. (1980). Cerebral atrophy in anorexia nervosa. *Journal of Paediatrics, 96,* 867–869.

Palazidou, E., Robinson, P., & Lishman, W.A. (1990). Neuroradiological and neurophysiological assessment in anorexia nervosa. *Psychological Medicine, 20,* 521–527.

Palla, B. & Litt, I. (1988). Medical complications of eating disorders in adolescents. *Paediatrics, 81,* 613–623.

Russell, G. (1985). Pre-menarcheal anorexia nervosa and its sequelae. *Journal of Psychiatric Research, 19,* 363–369.

Salardi, S., Orsini, L.F., Cacciari, E., Bovicelli, L., Tassoni, P., & Reggiani, A. (1985). Pelvic ultrasonography in pre-menarcheal girls: Relation to puberty and sex hormone concentration. *Archives of Disease in Childhood, 60,* 120–125.

Sheridan, P.H. & Collins, M. (1983). Potentially life-threatening hypophosphatemia in anorexia nervosa. *Journal of Adolescent Health Care, 4,* 44–46.

Sherman, B.M. & Halmi, K.A. (1977). Effect of nutritional rehabilitation on hypothalamic-pituitary function in anorexia nervosa. In R. Vigersky (Ed.), *Anorexia Nervosa* (p. 211). New York: Raven Press.

Stanhope, R., Adams, J., Jacobs, H.S., & Brook, C.G.D. (1985). Ovarian ultrasound assessment in normal children, ideopathic precocious puberty, and during low dose pulsatile gonadotrophin releasing hormone treatment of hypogonadotrophic hypogonadism. *Archives of Disease in Childhood, 60,* 116–119.

Swift, W. (1982). The long-term outcome of early onset anorexia nervosa: A critical review. *Journal of the American Academy of Child Psychiatry, 21,* 38–46.

Takahara, H., Hosogi, H., Hasimoto, K., et al. (1976). Hypothalamic pituitary adrenal function in patients with anorexia nervosa. *Japanese Journal of Endocrinology, 23,* 451.

Tanner, J.M., Whitehouse, R.H., & Takaishi, M. (1966). Standards from birth to maturity for height, weight, height velocity and weight velocity: British children 1965. Parts 1 and 2. *Archives of Disease in Childhood, 41,* 454–613.

Treasure, J.L., Wheeler, M., King, E.A., Gordon, P.A.L., & Russell, G.F.M. (1988). Weight gain and reproductive function: Ultrasonographic and endocrine features in anorexia nervosa. *Clinical Endocrinology, 29,* 607–616.

Tucker, M., Adams, J., Mason, W.P., & Jacobs, H.J.S. (1984). Infertility, megalocystic and polycystic ovaries: Differential response to LHRH therapy. *Journal of Medical Science, 89,* 43–46.

Umeki, S. (1988). Biochemical abnormalities of the serum in anorexia nervosa. *Journal of Nervous and Mental Disorders, 176,* 503–506.

Vigersky, R.A., Loriaux, D.L., Anderson, A.E. et al. (1976). Anorexia nervosa behavioural and hypothalamic factors. *Journal of Clinical and Endocrinology and Metabolism, 5,* 517.

Warren, M.P. & Vande Weile, R.L. (1973). Clinical and metabolic features of anorexia nervosa. *American Journal of Obstetrics and Gynaecology, 117,* 435.

Wilson, J.D. & Foster, D.W. (1985). *Williams textbook of endocrinology.* Philadelphia: Saunders.

Wu, J.C., Hagman, J., Buchsbaum, M.S., Blinder, B., Derrfler, M., Tai, W.Y., Hazlett, E., & Sicotte, N. (1990). Great left cerebral hemispheric metabolism in bulimia assessed by positron emission tomography. *American Journal of Psychiatry, 147,* 309–312.

CHAPTER FOUR

Epidemiology

Rachel Bryant-Waugh

INTRODUCTION

Anorexia nervosa and related eating disorders are most commonly diagnosed in adolescent girls and young women, and a number of researchers have investigated incidence and prevalence rates in this "high risk" group. It is far from clear how many people suffer from eating disorders, and most figures quoted in the literature are either estimates or figures relating to specific groups in specific localities. The scale of the problem as far as children are concerned is even less clear, as no good epidemiological research has been carried out with this population. Consequently, our knowledge about the numbers of children who may be affected remains limited.

SOME PROBLEMS IN EPIDEMIOLOGICAL RESEARCH ON EATING DISORDERS

In medical epidemiological research, information may be obtained from a variety of sources. Often, it is of interest to investigate both clinical and non-clinical populations. Clinical populations are usually those who have presented for treatment and have received a formal diagnosis. However, there may be further individuals who display some or all of the features of a disorder, but for one reason or another do not come to professional attention. In these instances, investigations of non-clinical populations or of non-referred populations (that is, groups of patients or clinic attenders who are not selected on the basis of diagnosis) might reveal whether there are significant numbers of affected people who would be missed if attention is focused solely on clinical populations.

In the case of eating disorders, it has been suggested that quite a sizeable number of individuals display some but not all the essential features, and do not receive formal diagnoses. Button & Whitehouse (1981) have suggested that around 5% of all teenage girls develop "subclinical" anorexia nervosa (mild anorexia nervosa that does not come to psychiatric attention) after reaching puberty. Clearly, if true, this represents a significantly large population, whose existence would not be identified from investigations of clinical populations alone. The actual number of such individuals is impossible to estimate, as there is no means of systematically documenting their presence. Some may present to their general practitioner for help, but many more may rely on families, friends or self-help groups.

Information about clinical populations may come from a variety of sources, such as national or regional statistics, or case-register studies. There are many problems in using such statistics as a basis for making statements about incidence. For example, the diagnosis may not have been appropriately applied and there is a relatively high chance that not all existing cases will have been included. Individuals who do not present for psychiatric treatment, and those who are seen only by their general practitioner, tend to be omitted. A further difficulty is that reports of large-scale epidemiological studies tend not to differentiate between younger and older patients, so that little impression can be gained of the incidence in one specific subgroup. For example, Nielsen's (1990) study of the incidence of anorexia nervosa in Denmark uses the national case register and includes children from the age of ten, but it is not clear what the estimated incidence is in children, distinct from the incidence in the total group.

As mentioned above, a further approach used by epidemiologists is the screening of non-referred populations, for example, general practice populations. King (1989) screened attenders at four London group practices using the Eating Attitudes Test (Garner & Garfinkel, 1979; Garner, Olmstead, Bohr, & Garfinkel, 1982) and found that of 720 subjects aged 16–35 included in the study, 76 obtained high EAT scores. All but seven of these were then interviewed to establish the presence or absence of a clinical eating disorder. Six females and one male received a diagnosis of bulimia nervosa, whereas there were no cases of anorexia nervosa. This study highlights a very important obstacle to the study of the incidence and prevalence rates of eating disorders: namely the fact that they are relatively rare, anorexia nervosa particularly so.

When a disorder is uncommon, it becomes difficult to detect it in large-scale surveys of non-referred populations. The positive predictive value of screening measures used (that is, the likelihood that someone who scores above the cut-off point on a particular measure will be a "true" case) is known to be relatively low in cases where the illness or disorder investigated has a low prevalence rate (Williams, Hand, & Tarnopolsky, 1982). The sensitivity and specificity of the measure needs to be high, which is difficult under such circumstances.

Populations of schoolgirls form another group of interest to epidemiologists studying eating disorders as they represent a "high risk" group because of their age and sex. Johnson-Sabine et al. (1988) screened 1010 London schoolgirls aged 14–16, again using the Eating Attitudes Test. All 83 obtaining high scores were interviewed and four cases of clinical eating disorder were identified (all bulimia nervosa). As with King's (1989) study, no diagnoses of anorexia nervosa were made. However, these authors suggest that there were two cases among individuals who had refused to be screened. This illustrates a further important obstacle to attempting to discover the scale of the problem of eating disorders. Such disorders are characterised by secretiveness, and, in the case of anorexia nervosa, often massive denial that there is any problem at all, which undoubtedly serves to hamper detection. The problem of denial of eating difficulty, and the effects this has on the completion of self-report questionnaires used as screening instruments, has been discussed in detail elsewhere (Vandereycken & Vanderlinden, 1983).

WHAT IS THE INCIDENCE OF ANOREXIA NERVOSA IN CHILDREN?

So what about the children? Can we learn anything about the incidence of anorexia nervosa and related eating disorders in children from studies of older individuals? Reviewing the epidemiological literature relating to eating disorders in adolescents and adults, it is striking how much reported incidence and prevalence rates vary. (Ledoux, Choquet, & Flament, 1991) have attributed such inconsistencies to three main causes.

First, different assessment methods have been used to define "caseness", and thus inclusion in the eating disorder population. As there have been no studies looking specifically at childhood populations it is not possible to compare the definitions used. However, the problem of appropriate assessment methods does exist for futures studies given that the screening tools most often used (e.g. the Eating Attitudes Test) were not developed for use with this age-group and are in many ways unsuitable (Lask & Bryant-Waugh, 1992). In addition, there remains inconsistency about the use of the term "anorexia nervosa" when applied to children. Some authors claim that very young children (as young as four years of age : DiNicola, 1989; Gislason, 1988) can have anorexia nervosa, whereas others (the Editors included) maintain that it is unlikely to occur in children younger than eight because of the developmental level necessary to experience the characteristic disturbances in cognitive functioning.

Second, the groups surveyed are not homogeneous. For example, some researchers concentrate on "high risk" populations (e.g. females aged 14–20), whereas others include total populations, or groups defined otherwise. Although the individual authors of reports of epidemiological surveys are usually clear in their statements—i.e. that they found a prevalence rate of X% in a population of Y individuals in a given age range—these figures unfortunately get taken out of context and used in the sense of anorexia nervosa having a prevalence rate of X%. This is clearly meaningless, as the group studied may not be at all representative of a wider population. Because of the tendency to focus on female adolescent populations, children until now have largely been overlooked. It is not possible to use existing estimates of incidence and prevalence in other groups to gain an impression of the numbers of children who may be affected.

Third, different diagnostic criteria are used. An example of how this may affect reported rates is provided by Ledoux et al.'s (1991) account of the incidence of bulimia in French boys and girls between the ages of 12 and 19. Using DSM III criteria (American Psychiatric Association, 1980) a rate of 1.3% was identified, while when using DSM III R criteria (American Psychiatric Association, 1987), which are more highly specific, a rate of 0.7% was obtained. In the case of children, this potentially poses a particular problem, as existing widely used diagnostic criteria have a number of inadequacies when applied to younger individuals (see chapter 2).

There is a strong body of opinion that rigid adherence to existing formal diagnostic criteria may result in an underestimation of the number of individuals who experience eating disorder symptoms. Hendren, Barber, and Sigafoos (1986) found that up to 18.6% of a schoolgirl population aged 12 to 18 had one or more major symptoms of an eating disorder, without necessarily meeting full diagnostic criteria. McSherry (1986) argues that the use of such rigorous criteria may be counterproductive because the disorder is recognised only in its most severe form, and proposes that more flexible criteria should be used to encourage detection in the early stages when intervention may be more likely to be successful. In the case of children this may be particularly relevant. When formal criteria are applied, many children with eating disorder symptoms may be excluded as such criteria are based on observations of older individuals. Bunnell et al. (1990) are of the opinion that younger subjects in particular may not fulfil formal criteria but may nevertheless present with considerable emotional, physical and behavioural disturbances.

In conclusion, the answer to the question of how many children develop anorexia nervosa or related eating disorders remains largely unknown. It does seem fair to say that there are far fewer eating disorder patients aged between 8 and 13 than there are in a similar age span of 14 to 19. Certainly, resources for these younger patients are very limited, reflecting perhaps that the demand has previously not been particularly high. Thankfully, anorexia nervosa in children appears to remain relatively rare.

WHAT ABOUT BULIMIA NERVOSA AND RELATED EATING DISORDERS IN CHILDREN?

Until now the discussion has focused mainly on anorexia nervosa in children. This may seem odd, given that most studies of adolescent and adult populations suggest that rates for bulimia nervosa are well in excess of those for anorexia nervosa. A typical example might be Whitaker et al.'s (1990) survey of 5596 schoolchildren (both boys and girls) aged between 13 and 18. They reported a lifetime prevalence of 2.5% for bulimia nervosa, compared with only 0.2% for anorexia nervosa. In our own clinical experience the onset of bulimia nervosa (as defined by DSM III R criteria—American Psychiatric Association, 1987) below the age of 14 is extremely rare (see further chapter 2). Similarly, "subclinical" or "partial syndrome" eating disorders are commonly believed to be much more prevalent than full syndrome eating disorders (partial syndrome anorexia nervosa has been described as including the essential psychopathological features of anorexia nervosa, but with persisting, irregular menstruation and weight remaining within normal limits) (Mann et al., 1983). The partial syndrome variant has yet to be described in children, and although it is certainly likely to exist, nothing can as yet be said about its incidence in the younger age group.

IS THE INCIDENCE OF EATING DISORDERS RISING?

There remains much debate and confusion over the issue of the extent to which the incidence of eating disorders is rising. At face value, many of the published statistics appear to suggest that the past two decades have seen a significant rise in incidence. There have been reports of anorexia nervosa reaching "epidemic" proportions, although this is refuted by those who have been concerned with epidemiological research (e.g. Ben-Tovim & Morton, 1990). Jones, Fox, Babigan, and Hutton's (1980) much-quoted study of the numbers of individuals receiving treatment for anorexia nervosa in Monroe County, New York, reported an incidence of 0.35 per 100,000 population in 1960–1969, compared to an incidence of 0.64 per 100,000 population in 1970–1976. Similarly, Szmukler, McCance, McCrone, and Hunter's (1986) study of the Aberdeen case register found an incidence of anorexia nervosa of 1.6 per 100,000 population in 1966–1969 compared to an incidence of 4.06 per 100,000 population in 1978–1982.

One interpretation of these findings is that the incidence of anorexia nervosa has indeed risen, resulting in an increase in the number of cases treated. However, this is by no means certain and the reported rise in figures may be a reflection of the fact that physicians have become more aware of eating disorders and are better at recognising them. In addition, changes in population size and structure may need to be taken into account. For example, in an investigation of all patients aged between 10 and 64 admitted to psychiatric facilities in England with a main diagnosis of anorexia nervosa from 1972 to 1981, Williams and King (1987) found a significant rise in the number of first admissions with time. Rather than taking this to be evidence of a rise in the incidence of anorexia nervosa, these authors suggest that this finding is more likely to be related to the increase in the number of young women in the general population over this nine-year period. Similarly, Lucas, Beard, O'Fallon, and Kurland (1988) found no significant increase in the incidence rate of anorexia nervosa over a 45-year period in Minnesota, after general population trends and other intervening variables had been taken into account.

A further factor which may have contributed towards the impression that there has been a rapid rise in incidence rates is that of re-admission. Studies based on the numbers of individuals treated at any one time may not differentiate between first and subsequent admissions. For example, Williams and King (1987) have noted that there has been an increase in the rate of re-admission of patients with an eating disorder, and suggest that this may have added to the impression that there has been an increase in the risk of morbidity. In such cases, incidence rates may appear higher than in reality as some individuals may be included more than once.

The situation regarding children is less clear. Given that there have been no good estimates of incidence and prevalence rates specifically in children below the age of 14, it is not possible to detect a rise in numbers. In our own experience it is true to say that we have witnessed a significant increase in the number of referrals to the Hospital for Sick Children over the past decade. The extent to which this reflects a rise in the number of children developing eating disorders, an increased awareness of the possibility that anorexia nervosa and related disorders can occur in children, or the knowledge that we offer a specialist service for such children, remains a subject for debate.

WHAT DO WE KNOW ABOUT CHILDREN WHO DEVELOP EATING DISORDERS?

Comparing the background characteristics of children reported in recent series of early onset anorexia nervosa patients, the following points emerge.

1. More Boys than Expected

Numbers of boys relative to girls are higher than might be expected on the basis of comparison with older patients. It is generally believed that in adolescents and adults around 5% to 10% of cases occur in males (Barry & Lippmann, 1990). However, in children, this figure appears to be much greater. In 1985, Hawley described a follow-up study of 21 children with anorexia nervosa aged 13 or younger at onset. The relatively high percentage of males (19%) was commented upon as being high in comparison to other studies (Hawley, 1985). In Jacobs and Isaacs' (1986) study of pre-pubertal anorexia nervosa, a pre-pubertal and a post-pubertal group of anorectics were compared with a control group. The sex ratio in the pre-pubertal group was 6:14 (male:female), whereas in the post-pubertal group the ratio was 1:19 (male:female). The numbers in each group were small (20), and the difference in sex ratio between the pre and post-pubertal groups did not reach statistical significance. Nevertheless, in Fosson, Knibbs, Bryant-Waugh and Lask's (1987) report of early onset anorexia nervosa in 48 children, 13 (or 27%) were male, a figure which supported Jacobs and Isaacs' earlier finding. Two years later, Higgs, Goodyer, and Birch, (1989) published a further study of anorexia nervosa and related eating disorders in children, 27 of whom met the criteria for anorexia nervosa. Eight (or 30%) were boys, again providing further support for the impression that in children, males form a greater proportion of those presenting with eating disorders than in older individuals. In the absence of larger scale studies, it is at present not clear whether this does represent a difference between early onset and later onset anorexia nervosa. Certainly, it is a finding of interest that requires further investigation.

2. Social Class Bias

Margo's (1985) report of anorexia nervosa in patients aged 12–18 reported that 27 out of the 40 subjects included in the study (or 67.5%), were from Social Classes 1 and II ([Office of Population Cencuses and Surveys.] Registrar General's Classification of Occupations, 1970). This figure was noted to be significantly in excess of what might be expected, given the population distribution of the area in which the study was carried out. There was however no differentiation between those below and above the age of 14, making it difficult to gain any impression of the social class distribution at the younger end of the age range. Fosson et al. (1987) reported that 22 (46%) of the 48 children included in their series (all aged 13 or under at the time of onset) were from Social Classes I and II, again biased towards higher social classes compared with the general population. Higgs et al. (1989) found that 14 or (54%) of the 27 early onset anorexia nervosa patients included in their series had a "middle-class" background, but did not define this in terms of social classes. Finally, Gowers, Crisp, Joughin, and Bhat (1991) reported that 80% of 30 individuals with pre-menarcheal onset had Social Class I and II backgrounds. Thus it appears that in children presenting for treatment of anorexia nervosa, higher social classes are overrepresented.

Anorexia nervosa in adolescents and adults has long been associated with middle-class backgrounds, and continues to be reported as being overrepresented in Social Classes I and II (Szmukler et al., 1986). However, some authors maintain that the past decade has seen a change, with the social class bias becoming less pronounced (Garfinkel & Garner, 1982). Again, caution is required in the interpretation of reported figures. Social class structure varies between different areas and countries, and different institutions may have a long history of a particular distribution of clientele. In addition, it is often suggested that middle-class families are better at making use of facilities open to them, although there does not appear to be any research to substantiate this in the context of eating disorders.

In conclusion, because of the limited number of published studies of early onset anorexia nervosa it would not be appropriate to state that there is a social class bias in the incidence of the disorder in this age-group. However, the few relatively small-scale studies that do exist, suggest that there is such a tendency—again a point that requires further investigation before any firm statements can be made.

3. Anorexia Nervosa Can Occur in Children from
Various Cultural Backgrounds

Until relatively recently, anorexia nervosa has been associated with people of white ethnic origin. However, over the last decade an increasing number of reports have appeared in the literature describing the development of eating disorders in individuals from different ethnic backgrounds. Anorexia nervosa and bulimia nervosa have now been identified in people of both African and Asian racial background, both in their countries of origin and elsewhere. Bryant-Waugh and Lask (1991) have reviewed this literature and report the occurrence of anorexia nervosa in a group of Asian children living in Britain. Bhadrinath (1990) describes three Asian adolescents, and argues that, in view of the increasing number of such reports, there is now a need to attempt to understand culture-specific attitudes towards food and eating and to explore their role in eating disorders in individuals from other ethnic groups. Mumford and Whitehouse (1988) also noted the occurrence of bulimia nervosa in a slightly older group of Asian girls, and suggest that exposure to Western culture may be important in the aetiology of eating disorders in immigrant families.

It is our clinical impression that it may be less the exposure to Western culture *per se* that precipitates the onset of the eating disorder (as there are many who do *not* suffer from eating disorders under similar circumstances), but more the difficulty in attempting to reconcile elements from two very different cultures. In our experience, children from different ethnic backgrounds who develop anorexia nervosa tend to be those whose families maintain their own beliefs and practices, and socialise primarily with others of the same racial origins. Thus, it appears that it is not the more Westernised families who are at risk, but those where the children struggle to accommodate their experience at school and elsewhere with their home life and the expectations that go with this. In epidemiological terms we can therefore no longer view anorexia nervosa as a culture-bound disorder.

FINALLY: A WORD ABOUT DIETING,
DANCING AND MODELLING

It is common knowledge that eating disorders tend to occur at different rates in different groups, being most common in females, with the peak age of the onset of anorexia nervosa at around 14–18 years, and that of bulimia nervosa in the early 20s. However, certain subgroups have been identified which appear to represent particularly "high risk" groups. Ballet dancers and models appear to be especially prone to eating disorders with reports of 4–6% developing anorexia nervosa (Farmer, Treasure, & Szmukler, 1986). Most of this research has been carried out on adults (e.g. Hamilton, Brooks-Gun, & Warren, 1985), although there are some studies of adolescent dancers aged between 14 and 18 (Brooks-Gun, Burrow, & Warren, 1988; Garner, & Garfinkel, 1980). Eating disorder symptoms have been found to be uniformly high in all these published studies.

With the exception of one study (Garner, Garfinkel, Rockert, & Olmstead, 1987), there has been very little research specifically looking at very young ballet students (for example the 10–12-year-olds), so that it is not possible to say with any certainty whether the same situation is found in children who dance. Garner et al. (1987) studied a group of 11–14-year-old dancers receiving professional ballet training. They found that at two-year follow-up 11 of the original 55 had anorexia nervosa, and a further five had another form of eating disorder.

Over the past few years we have had a number of referrals of very promising young dancers presenting with anorexia nervosa. These children are subject to the same pressures to be small and slim as their older colleagues, and it is our impression that this places them at greater risk of developing an eating disorder than might otherwise be the case. As far as children who model are concerned, the same may apply, but to my knowledge there has been no research in this area.

The question about dieting is becoming of increasing interest. Anorexia nervosa has traditionally been referred to in the popular press by the dreadful term "slimmer's disease". This unfortunate term is misleading because it implies that anorexia nervosa is simply dieting gone wrong. Clearly, it is much more complex, and the aetiology of eating disorders is explored in greater depth in chapter 5. Nevertheless, many patients who have eating disorders claim they began with a "normal" diet, and Patton et al. (1990) have suggested that in female adolescents, dieters run eight times the risk of developing an eating disorder compared to non-dieters. This may to some extent be a reflection of the reasons why a diet is started in the first place, but such information is very difficult to obtain. There is no doubt at all that dieting behaviour is extremely common in the female adolescent population, and Hill, Oliver, and Rogers (1991) have recently suggested that it is increasing among younger children, with girls as young as nine engaging in a wide range of dieting behaviours.

The precise link between dieting and the onset of an eating disorder is incompletely understood, and is a subject for much debate. Hsu (1990) proposes that eating disturbances can best be viewed using a continuum model ranging from simple dieting to clinical eating disorders. A consequence to adopting such a model is Hsu's contention that the prevalence of eating disorders is then directly proportional to the prevalence of dieting behaviour (within a given population). If we accept this, and believe reports of dieting behaviour increasing in children, we might expect to see an increase in the number of children presenting for treatment of an eating disorder.

SUMMARY

This chapter has been concerned with the epidemiology of anorexia nervosa and related eating disorders in children. This is a much neglected area of research, with no good studies of childhood populations upon which to base estimates of incidence. Studies that include children in the population surveyed have so far failed to differentiate between incidence rates in early onset patients and older individuals.

Problems related to epidemiological research in this context, such as the lack of reliable statistics, the relative rarity of eating disorders, and the likelihood that a significant number of individuals may be missed, have been discussed. The wide range of variation in published incidence and prevalence rates for eating disorders in adults and adolescents can be understood in the face of the many methodological problems inherent to this type of research. The conclusion is reached that we do not know how many children suffer from true clinical eating disorders, how many have "subclinical" or "partial syndrome" forms, or how many experience distressing eating disorder symptoms. On the basis of demand for services, it seems likely that the number of children with the full syndrome of anorexia nervosa is relatively small compared to older individuals, and that bulimia nervosa is very rare indeed in children below the age of 14.

Attention has also been focused on the question of whether the incidence of eating disorders is rising. The general consensus is that reports of a dramatic increase are exaggerations, and what we may be seeing is an increased demand on and use of services rather than a true increase in morbidity. This remains, however, a much-debated point. As far as children are concerned the picture is unclear, but we are certainly seeing an increasing number of patients in our own clinic for 8 to 14-year-olds.

Finally, a number of comments are made about those children who have been documented in various studies of early onset anorexia nervosa. In particular, the higher than expected ratio of boys to girls, the apparent social class bias, and the fact that such children are not confined to white Western backgrounds are discussed. It seems that children may also belong to the "high risk" groups identified by researchers investigating older populations, with dieting and dancing carrying perhaps an added risk for precipitating even children into an eating disorder. The impression that emerges is that we don't know very much, but the outlook does not look too good. The incidence of anorexia nervosa in children is almost certainly *not* decreasing.

REFERENCES

American Psychiatric Association. (1980). *Diagnostic and statistical manual of mental disorders* (3rd ed.). Washington, DC: American Psychiatric Association.

American Psychiatric Association. (1987). *Diagnostic and statistical manual of mental disorders* (3rd ed. rev.). Washington, DC: American Psychiatric Association.

Barry, A. & Lippmann, B.B. (1990). Anorexia in males. *Postgraduate Medicine, 87,* 161–65.

Ben-Tovim, D.I. & Morton, J. (1990). The epidemiology of anorexia nervosa in South Australia. *Australian and New Zealand Journal of Psychiatry, 24,* 182–186.

Bhadrinath, B.R. (1990). Anorexia nervosa in adolescents of Asian extraction. *British Journal of Psychiatry, 156,* 565–568.

Brooks-Gunn, R., Burrow, C., & Warren, M.P. (1988). Attitudes towards eating and body weight in different groups of female adolescent athletes. *International Journal of Eating Disorders, 7,* 749–757.

Bryant-Waugh, R. & Lask, B. (1991). Anorexia nervosa in a group of Asian children living in Britain. *British Journal of Psychiatry, 158,* 229–233.

Bunnell, D.W., Shenker, I.R., Nussbaum, M.P., Jacobson, M.S., & Cooper, P. (1990). Subclinical versus formal eating disorders: Differentiating psychological features. *International Journal of Eating Disorders, 9,* 357–362.

Button, E.J. & Whitehouse, A. (1981). Subclinical anorexia nervosa. *Psychological Medicine, 11,* 509–516.

DiNicola, V.F. (1989). Eating and mood disorders in young children. *Psychiatric Clinics of North America, 12,* 873–893.

Farmer, A., Treasure, J., & Szmukler, G. (1986). Eating disorders: A review of recent research. *Digestive Diseases, 4,* 13–25.

Fosson, A., Knibbs, J., Bryant-Waugh, R., & Lask, B. (1987). Early onset anorexia nervosa. *Archives of Disease in Childhood, 62,* 114–118.

Garfinkel, P.E. & Garner, D.M. (1982). *Anorexia nervosa: A multidimensional perspective.* New York: Basic Books.

Garner, D.M. & Garfinkel, P.E. (1979). The eating attitudes test: An index of the symptoms of anorexia nervosa. *Psychological Medicine, 9,* 273–279.

Garner, D.M. & Garfinkel, P.E. (1980). Socio-cultural factors in the development of anorexia nervosa. *Psychological Medicine, 10,* 647–656.

Garner, D.M., Olmstead, M.P., Bohr, Y., & Garfinkel, P.E. (1982). The eating attitudes test: Psychometric features and clinical correlates. *Psychological Medicine, 12,* 871–878.

Garner, D.M., Garfinkel, P.E., Rockert, W., & Olmstead, M.P. (1987). A prospective study of eating disturbances in the ballet. *Psychotherapy and Psychosomatics, 48,* 170–175.

Gislason, I.L. (1988). Eating disorders in childhood (ages 4 through 11 years). In B.J. Blinder, B.F. Chaitin, & R. Goldstein (Eds.), *The eating disorders.* PMA Publishing Corp. (1988).

Gowers, S.G., Crisp, A.H., Joughin, N., & Bhat, A. (1991). Pre-menarcheal anorexia nervosa. *Journal of Child Psychology and Psychiatry, 32,* 515–524.

Hamilton, L.H., Brooks-Gunn, J., & Warren, M.P. (1985). Sociocultural influences on eating disorders in female professional dancers. *International Journal of Eating Disorders, 4,* 465–467.

Hawley, R.M. (1985). The outcome of anorexia nervosa in younger subjects. *British Journal of Psychiatry, 146,* 657–660.

Hendren, R.L., Barber, J.K., & Sigafoos, A. (1986). Eating-disordered symptoms in a non-clinical population: A study of female adolescents in two private schools. *Journal of the American Academy of Child Psychiatry, 25,* 836–840.

Higgs, J.F., Goodyer, I.M., & Birch, J. (1989). Anorexia nervosa and food avoidance emotional disorder. *Archives of Disease in Childhood,64,* 346–351.

Hill, A.J., Oliver, S., & Rogers, P. (1992). Eating in the adult world: The rise of dieting in childhood and adolescence. *British Journal of Clinical Psychology, 31,* 95–105.

Hsu, L.K.G. (1990). *Eating disorders.* New York: The Guilford Press.

Jacobs, B. & Isaacs, S. (1986). Pre-pubertal anorexia nervosa: A retrospective controlled study. *Journal of Child Psychology and Psychiatry, 27,* 237–250.

Johnson-Sabine, E., Wood, K., Patton, G., Mann, A., & Wakeling, A. (1988). Abnormal eating attitudes in London schoolgirls–a prospective epidemiological study: Factors associated with abnormal response on screening questionnaires. *Psychological Medicine, 18,* 615–622.

Jones, D.J., Fox, M.M., Babigan, H.M., & Hutton, H.E. (1980). Epidemiology of anorexia nervosa in Monroe County, New York: 1960–1976. *Psychosomatic Medicine, 42,* 551–558.

King, M.B. (1989). Eating disorders in a general practice population. Prevalence, characteristics and follow-up at 12 to 18 months. *Psychological Medicine Monograph Supplement,* 14.

Lask, B. & Bryant-Waugh, R. (1992). Early onset anorexia nervosa and related eating disorders. *Journal of Child Psychology and Psychiatry Annual Research Review,* 3.

Ledoux, S., Choquet, M., & Flament, M. (1991). Eating disorders among adolescents in an unselected French population. *International Journal of Eating Disorders,10,* 81–89.

Lucas, A.R., Beard, C.M., O'Fallon, W.M., & Kurland, L.T. (1988). Anorexia nervosa in Rochester, Minnesota: A 45-year study. *Proceedings of the Mayo Clinic, 63,* 433–442.

Mann, A.H., Wakeling, A., Wood, K., Monck, E., Dobbs, R., & Szmulker, G. (1983). Screening for abnormal eating attitudes and psychiatric morbidity in an unselected population of 15-year-old schoolgirls. *Psychological Medicine, 13,* 573–580.

Margo, J.L. (1985). Anorexia nervosa in adolescents. *British Journal of Medical Psychology, 58,* 193–195.

McSherry, J.A. (1986). Progress in the diagnosis of anorexia nervosa. *Journal of the Royal Society of Health, 106,* 8–9.

Mumford, D. & Whitehouse, A. (1988). Increased prevalence of bulimia nervosa among Asian schoolgirls. *British Medical Journal, 297,* 718.

Nielsen, S. (1990). The epidemiology of anorexia nervosa in Denmark from 1973–1987: A nationwide register study of psychiatric admission. *Acta Psychiatrica Scandinavia, 81,* 507–514.

Office of Population Censuses and Surveys. (1970). *Registrar General's classification of occupations. A social and socio-economic classification.* Appendix B1. London: Her Majesty's Stationery Office.

Patton, G.C., Johnson-Sabine, E., Wood, K., Mann, A.H., & Wakeling, A. (1990). Abnormal eating attitudes in London schoolgirls—a prospective epidemiological study: Outcome at twelve month follow-up. *Psychological Medicine, 20,* 383–394.

Szmukler, G., McCance, C., McCrone, L., & Hunter, D. (1986). Anorexia nervosa: A psychiatric case register study from Aberdeen. *Psychological Medicine, 16,* 49–58.

Vandereycken, W. & Vanderlinden, J. (1983). Denial of illness and the use of self-reporting measures in anorexia nervosa patients. *International Journal of Eating Disorders, 2,* 101–107.

Whitaker, A., Johnson, J., Shaffer, D., Rapoport, J.L., Kalikow, K., Walsh, B.T., Davies, M., Braiman, S., & Dolinsky, A. (1990). Uncommon troubles in young people: Prevalence estimates of selected psychiatric disorders in a non-referred psychiatric population. *Archives of General Psychiatry, 47,* 487–496.

Williams, P., Hand, D., & Tarnopolsky, A. (1982). The problems of screening for uncommon disorders—A comment on the eating attitudes test. *Psychological Medicine,12,* 431–434.

Williams, P. & King, M. (1987). The "epidemic" of anorexia nervosa: Another medical myth? *Lancet, i,* 205–207.

CHAPTER FIVE

Aetiology

Bernadette Wren and Bryan Lask

INTRODUCTION

The search for a single cause for eating disorders has largely been abandoned. Anorexia nervosa and related eating disorders now tend to be viewed as multi-determined syndromes, with a variety of interacting factors—physical, psychological, family and socio-cultural—thought to be of causal significance.

But simply compiling a list of possible aetiological factors is insufficient explanation of causation, unless a picture emerges of the ways in which the different factors bear on each other. It is widely held, for instance, that achievement-orientated adolescent girls from conflict-avoiding families are at risk from an eating disorder. But as Garfinkel and Garner (1982) point out, not all individuals at risk will develop the disorder. In those who do, only some risk factors may be present in any individual and for each of those individuals the exact nature of, and relationship between, predisposing factors will vary.

To further complicate the picture, the development of self-starvation is a process over time. This means that the exact causal relevance of the reported personality traits, cognitive functioning and familial interaction of eating disordered children remains unclear, since these features will no longer be identifiable independently of the impact on them of the illness.

The effort to understand the aetiology of eating disorders lies therefore not in pinning down a single pathogenesis nor simply identifying risk factors, but in understanding how the various predisposing, precipitating and perpetuating factors interact and develop over time to produce the condition.

In this chapter, a number of factors widely considered to make a major contribution to aetiology will be described and a preliminary attempt made to suggest ways in which they interact. Little is known about the difference in aetiology in the early onset age range, and most of what follows relates to eating disorders in general. Relevant specific reference is made to the younger age group.

BIOLOGICAL FACTORS

A number of possible biological factors have been postulated to contribute to the aetiology of eating disorders: genetic, hypothalamic dysfunction, malnutrition, and disorders of gastric emptying.

1. Genetic Factors

There is now convincing evidence that genetic factors are relevant in eating disorders. Three studies are of particular significance. Theander (1970) has demonstrated that the incidence of anorexia nervosa in sisters of patients with it is 6%. This is approximately six times greater than even the highest reported incidence figure in population surveys (e.g. Crisp, Palmer, & Kalucy, 1976), and is matched only by figures for ballet students (Garner & Garfinkel, 1980).

Holland, Sicotte, and Treasure (1988) have found in a study of 45 twin pairs that the concordance rate for anorexia nervosa in dizygotic twins was 5%, while that for monozygotic twins was 56%. This finding lends considerable weight to the view that genetic factors play a significant part in the aetiology of anorexia nervosa.

Strober et al., (1990) have demonstrated that anorexia nervosa clusters in families with intergenerational transmission. They found it to be roughly eight times more common in female first-degree relatives of patients with anorexia nervosa than in the general population, and absent in relatives of probands with other types of disorder.

In conclusion, these family studies strongly suggest that there may be some genetic component contributing towards the development of an eating disorder. However, the precise nature of this is not yet known and on the basis of current knowledge little more can be said than that there appears to be some inherited vulnerability or predisposition. Whether this is specific to eating disorders is as yet unclear.

2. Hypothalamic Dysfunction

There is no doubt that a hypothalamic disorder occurs in anorexia nervosa (Russell, 1985), manifested by an endocrine disturbance involving the hypothalamic-pituitary-gonadal axis. Whether this endocrine disorder is primary or secondary to the eating problem remains to be ascertained.

A number of possibilities have been considered. First, damage to the hypothalamic centres regulating eating and reproduction may act as a predisposing factor to anorexia nervosa, and become relevant when circulating reproductive hormones begin to increase towards the end of the first decade of life. Second, a similar process may occur in the context of anomalous connections between neurones in the hypothalamus. Third, anorexia nervosa may be the clinical manifestation of an aberrant maturation process in a hypothalamus that had previously functioned normally. Fourth, hypothalamic tissue may be an unusually susceptible biological substrate in some individuals, and the dysfunction is only manifested at times of stress (see Weiner, 1985 for a fuller review).

At present there remains a lack of consensus on this issue, with as yet insufficient evidence to be able to state that the characteristic hypothalamic dysfunction plays a direct role in the aetiology of the eating disorder.

3. Malnutrition

While malnutrition clearly contributes to the overall clinical picture in eating disorders there is no evidence that it plays a primary part. Some researchers have suggested that zinc deficiency may cause anorexia nervosa through its clinical features of loss of appetite, loss of taste and depression. The fact that many children with anorexia nervosa are indeed zinc deficient (Lask, Fosson, Thomas, & Rolfe, 1993) is very likely to be due to the inadequate diet characteristic of the disorder. Further, zinc supplementation has not been found to improve the course of the illness, indicating that zinc deficiency is not of primary importance. Nor is there any evidence that any other dietary deficits are of aetiological significance.

4. Disorders of Gastric Emptying and the Role of Gastro-intestinal Hormones

There is much that has yet to be understood with regard to the regulatory mechanisms of gastric emptying. There are a large number and variety of regulatory mechanisms, both neurological and chemical.

Gastrointestinal hormones such as gastrin, secretin, cholecystokinin and gastric inhibitory polypeptide all slow gastric emptying, as do hydrochloric and fatty acids (Muller, 1988). Given the frequent complaint of children with anorexia nervosa that they feel full, and some recent anecdotal reports that such children have delayed and irregular gastric emptying, it is possible that a disturbance in gastric emptying could play a significant part in aetiology. Such a hypothesis has an added attractiveness when it is recalled that one of the gastrointestinal hormones, cholecystokinin, has both a peripheral (gastric) and a central mode of action. In other words it is feasible that an abnormality of cholecystokinin functioning could contribute to the pathogenesis of anorexia nervosa through both central and peripheral actions. Similar points can be made with reference to another hormone, vasoactive intestinal polypeptide (VIPS).

Alderdice, Dinsmore, Buchanan, and Adam (1985) have proposed a mechanism that could involve these hormones in eating disorders. They suggest that in some individuals food, especially carbohydrate, might produce an exaggerated release of one or most of these regular peptides. The high level of hormone may leak across the blood-brain barrier and act on receptor sites in the hypothalamus, resulting in a response of satiety, and a distaste for further eating. Alternatively, abnormal levels may trigger a bulimic episode.

Currently the most convincing evidence for a primary biological cause of eating disorders is that arising from genetic studies, but as bio-scientific methods of investigation become yet more sophisticated it is possible that other biological factors will come to the fore. It is likely that physiological vulnerability or damage acts as a necessary and predisposing component for the development of the disorder. In the context of this specific physiological substrate, other non-organic factors may then assume a particular importance. The role of these non-organic factors should now be considered.

PSYCHODYNAMIC MODELS

The understanding of the causes of eating disorders in the psycho-analytic literature has undergone a major shift in the last 50 years reflecting a wider change in the focus of psychoanalysis towards ever earlier phases of development in infancy. Work in the 1930s and 1940s favoured an account of anorexia nervosa as the result of unresolved Oedipal conflicts reactivated in adolescence. The symbolic nature of eating problems was emphasised, as in the paper by Waller, Kaufman, and Deutsch (1940) in which anorexia nervosa was characterised as the fear of oral impregnation. More recently, this type of sexual anxiety has been regarded less as the *cause* of various developmental disturbances, but rather as a manifestation of such a disturbance.

For Bruch (1974), the refusal to eat and fear of fatness are secondary to an underlying personality disturbance which has its roots in early mother/child interactions. She distinguishes a "why?" and "how?" question: Why do certain individuals "misuse the eating function in their efforts to solve or camouflage problems of living that to them appear otherwise insoluble?" From a psychoanalytical point of view, disturbed eating can have a vast range of symbolic meanings (e.g. expressing rage and hatred, a superior sense of power, rejection of parents, etc.). But it is the "how?" question that has been neglected: How has it been possible for eating to develop in such a way that it could be misused to such an extent to deal with complex emotional and interpersonal problems? Bruch's answer is that something has gone wrong in the early experiential and interpersonal processes surrounding the satisfaction of nutritional and other bodily needs.

Bruch has described the way in which gratifying early experiences with feeding create for the infant a trust, both in the mother's responsiveness to cues, and in the accuracy of the infant's own internal sensations of hunger and other appetites. When appropriate confirming responses from the mother are persistently lacking (such as when the mother feeds the child to suit her own needs and rhythms) the child becomes uncertain about her ability to discriminate her inner states and about her capacity to be looked after. The child does not learn to identify hunger correctly or to distinguish it from other states of bodily need or emotional arousal. Neither the world nor herself seem trustworthy. In Bruch's analysis this lack of emotional containment leads the child in desperation to be utterly compliant with what she takes to be her mother's needs, in order to maintain what feels like a frail connection with the mother. Hence the typical profile of the "good girl" anorectic patient—likeable, well-behaved, cheerful, with no history of previous problems. As she grows up she fails to develop a sense of herself as independent or entitled to take the initiative, but rather continues to win approval by her compliance and develops a "paralysing sense of ineffectiveness" (Bruch, 1974). Such an individual may feel helpless under the impact of her bodily urges. She may feel controlled from the outside and rely on safe, predictable routines to determine her behaviour.

Influenced by the writing of Melanie Klein, Chernin (1986) has described how the infant can feel overwhelmed by anxiety about how to survive her aggressive, greedy, jealous impulses towards the feeding caretaker. If the caretaker is not in touch with the baby's needs, not tuned-in to her distress and her wishes, the baby's aggressive impulses are heightened. She may then disown her feelings of dependency and employ a variety of powerful psychic defences to hold her emotional self together, e.g. denial of need, pseudo-independence, omnipotence. Chernin emphasises the extent to which the infant feels guilt and remorse over the strength of her oral rage at the mother, believing that her greed has diminished and damaged her mother. The setting conditions for the development of an eating disorder, she argues, are in the replay of oral rages coupled with anxiety and remorse when certain needs, reminiscent of childhood, make themselves felt again later in life. "An eating obsession comes into existence so that the need, rage and violence of the mother/daughter bond can be played out in a symbolic form that spares the mother."

Palazzoli (1974) sees a further implication of this attempt to renounce the hostility and aggression towards the mother. She describes the child as learning to project the hostility on to significant people around her and thus to see the world to an even greater degree as untrustworthy and menacing.

What is common to the different versions of the psychodynamic account is the notion that the angry, disappointed and frustrated child feels unable ultimately to condemn the so-much-needed caretaker. She thereby takes into herself the idea that it is not the responses of the caretaker that are inadequate, but rather the needs themselves are seen as inappropriate and must be denied. The child learns to present to the world a coping, obliging self, while "the unnurtured real self has been split off and repressed" (Orbach, 1986).

Recently, several writers combining psychodynamic insights with socio-cultural analysis have tried to spell out differences in the early psychological development of girls and of boys which could begin to account for the vastly greater number of eating disorder females than males. Eichenbaum and Orbach (1983) discuss the mother's differential response to the male and female baby. With a son, because he is "different", the mother will try to get to know his wants and needs. Since girls are "the same" the mother assumes she knows what the baby girl wants. So it is the girl who is more vulnerable to a sense of her real needs not being recognised and met. It is the girl who is more likely to deny her legitimate demands.

Linked to this is the notion that at the centre of female development is the pressure to make and sustain relationships while boys are encouraged to be more autonomous and self-directed. For male children, writes Gilligan (1982), failures in the relationships with mother are less threatening. When maternal empathy lapses, the boy is more likely to respond with greater renunciation of the maternal tie while the girl will respond empathically by trying to repair the tie, by compliance and, if necessary, by denial of her real needs. It follows on from this thesis that the males who do develop eating disorders are males who build a self, not upon a sense of otherness, but on a close identification with the mother, concerning themselves closely with her life and expressing their imperfect separation through food.

"REGRESSION" MODELS

The psychoanalytic account has placed centrally the eating disordered individual's struggle for a sense of identity, competence and effectiveness. For those who have generally been extremely eager and obedient children, the need for self-reliant independence which confronts every adolescent seems to cause an insoluble conflict. From the psychodynamic viewpoint all adolescents struggling for independence have long been seen as experiencing a powerful pullback to a child-like state. Typically adolescents try to deny this helplessness and the need for powerful mother and father figures, often by acting in an exaggeratedly defiant way. Since part of the process of maturity for the adolescent involves moves in the direction of the verbal expression of emotions, an eating disorder can be seen as a regressive stage in which the sufferer returns to earlier mechanisms for dealing with feelings. Edelstein (1989) describes such patients as individuals in whom emotions such as anger, anxiety, even happiness, are overtly connected with and expressed in terms of physical sensations.

Crisp (e.g. 1983) from a very different perspective has also elaborated the view that anorexia nervosa is an illness of individuals who experience particular difficulty in negotiating their way into the adult world. He sees them as "solving" the crisis by opting out, by regressing to the known, safe world of pre-puberty. This is a view based on the understanding that anorexia nervosa usually occurs within a few years of puberty and usually involves a clear reversal of the characteristic pubertal hormonal changes. For Crisp the fear of weight gain expresses a desperate avoidance of the normal physical development associated with puberty and its attendant alterations in role requirements.

Why certain individuals, faced with the inevitable adolescent problems of autonomy and separation, are vulnerable to displaying such regressive behaviour, is accounted for by an understanding of the setting conditions that form the background to the child's entry into adolescence. The family, for example, may feel particularly threatened by the child's emerging sexuality or the parents may be dependent on the continued presence of children for the survival of their marriage. "Within such contexts," writes Crisp (1983), "many adolescents beneath their bravura seek for greater control and security ... and in a society where institutionalised and moral limits are decreasing, possibly the internal controls of the more conflict-ridden adolescent need to become stronger. For the teenage girl this might well include the curbing of 'fatness' and all its implications by dieting."

The view of anorexia nervosa as essentially a state of biological and psychological regression is a popular and appealing explanation of many features of the associated characteristic behaviour. But it has several weaknesses. It cannot explain the emergence of eating disorders well before or after the onset of puberty. It also fails to acknowledge the existence of powerful internal tensions and contradictions. While the patient usually does pull back from assuming age-appropriate responsibility for her physical well-being, refuses to assume adult sexuality, and delays the development of adult body characteristics, there is also much in her behaviour that is a struggle for more control, independence and autonomy. Palazzoli (1974) has identified the anorectic's "message" to the family as embodying a series of contradictions. She rebels without appearing to be rebellious; she revenges herself without appearing to be revengeful; she punishes without appearing to punish. The "regression" hypothesis too easily accepts at face value the picture of the "good girl" anorectic and neglects this tension. Lawrence (1984) has described "the control paradox" of the anorectic who experiences herself as powerless and out-of-control, and cannot integrate the powerful and controlling sides of herself. Anorexia nervosa can therefore be understood as an expression of powerlessness and an unsuccessful attempt to reject and overcome this state.

THE POSSIBLE ROLE OF ADVERSE SEXUAL EXPERIENCES

It is a popular view that fear of fatness may be related to avoidance of psychosexual maturity. Nevertheless, actual instances of sexual trauma or abuse have until recently been generally neglected in the literature. It has taken a new awareness of the prevalence of sexual abuse in childhood (e.g. Finkelhor, 1986; Nash & West, 1985) to invoke a reconsideration of the possibility of early sexual trauma in histories of eating disordered children and adults.

Browne and Finkelhor (1986) have reported that the consequences of childhood sexual abuse in later life include problems with sexual confidence, personal relationships and self-esteem. Disturbances of eating are also described for children who have suffered sexual abuse and for sexually abused women (Finkelhor, 1984). In the words of Palmer et al. (1990), "the individual's response to biological maturity and to the psychological and social demands of sexual development are widely invoked as being especially relevant (in the pathogenesis of anorexia nervosa and bulimia nervosa). Events which disrupt that development or make premature demands upon the person might be expected to increase the risk of eating disorders."

It is not only "regressive" symptoms of eating disorders that can be perceived in a new light if the possibility of early sexual trauma is considered more seriously. A variety of psychological features described in psychodynamic formulations—ambivalent love for mother, desire for autonomous control over the body, self-punishment—have potential "links of meaning" (Palmer et al., 1990) to the experience of early sexual trauma. Sloan and Leichner (1986) write: "It has long been considered that any or all of these dynamic factors in various combinations may be present in many patients as a consequence of actual past sexual assault or violence, or actual incestuous relationships involving various degrees of voluntary participation."

Clearly, as Sloan and Leichner point out, sexual abuse is neither necessary nor sufficient for the development of eating disorders. Furthermore, there are major problems regarding the specificity and causal relevance of findings in this area especially since it may be that a substantial proportion of non-eating-disordered female psychiatric patients give histories of childhood sexual abuse (Jacobson and Richardson, 1987). But evidence is growing that early sexual trauma may well be one of the contributory factors in the aetiology of eating disorders in a significant number of individuals.

Palmer et al. (1990) report that of 158 women seen in an Eating Disorders Clinic, questioned about their sexual experience with adults before the age of 16, a third reported non-trivial events in childhood. Over half also reported a variety of later adverse sexual experiences. Hall et al. (1989) reported even higher figures with similar numbers of eating-disordered subjects. In Calam and Slade's (1989) study of female undergraduates there was a higher-than-chance co-occurrence of sexual abuse as a trigger for the development of eating disorders. These authors understand sexual abuse as a trigger for the development of eating disorders in particular "setting conditions" and they hypothesise the link between childhood sexual abuse and eating disorders to be mediated by disgust for femininity and sexuality, expressed in concern for body image. In fact, in a later unpublished questionnaire study they found that body dissatisfaction did not look to be as salient a mediating variable as the perceived quality of relationship with parents. Their findings suggest the individuals most vulnerable to eating disorders and potentially abusive situations are those whose self-esteem is low, associated with a perceived lack of parental care and affection—even in the presence of over-protectiveness.

Many of the obviously eating-disordered patients interviewed by Hall et al. (1989) were clear about their wish to be skeletally thin because of the safety their appearance offered from further sexual assaults. Although this fits with the "regression" hypothesis, the authors see the motivation as more complex. The patients seem to want to "disgust" the individual who committed the assault, in large part as a way of breaking the emotional bond between themselves and the perpetrator.

FAMILY MODELS

Perhaps the most powerful and generative model for the understanding and treatment of eating disorders in the last 15 years has been the "family model". A central idea to the family approach to eating disorders is that it is not helpful to see one or even several family members as disordered; rather it is the organisation of the family which is dysfunctional.

Minuchin, Rosman, and Baker (1978) studied families with a variety of "psychosomatic" disorders including anorexia nervosa. They described the development of such an illness in terms of a pre-existing physiological vulnerability coupled with a particular type of family functioning. In "psychosomatic" families, members are described as over-involved and over-protective. They present as not needing or wanting change, preferring repeatedly to use a narrow range of ineffective strategies to cope with problems and avoiding tackling any issues that would lead to open conflict. Autonomy and independence are restricted, growing up and separating from the family are discouraged. The kind of environment fostered by such families encourages passive methods of defiance and makes it difficult for members to assert their individuality.

Palazzoli (1974) describes the families of anorectics whom she has treated as "rigid homeostatic systems ... governed by secret rules that shun the light of day and bind the family together with pathological ties" and she notes that psychiatric symptoms like self-starvation arise when the system is seriously threatened by the challenge of change, from within the family or from outside. A child's entry into adolescence is the point of change widely associated with the onset of an eating disorder.

Dare (1985) has commented on the common co-occurrence of critical transitional stresses in several family members at the onset of anorexia nervosa, constituting a strong demand for new attitudes and interests, and the giving-up of others appropriate to a preceding life-stage. He has suggested that anorexia nervosa may provide a respite to a family which, rather than negotiate change, utilises and supports the symptom to maintain the family system as it is.

The existing family system often involves, as both Minuchin and Palazzoli with their colleagues have observed, the child with anorexia nervosa occupying a triangulated position between the parents when the parents experience mutual difficulties in intimacy and trust (Palazzoli's "three-way matrimony"). Spouse conflict will not be acknowledged but masked by a façade of loyalty and smooth functioning with each spouse competing to make the greatest sacrifices in the course of duty. Palazzoli goes on to argue that to the extent that loyalty, cohesion and self-sacrifice are idealised in the families of children with anorexia nervosa, it is likely that betrayal, escape and self-centredness are bound to be highly tempting and deeply feared.

A "weaker" causal version of the family account sees the symptom as the patient's attempt to "solve" problems generated in families where major problems cannot be tackled directly or honestly. Haley (1976) has popularised the notion that symptoms are strategies for control in human relationships. A child's illness, for example, may be a strategy for bringing a marginal father back into family life or providing a depressed mother with a meaning to her day. This account allows for the inclusion of other individual psychological and biological factors as relevant in the development of the eating disorder. Alternatively, as Dare (1985) has noted, the vulnerable individual may develop an eating disorder for a host of other reasons unrelated to family organisation, but find his or her symptoms utilised and maintained by the family for its own purposes.

Is it possible to draw conclusions about the aetiological significance of family organisation in the development of an eating disorder from this work? No controlled examination of the pervasiveness of these characteristics in eating-disordered families has been conducted, although many clinicians and researchers agree that they quite appropriately describe the transactional patterns of many such families (e.g. Garfinkel & Garner, 1982) and the description has been an important lead in the development of a family-based approach to treatment. However, it is always possible that much of the apparent psychopathology in these families is a *result* rather than a *cause* of the problem. There is certainly no evidence that this dysfunctional kind of organisation is directly causative, although this assumption is sometimes made inappropriately when therapy which tackles these areas of functioning is successful.

CULTURAL EXPLANATIONS

Any model of the aetiology of anorexia nervosa and related eating disorders is incomplete if it fails to provide an adequate answer to the question of why they predominantly occur in females in "developed" Western societies. Many writers from diverse perspectives have argued that the cultural pressure on women to be thin is an important setting condition for the development of eating disorders (e.g. Bruch, 1974; Crisp, 1983; Garfinkel & Garner, 1982). Being thin has become almost synonymous with being good in a society that worships the bulge-free female form, and many anorectics begin their career in self-starvation after hearing a chance critical remark concerning their body shape or size.

In recent years theorists from outside mainstream psychiatry have put this fact at the forefront of their analysis and have viewed eating disorders in their relation to the current cultural preoccupation with thinness and to the position of women as objects to be looked at. Cultural historian Brumberg (1988) notes that prior to this interpretation, "women's dieting and weight concerns were once trivialised or interpreted as masking a strictly individual psychological problem without consideration for ways in which culture stimulated, exacerbated, and gave shape to a pattern of problematic behaviours".

The "cultural" approach recognises that throughout history the passive, depersonalised female form has been an object of pleasure for men and that this aspect of femininity is absorbed into each woman's experience of herself. The pressure experienced by teenage girls to conform to a fashion dictate that stresses the achievement of improbable shapes and weights is well documented. In a group of British schoolgirls, for example, only 4% of whom were overweight, almost half considered themselves so (Davies & Furnham, 1986). The cultural imperative is unlikely to be the sole explanation for the development of severe eating disorders. Most women live with a sense of body insecurity, dieting intermittently and usually unsuccessfully, but without resorting to damaging self-starvation. Further factors drive others to refuse food to a pathological degree, as if their acceptability as human beings, indeed their very identity, were attached to their capacity to be thin.

The cultural analysis, in attempting to set eating disorders in the complex interrelationships between culture, gender and food, acknowledges that it is still a fact that the vast majority of meals are purchased, prepared and served by women. Throughout history, Orbach (1986) reminds us, women have occupied the dual role of feeding others while denying themselves. Once an economic necessity, today it is a social demand. As Edwards (1987) summarises it, "For women, socially identified with their bodies and stereotypically linked to food and the kitchen, the struggle for control is naturally expressed through eating disorders."

The cultural model partly depends for its power, not just on the fact that eating disorders are predominantly female problems but also on the belief that the incidence of eating disorders is steadily increasing. The hypothesis is that the dieting female is struggling to transform her body in an attempt to deal with the contradictory requirements of her role in late-twentieth century Western societies. She faces contradictory problems and may be confused about her authentic needs and wishes. Culturally and psychologically, she is prepared for a life in which she should continue to service the needs of others (emotional, sexual, nutritional). At the same time she is teased with the possibility of a more autonomous and self-determined life. Working with girls from rural families who have moved to the city, Palazzoli (1974) argued that sufferers from anorexia nervosa typically come from families in the midst of cultural transition. An era of changing opportunities and expectations for women may similarly be a fertile ground for the development of anorexia nervosa, conceptualised essentially as a struggle for autonomy and individuality. The struggle finds expression in the paradoxical stance of the powerful but passive anorectic (her wish to be ultra-feminine, coupled with her rejection of femininity).

Lawrence (1984) sees this struggle played out in the field of education. She views education for women as bringing with it a whole set of difficulties which often push the educated female into a series of uneasy compromises with herself. The "middle-class bias" often referred to in accounts of anorexia nervosa (e.g. Palmer et al., 1980) she interprets as essentially an education bias. Indeed a clear coincidence of anorexia nervosa and educational achievement is identified in the literature (Dally & Gomez, 1979). But this striving for excellence can be problematic for girls. Bruch (1973) writes: "Growing girls can experience ... liberation as a demand and feel that they have to do something outstanding. Many of my patients have expressed the feeling that they are overwhelmed by the vast number of potential opportunities available to them ... and [that] they have been afraid of not choosing correctly." Girls, according to Lawrence (1984), may feel that they are compromising their feminine identity by achieving at school and they may strive to conform as a conventional young woman by achieving slimness. All the effort and self-denial that might have gone into school work is put into the struggle to be thin. Other writers have emphasised that the scholastic excellence noted in many groups of eating-disordered women is the product of a need to please others, rather than of a generally high natural endowment (e.g. Bruch, 1973; Garfinkel & Garner, 1982). To this picture of identity conflict, Chernin (1986) adds the extra problem for a female of accepting advantages and opportunities denied to her mother. Girls who cross into the male sphere of self-development and social power may experience profound ambivalence and guilt.

It was noted earlier that the "cultural" model depended for its power partly on the belief that the incidence of eating disorders is increasing. But is this so? Depending on diagnostic criteria, the population under study, and the manner of collecting data, researchers have come up with conflicting views on the incidence of eating disorders over the last 20 years. The evidence of an increase in the number of new cases of anorexia nervosa in women in both case-register studies (e.g. Jones, Fox, Babigan, & Hutton, 1980) and hospital admission data (Halmi, 1974) has been challenged on the grounds that any increase is due to greater numbers of young women in the population (Williams & King, 1987) (see further chapter 4). Interestingly there is greater consensus on the absence of any significant increase in the number of male cases. We therefore need to ask how far the contemporary cultural milieu plays a part in the aetiology of anorexia nervosa, if its incidence has not altered a great deal since its emergence as a modern disease in the early nineteenth century?

Brumberg (1988) suggests an answer by arguing that even in the last century anorexia nervosa mirrored the deepest preoccupations of the culture, with eating becoming a highly charged, emotional and social undertaking for women. With the reversal of the traditional view that a well-rounded women reflected the prosperity of her man, the fashion developed for debility and indolence in women, and the denial of "gross" appetites. Thinness became a sign of social status. In this cultural context girls became anorectic, says Brumberg, in an attempt to express an ideal of female perfection and moral superiority through denial of appetite. If there have been changes in incidence over the last couple of decades it may simply be because this aspiration is no longer a middle-class privilege.

Currently the "cultural" hypothesis is being challenged by an increasing number of reports that eating disorders are beginning to appear outside the Western world and among people of various ethnic origins. Anorexia nervosa is now well-documented in Japan (Suetmatsu, 1985) and has been described in blacks in the US (Robinson & Anderson, 1985), Britain (Holden & Robinson, 1988), and in Africa (Nwaefuna, 1981), and in Asians in Singapore (Ong, Tsoi, & Cheah, 1982), and now also in Asian children in Britain (Bryant-Waugh & Lask, 1991).

These atypical representations occur largely among migrants, and in societies undergoing rapid economic and socio-cultural change. It seems that as new populations adopt consumerist and individualistic values, they also grasp the novel and paradoxical relationship between the abundance of food and body weight. The individuals who are specifically vulnerable to developing an eating disorder may be those who experience more acutely the conflicts inherent in such a culture change.

TOWARDS AN INTEGRATION

Much of the theorising about the aetiology of eating disorders focuses on events and experiences in the lives of patients prior to (or sometimes coincident with) the onset of the problem. A virtue of Slade's (1982) lucid model of the evolution of anorexia nervosa is that it pays close attention to the changes over time which are a notable feature of eating disorders. His model stresses the importance of exploring not just the *antecedent* events in understanding aetiology, but also the *consequences* of the anorectic individual's behaviour at various stages in the development of the illness. These consequences can maintain existing psychological and physical symptoms in a continuous feedback loop as well as pushing the individual on to new stages of the disorder. According to Slade's model, dieting and weight loss are triggered by specific psychosocial stimuli given certain necessary setting conditions. If the dieting behaviour leads to feelings of success and "being in control" it is reinforced both by those feelings and (negatively) through fear of weight gain and avoidance of other problems. If the reinforcements are sufficiently powerful then the food avoidance is intensified to a pathological level leading to full-blown anorexia nervosa.

Slade's model shows the usefulness of a schematic approach in trying to imagine an integration of the various factors that seem important in the aetiology of eating disorders. Any formulation of anorexia nervosa and related eating disorders should aim to reflect the complex interplay over time of the major causative and maintaining factors. These are summarised below.

1. Predisposing Factors

From an organic perspective, a genetic predisposition to develop anorexia nervosa has been identified, and it may be that soon the relevant physiological vulnerability will be specified.

Among the essential predisposing factors, from a psychological perspective, identified by Slade (1982) is a "general dissatisfaction with life and self". This state may be created when adolescent conflicts over autonomy are particularly powerful—for example, within a family where the child is "triangulated" in a poor marriage. These are the features of family life which, as we have seen, are widely recognised as important predisposing factors. Other predisposing factors contributing to the general dissatisfaction with life and self may be stress and failure experiences, e.g. the pressure to achieve academically, which we have seen is a feature in the lives of many anorectic girls. A tendency to perfectionism is another predisposing factor for which there is significant research evidence (e.g. Halmi et al., 1977). The perfection-istic and dissatisfied adolescent may turn to self/bodily control, to attain a sense of success or achievement in some area. Adverse sexual experiences may also predispose the individual to that combination of low self-esteem, internal conflict and a wish for control which seems central to the development of eating disorders.

2. Precipitating Factors

Precipitating factors determine the time of the onset of an illness. An important trigger for the onset of intense dieting is popularly thought to be a comment on the individual's weight or shape, or the observation that a peer is dieting. Research has identified a broader range of precipitants (although it needs to be noted that the individual sufferer or close observer may find it hard to identify a trigger in retrospect, while for researchers the line between "triggers" and "setting conditions" can be a fine one). Halmi (1974) and Morgan & Russell (1975) found that over half their patients identified an external precipitant. Garfinkel and Garner (1982) succinctly summarise the research in this area and note that whatever the precipitating event, the individual perceives it as representing "a threat of loss of self-control and /or a threat of an actual loss of self-worth". Separations and losses have frequently been identified as precipitating factors in anorexia nervosa—from bereavement, to parental divorce, to leaving home for college. Such events disrupt familiar expectations and may provide a grave threat to an individual with a poor sense of self-reliance and self-worth. Such disruptions of known demands may also occur when an individual is involved in her first intimate or sexual contact. Certainly, the transition into adolescence can create a host of conflicts (usually centred around the issue of autonomy) which can be heightened by difficulties in the family and social matrix. These may serve both as predisposing or precipitating factors.

3. Perpetuating Factors

Once an eating disorder has developed, whatever its origins, the body's adaptation to it and the patient's attempts to deal with the symptoms can lead to an elaboration and perpetuation of the condition in a variety of ways.

Several of the physiological features of eating disorders, and of anorexia nervosa in particular, which may be secondary to starvation, are likely to have a role in perpetuating the disorder. For instance, delayed gastric emptying at low weight produces an unpleasant feeling of fullness after small meals, and can lead to a further reduction of food intake, to an increased preoccupation with food, and possibly to a greater distortion of the body image.

The increased social isolation and abandonment of old interests and activities, characteristic of the lives of seriously disturbed eaters, can lead to depressed mood and the further reduction of self-esteem. Typically the eating-disordered patient will respond to this by renewed efforts at weight control in a self-perpetuating cycle.

The weight control achieved by dieting can, for vulnerable individuals, be highly rewarding and produce an intense sense of success and internal power. A strength of Slade's (1982) model is its acknowledgement of how the sense of being-in-control acquires an over-valued importance for individuals who perceive themselves as failures in all other areas of functioning, and so leads to continued self-starvation in a vicious cycle where a more intense denial is needed to generate success experiences of the required potency. Crucially built into this feedback loop is a further consequence of the obsession with self-starvation: the avoidance of the various interpersonal problems and stresses that formed the major motivation for dieting in the first place. Thus the internal conflicts that serve to predispose to illness are seen to serve later as powerful maintaining forces once food refusal becomes established.

For the patient's family, too, the continuation of the eating disorder may distract from attempts to resolve family problems (problems which may have played a role in the development of the disorder). There may also be aspects of the family's adaptation to the conditions which serve to sustain it, such as greater involvement in family life by father, or attention given to the patient at the expense of siblings.

CONCLUSION

The challenge in understanding the aetiology of anorexia nervosa and related eating disorders lies not in identifying a single cause nor even in documenting a list of all risk factors, but rather in understanding the particular ways in which the various contributory factors are likely to interact at different stages in the evolution of the illness.

It is not enough, for example, to see familial over-protection and conflict avoidance as co-existing as causal factors with societal pressure for slimness. Rather it becomes important to try to elucidate how the wider culture is transmitted through the family: how, for instance, Minuchin's "anorectic families" teach their daughters the most conventional social attitudes to femininity (Edwards, 1987).

The cultural objectification of the female body can also be seen as contributing to the widespread incidence of childhood sexual abuse which, as discussed earlier in this chapter, often has an important, if imperfectly understood, role in the development of eating disorders. The causal significance of the wish to reverse the development of normal puberty may, for some individuals, be linked to traumatic sexual experiences.

A third example of the need to understand the interactions between causal factors is the way in which the "middle-class bias" in anorexia nervosa may turn out to be better understood as an education bias, which can in turn be seen as implicated in the psychological features of over-compliance and the lack of inner directiveness emphasised by some psychodynamic writers (e.g. Bruch, 1974).

We can anticipate the advent of increasingly complex models of the aetiology of eating disorders but there are two caveats to that proposal. First, it is likely that the precise interaction of the many predisposing, precipitating and perpetuating factors important in the evolution of eating disorders can never be fully delineated. Nor may it even be entirely clear what characteristics protect some apparently vulnerable individuals. The second caveat is that the richness and complexity of the models we build should not obscure the need for a central organising idea. A number of authors from very diverse perspectives share an understanding of anorexia nervosa as essentially a syndrome of pathological self-control (Bruch, 1974; Slade, 1982; Crisp, 1983; Lawrence, 1984). Crucially, this shifts the wish to be thin from the centre of the phenomenological picture and gives clearer shape to the search for coherence in understanding the relationship between causal forces. As Bruch (1974) lucidly expresses it: "The main issue is a struggle for control, or a sense of identity, competence and effectiveness. Many of these youngsters had struggled for years to be 'perfect' in the eyes of others. Concern with thinness and food refusal, are late steps in this maldevelopment."

REFERENCES

Alderdice, J., Dinsmore, W., Buchanan, K., & Adam, C. (1985). Gastrointestinal hormones in anorexia nervosa. *Journal of Psychiatric Research, 19*, 207–213.

Browne, A. & Finklehor, D. (1986). Impact of child sexual abuse: A review of the research. *Psychological Bulletin, 99*, 66–67.

Bruch, H. (1973). *The golden cage: The enigma of anorexia nervosa.* London: Open Books.

Bruch, H. (1974). *Eating disorders: Obesity, anorexia nervosa and the person within.* London: Routledge & Kegan Paul.

Brumberg, J.J. (1988). *Fasting girls.* Cambridge, Massachusetts: Harvard University.

Bryant-Waugh, R. & Lask, B. (1991). Anorexia nervosa in a group of Asian children living in Britain. *British Journal of Psychiatry, 158,* 229–233.

Button, E.J. & Whitehouse, A. (1981). Subclinical anorexia nervosa. *Psychological Medicine, 11,* 509–516.

Calam, R.M. & Slade, P.D. (1989). Sexual experience and eating problems in female undergraduates. *International Journal of Eating Disorders, 8,* 391–397.

Chernin, K. (1986). *The hungry self.* London: Virago.

Crisp, A.H. (1965). Some aspects of the evolution, presentation and follow-up of anorexia nervosa. *Proceedings of the Royal Society of Medicine, 58,* 814–820.

Crisp, A.H. (1983). Anorexia nervosa. *British Medical Journal, 287,* 855–858.

Crisp, A., Palmer, R., & Kalucy, R. (1976). How common is anorexia nervosa? A prevalence study. *British Journal of Psychiatry, 128,* 549–554.

Dally, P. & Gomez, J. (1979). *Anorexia nervosa.* London: Heinemann.

Dare, C. (1985). The family therapy of anorexia nervosa. *Journal of Psychiatric Research, 19,* 435–443.

Davies, E. & Furnham, A. (1986). The dieting and body shape concerns of adolescent females. *Journal of Child Psychology and Psychiatry, 27,* 417–428.

Edelstein, E.L. (1989). *Anorexia nervosa and other dyscontrol syndromes.* Berlin: Springer-Verlag.

Edwards, G. (1987). Anorexia and the family. In M. Lawrence (Ed.), *Fed up and hungry: Women, oppression and food.* London: Women's Press.

Eichenbaum, L. & Orbach, S. (1983). *Understanding women: A feminist psychoanalytic approach.* London: Penguin.

Finkelhor, D. (1984). *Child sexual abuse: New theory and research.* New York: Free Press.

Finkelhor, D. (1986). *A sourcebook on child sexual abuse.* London: Sage.

Garfinkel, P.E. & Garner, D.M. (1982). *Anorexia nervosa: A multi-dimensional perspective.* New York: Brunner Mazel.

Garner, A. & Garfinkel, P. (1980). Sociocultural factors in the development of anorexia nervosa. *Psychological Medicine, 10,* 647–656.

Gilligan, C. (1982). *In a different voice.* Cambridge, Massachusetts: Harvard University.

Haley, J. (1976). *Problem-solving therapy.* New York: Harper and Row.

Hall, R.C.W., Tice, M.S.W., Beresford, T.P., Wooley, B., & Hall, A.K. (1989). Sexual abuse in patients with anorexia and bulimia. *Psychosomatics, 1,* 73–79.

Halmi, K.A. (1974). Anorexia nervosa: Demographic and clinical features in 94 cases. *Psychosomatic Medicine, 36,* 18–25.

Halmi, K.A., Goldberg, S.C., Eckert, E., Casper, R., & Davis, J.M. (1977). Pretreatment evaluation in anorexia nervosa. In R.A. Vigersky (Ed.), *Anorexia nervosa.* New York: Raven.

Holden, N. & Robinson, P. (1988). Anorexia nervosa and bulimia nervosa in British blacks. *British Journal of Psychiatry, 152,* 544–549.

Holland, A., Sicotte, N., & Treasure, J. (1988). Anorexia nervosa—evidence for a genetic basis. *Journal of Psychosomatic Research, 32,* 549–554.

Jacobson, A. & Richardson, B. (1987). Assault experiences of 100 psychiatric in-patients: Evidence of the need for routine enquiry. *American Journal of Psychiatry, 144,* 908–913.

Jones, D.J., Fox, M.M., Babigan, H.M., & Hutton, H.E. (1980). Epidemiology of anorexia nervosa in Munroe County, New York: 1960–1976. *Psychosomatic Medicine, 42,* 551–558.

Klein, M. (1975). *Envy and gratitude and other works.* London: The Hogarth Press.

Lask, B., Fosson, A., Thomas, S., & Rolfe, U. (1993). Zinc deficiency in children with anorexia nervosa. *Journal of Clinical Psychiatry.*

Lawrence, M. (1984). *The anorectic experience.* London: The Woman's Press.

Minuchin, S., Rosman, B.L., & Baker, L. (1978). *Psychosomatic families: Anorexia nervosa in context.* Cambridge, Massachusetts: Harvard University Press.

Morgan, H.G. & Russell, G.F.M. (1975). Value of family background and clinical features as predictors of long-term outcome in anorexia nervosa: Four year follow-up study of 42 patients. *Psychological Medicine, 5,* 355–371.

Muller, A. (1988). *Harries paediatric gastroenterology,* P. Milla & A. Muller (Eds.). London: Churchill Livingstone.

Nash, C.L. & West, D.J. (1985). Sexual molestation of young girls: A retrospective survey. In D.J. West (Ed.), *Sexual Victimisation.* Aldershot: Gower.

Nwaefuna, A. (1981). Anorexia nervosa in a developing country. *British Journal of Psychiatry, 138,* 270–271.

Ong, Y.L., Tsoi, W.F., & Cheah, J.S. (1982). A clinical and psychosocial study of seven cases of anorexia nervosa in Singapore. *Singapore Medical Journal, 23,* 255–261.

Orbach, S. (1986). *Hunger strike.* Harmondsworth: Penguin.

Palazzoli, M.S. (1974). *Self-starvation.* London: Chancer.

Palmer, R.L. (1980). *Anorexia nervosa: A guide for sufferers and their families.* Harmondsworth: Penguin.

Palmer, R.L., Oppenheimer, R., Dignon, A.L., Chaloner, D.A., & Howells, K. (1990). Childhood sexual experiences with adults reported by women with eating disorders: An extended series. *British Journal of Psychiatry, 156,* 699–703.

Robinson, P. & Anderson, A. (1985). Anorexia nervosa in American blacks. *Journal of Psychiatric Research, 19,* 183–188.

Russell, G. (1985). Anorexia and bulimia nervosa. In M. Rutter & L. Herson (Eds.), *Child and adolescent psychiatry.* Oxford: Blackwell Scientific Publications.

Slade, P.D. (1982). Towards a functional analysis of anorexia nervosa. *British Journal of Clinical Psychology, 21,* 167–179.

Sloan, G. & Leichner, P. (1986). Is there a relationship between sexual abuse or incest and eating disorders? *Canadian Journal of Psychiatry, 31,* 656–660.

Strober, M., Lampert, C., Morrell, W., Burroughs, J., & Jacobs, C. (1980). A controlled family study of anorexia nervosa. *International Journal of Eating Disorders, 9,* 239–253.

Suetmatsu, H. (1985). The concept and definition of anorexia nervosa. In H. Suetmatsu (Ed.), *Anorexia nervosa,* (pp. 2–11). Tokyo: Igakoshoin.

Theander, S. (1970). Anorexia nervosa: A psychiatric investigation of 94 female patients. *Acta Psychiatrica Scandinavica,* Suppl. 214.

Waller, J.V., Kaufman, R.M., & Deutsch, F. (1940). Anorexia nervosa: A psychosomatic entity. *Psychosomatic Medicine, 2,* 3–16.

Weiner, H. (1985). The physiology of the eating disorders. *International Journal of Eating Disorders, 4,* 347–388.

Williams, P. & King, M. (1987). The "epidemic" of anorexia nervosa: Another medical myth? *Lancet, i,* 205–207.

CHAPTER SIX

Prognosis and Outcome

Rachel Bryant-Waugh

INTRODUCTION

There are hundreds of reports of follow-up studies of patients treated for an eating disorder. The results of these studies vary considerably, and are often contradictory. Consequently there is a very confusing body of data, with no clear picture emerging of prognosis and outcome in eating disorders. The majority of follow-up studies have been carried out with people treated for anorexia nervosa. There remain at present fewer outcome studies of bulimia nervosa, primarily because this has only relatively recently been identified as a disorder distinct from anorexia nervosa, but new research findings in this area continue to be published. In the case of children, outcome studies focus exclusively on anorexia nervosa, with the exception of one study, which includes children with food avoidance emotional disorder (Higgs, Goodyer, & Birch, 1989; see further chapter 2).

Steinhausen & Glanville (1983) have provided a clear overview of 45 follow-up studies of adolescent and adult anorectic patients published between 1953 and 1981. The majority of these studies were concerned with one of two main questions: What is the effectiveness of different treatment techniques, and which prognostic indicators can be identified? The most striking point to emerge from these studies is the very wide discrepancy between results obtained. Hsu (1980) carried out a similar review of studies of the outcome of anorexia nervosa, including

16 studies published between 1954 and 1979. He also found a large amount of variation in results obtained, and cautiously suggested that at 4–8-year follow-up, approximately 75% of all the subjects included in the studies were "better at follow-up than at initial presentation in terms of body weight". However, results in the areas of menstrual functioning and psychiatric status were found to be more unsatisfactory, and of the 75% whose weight had improved, a significant percentage continued to struggle in one or more areas of their life. The available literature suggests ever more convincingly that complete recovery from anorexia nervosa is probably the exception rather than the rule, and the depressing reality is emerging that the probability of relapse or symptom substitution is relatively high.

THE IMPORTANCE OF OUTCOME RESEARCH

There are many good reasons for conducting follow-up studies of particular groups of patients treated for similar disorders in a specific setting. Most clinicians would express an interest in finding out how their patients have fared in the longer term, and might hope to learn from interviewing such individuals. Ex-patients are a useful source of comment and criticism about treatment methods offered, and clinical practice may benefit from contact with them. However, well-designed outcome research has many further potential benefits besides satisfying the clinician's curiosity. These have been summarised by Hsu (1990) as including the following:

1. A distinction can be made between short-term improvement and long-term recovery. (This point is discussed in more detail in the section entitled "Adequate Length of Follow-up" later in this chapter.)
2. Treatment efforts can be evaluated and compared against the natural course of the illness. This represents a somewhat neglected area in research, as it is ethically very difficult to conduct a study comparing a treated and non-treated group of patients. Crisp et al. (1991) have perhaps come the closest to this by including a "no-treatment" group in a recent follow-up study of anorexia nervosa patients. Good treatment-outcome studies, that is studies designed to assess the effectiveness of specific treatment components, are relatively rare in the eating-disorders literature. Only one major study to emerge has specifically addressed treatment in younger patients: Russell, Szmukler, Dare, and Eisler (1987) found that family

therapy appears to be a more useful mode of therapeutic intervention than individual psychotherapy in people below the age of 18 with anorexia nervosa of less than three years duration.

3. Prognostic indicators can be identified, which may allow a more accurate prediction of the course the illness is likely to take in any one individual. Identification of prognostic indicators may also allow for treatment to be more effectively targeted. Unfortunately, there is much inconsistency in prognostic indicators reported in the literature, with no factors being universally found to have a positive or a negative influence on outcome. (See further the section on "Prognostic Indicators in the Early Onset Population" later in this chapter.)

4. The confusion about the identity and classification of the various eating disorders may be clarified. There remains much debate about the relationship between, for example, restricting anorexia nervosa, anorexia nervosa accompanied by purging and vomiting, bulimia nervosa, etc. It may be that consistent findings at outcome of patients with different diagnoses may shed some light on the interrelationships involved.

METHODOLOGICAL CONSIDERATIONS IN OUTCOME RESEARCH

Few of the existing follow-up studies attempting to assess the outcome of anorexia nervosa and related eating disorders are free from methodological weaknesses. Essential requirements of good outcome studies include the following:

1. Clear Definitions of Disorders Studied and Descriptions of Subjects Selected

It is clearly important that basic information is provided about the subjects included in any follow-up study. Inclusion criteria must be listed, with mention of any formal diagnostic criteria that have been used, such as those of DSM III R (American Psychiatric Association, 1987). In order for studies to be useful for comparison purposes it is necessary to distinguish between the different types of eating disorder (i.e. anorexia nervosa, bulimia nervosa), and where terms such as "partial syndrome" or "sub-clinical" are used, a clear operational definition must be provided.

In addition, some mention should be made about the relative severity of illness in the group as a whole. This may be rather difficult, but clearly the outcome in two groups of patients with anorexia nervosa may be expected to differ if one group represents a more severely ill group at the time of the index treatment. Severity of illness is usually expressed in terms of length of illness prior to treatment, degree of weight loss, previous hospital admissions in the context of an eating disorder, etc. Part of the problem with the existing outcome literature is that there are many different studies measuring different features in non-comparable groups of patients. It is therefore not surprising that results are so varied.

2. Multiple Outcome Parameters

Anorexia nervosa and other eating disorders are multi-determined, multi-faceted disorders. Any attempt to describe outcome in meaningful terms must therefore involve assessment using multiple outcome parameters. The most obvious, and most commonly reported, are body weight (usually expressed as a percentage of average body weight), eating behaviour (rather more difficult to define) and in females, menstrual functioning. Where deaths occur, mortality rates are reported; in most cases these are expressed as a percentage of the patient series studies. Of arguably equal importance are the individual's general mental state, including the presence of any psychopathology at follow-up, attitudes to weight and eating, sexual adjustment and social functioning, which might include the nature and quality of personal relationships. In patients with early onset anorexia nervosa, height should also be added to the list, given the suspension of growth that typically occurs in this age group. Findings from studies investigating outcome in early onset patients in the above areas are summarised later in this chapter.

Clearly, the outcome on any one of these parameters will not give a reliable impression of whether an individual has "recovered" or not. Studies that simply state the numbers of subjects whose outcome is "good", "intermediate" or "poor", without indicating how this has been defined, are of limited usefulness, and do not really allow a clear impression to be gained of the degree of improvement or deterioration that may have taken place in different areas of the patients' functioning. Authors who use global outcome measures as the main means of expressing outcome have been criticised by their peers for this reason (e.g. Kreipe, Churchill, & Strauss, 1989; Woodside, 1990).

3. Reliable Data Base

Because of the now well-known problem of denial in eating disorders (Vandereycken & Vanderlinden, 1983), follow-up studies that rely on information obtained from telephone interviews or postal questionnaires, must be viewed as inadequate. Hsu (1990) has pointed out that not only do indirect methods usually result in inaccurate information being recorded, but it is also impossible to detect minor morbidity. Face-to-face interviews of patients are the best means of gathering information, and also allow an assessment of mental state. Interviewing parents, partners, or other "significant others" as a means of obtaining corroborative information is valuable. It is, of course, essential that adequate description should be provided of the means employed to obtain follow-up information.

The assessment of mental state at follow-up is clearly of major importance in outcome studies of eating disorders. Some authors have made a plea for this assessment to be made by means of a standardised structured, or semi-structured, interview such as the Present State Examination of Wing, Cooper, and Sartorius (1974) (e.g. Hsu, 1990; Walford & McCune, 1991). The rationale for this is to eliminate the variation in different clinicians' opinions of any one individual's mental state. It is generally considered preferable for follow-up interviews to be conducted by someone who has not been actively involved in the patient's treatment, as this may bias results. However, Martin (1985) has suggested that regular follow-up appointments on a six-to twelve-month basis over a period of some years may serve to improve outcome because of the ongoing supportive relationship with the therapist. This view incorporates longer term follow-up as part of the treatment process, and interviews are not sprung upon discharged patients for research purposes.

4. Adequate Length of Follow-up

Much has been written about what constitutes an "adequate" follow-up interval. It is generally agreed that follow-up shortly after treatment has been terminated will give the best results, although Martin (1985) has reported that results obtained at five-year follow-up were better than at the end of treatment in the group of adolescent patients she studied. Many authors have followed the recommendation set out in Morgan & Russell's (1975) paper, first mentioned by Russell (1970), that there should be a minimum period of four years before any reliable impression emerges about outcome in any one individual. However, there is much inconsistency in defining the length of the follow-up interval. Some authors take the period between discharge from hospital and follow-up, while others use time of presentation or initiation of treatment, or time of onset of the eating disorder. As long as there is no agreed way to measure this interval, the means used to arrive at a figure for length of follow-up should be stated.

Russell (1977) has stated that anorexia nervosa is an illness that must run its course, and one that is characterised by cycles of recovery and relapse. When outcome is measured before the illness has completed its course, misleading results may be obtained. This is clearly illustrated by Theander's long-term follow-up study of 94 females hospitalised for anorexia nervosa between 1931–1960. Two follow-up studies were carried out on this population, the first in 1966 (Theander, 1970) and the second in 1984 (Theander, 1985). In the latter the observation period for all patients was 24 years or more. Compared to the first study more were deemed to have recovered, but the mortality rate was also found to be higher, with most deaths occurring from suicide or causes related to the eating disorder. Of the ten early onset patients in this series, three had a recurrence of anorexia nervosa after a remission of between two and six years during which they had normal weight and menstruation. Hsu (1990) has suggested that a distinction might be made between intermediate-term follow-up studies (e.g. 4–8 years) and long-term follow-up studies (more than 20 years) to allow account to be taken of the apparently lengthy course of the illness. This suggestion leaves a question mark over what to call studies with a follow-up period of 9–20 years, but some such system of classification may prove to be very useful.

5. Description of Treatment Received

For comparison purposes it is necessary to have access to a clear description of the treatment received by the subjects included in any outcome study. While the majority of follow-up investigations are not treatment outcome studies, i.e. they do not set out to discover the relative effectiveness of different treatment components, it is useful to have some information about the therapy received. This may allow an impression to be gained of how patients in one treatment environment fare in comparison to those in another (given comparable groups of subjects), but it does not allow statements to be made along the lines of "day-patient care is preferable to in-patient care". In order to be able to do this, specifically designed treatment-outcome studies are necessary. Most follow-up studies do not attempt to separate out the effect of different treatment components.

Related to the need to describe treatment received is the requirement that the number of patients not engaging in, or dropping out of, treatment should be specified (Hsu, 1990). This group represents a neglected area in terms of research, and we have very little idea about the longer term course of their illness.

6. Taking Account of "Refusers" and "Failure-to-trace" Subjects

Most researchers who have tried to conduct a follow-up study of patients treated for anorexia nervosa will be familiar with the reluctance of a significant number of individuals to attend for interview. It has often been suggested that in the case of eating disorders, patients who are still ill will be less likely to co-operate (e.g. Hsu, 1980). This will clearly affect the results obtained, biasing them in the direction of a more favourable overall outcome. It is therefore essential that the percentage of subjects refusing to participate in the follow-up investigation is specified. If possible, information should be sought about these patients via means other than face-to-face interview. However, such patients are often insistent in their wish not to comply with requests and refuse telephone interviews, postal questionnaires, or access to partners or families. In such instances the patient's right to privacy must be respected.

Similarly, the percentage of patients lost to follow-up because they have moved away, or are otherwise inaccessible, must be stated. It might be argued that this group is more likely to include patients with a range of outcomes when compared to the group of refusers. Nevertheless, outcome in these patients remains a question mark and the more there are of them, the less reliable a picture is obtained from the group who do attend for interview. The aim is ultimately to follow the progress of as many patients as possible to ensure accuracy in the results reported.

OUTCOME IN EARLY ONSET EATING DISORDER PATIENTS

Relatively few studies have been carried out specifically investigating the outcome in childhood onset eating disorder patients, and of those which have, very few stand up to methodological criticism. Swift (1982) reviewed seven early onset follow-up studies published between 1960 and 1978, and concluded that only two were relatively free from flaws in research design (Cantwell et al., 1977; Warren, 1968). The remaining five were considered to have significant methodological faults (Goetz, Succop, Reinhart, & Miller, 1977; Lesser, Ashenden, Delruskey, & Eisenberg, 1960; Minuchin, Rosman, & Baker, 1978; Rowland, 1970; Valanne et al., 1972). The fact that the two studies with a more satisfactory design report quite different overall results, and consequently that their authors draw different conclusions about prognosis and outcome in younger eating disorder patients, is indicative of the confusing nature of outcome research. Since Swift's (1982) review a number of other follow-up studies have been published (some of which are described in more detail below), but the overall impression remains one of wide variation in findings.

Mortality

It has long been recognised that anorexia nervosa in children is a serious disorder which is potentially fatal (Blitzer, Rollins, & Blackwell, 1961; Warren, 1968). Mortality rates reported in the early onset literature vary from 0% to 18% (Swift, 1982), and are generally placed around 0–5%, although Lucas, Duncan, & Piens (1976) reported an exceptionally high mortality rate of 22%, and Theander (1988) reports that two of ten early onset patients had died by the time of long-term follow-up. Most deaths are reported as occurring in the first eight years after the initial consultation, and particularly in the first four. As in the outcome literature on older age at onset patients, the main causes of death appear to be suicide and causes secondary to starvation.

Hsu (1990) has proposed that mortality should be expressed in terms of a standardised mortality ratio to allow comparison between different studies and with age and sex specific mortality rates for the general population. He quotes Patton (1988) as claiming that the standard mortality ratio for anorexia nervosa (in older patients) represents a 600% increase in mortality when compared to the expected ratio in the normal population, and that this figure is even higher for bulimia nervosa. Mortality rates reported in the early onset literature are in general similar to those reported for older patients, and there is no reason to believe that younger patients are less likely to die. Clearly this is a situation that gives rise to considerable concern.

Weight and Nutritional Status

Weight at follow-up is usually expressed in terms of the percentage of average body weight, which is defined according to actuarial tables or, in the case of adolescents, standard measures of growth and development (Tanner, Whitehouse, & Takaishi, 1966). Findings of weight at follow-up in early onset patients include the following. Kreipe et al. (1989) found that 65% of 49 adolescents treated in an intensive in-patient unit for anorexia nervosa were 90% or more of ideal body weight at an average of 6.5 years after hospitalisation. Bryant-Waugh et al. (1988) reported that 50% of 30 early onset patients with a mean follow-up period of 7.2 years had regained normal body weight, 17% were underweight and 3% overweight. Outcome in terms of weight was reported to be good (within 15% of average body weight during the preceding six months) in 66% of the 15 early onset cases followed up by Walford and McCune (1991) and in 67% of Hawley's (1985) 21 early onset patients. A further 20% of Walford and McCune's patients were reported to be underweight. These findings are remarkably similar to those reported in outcome studies of older patients; Hsu's (1990) review of five intermediate outcome studies published between 1975 and 1984 revealed that 50–62% of subjects had regained normal weight, 11–20% were markedly underweight, and 2–10% were overweight at the time of follow-up.

Eating Difficulties, Concerns about Weight and Continuing Eating Disorder

This represents a rather under-reported area, with many studies failing to mention what proportion of subjects continue to experience abnormal attitudes and behaviour concerning food, weight and eating. It is certainly not the case that improvement in body weight is necessarily associated with normalisation in eating behaviour. Kreipe et al. (1989) report that 44% of their series had few or no eating-disorder symptoms at follow-up, 25% had some symptoms, and 25% were actively ill (approximately six and a half years after hospitalisation). They also found that 49% of the 49 subjects included in the study had developed bulimia nervosa after or during recovery from anorexia nervosa, but that by the time of follow-up this had remitted in about half. Vilsvik and Vaglum, (1990) report that at the end of treatment eating difficulties persisted in 65% of 17 teenage anorectics (mean age at referral 15 years). Maloney and Klykylo (1983) have suggested that follow-up studies of eating disorders in children and adolescents indicate that after five years only around 35% of patients are found to be eating normally. Again, this seems similar to the situation in older patients, where approximately two thirds of subjects are found at follow-up to continue to be preoccupied with weight and diet, with bulimia nervosa being commonly reported, while only around one third have a normal regular pattern of eating (Hsu, 1990).

Menstrual Functioning

Here again, results vary considerably and account needs to be taken of the extent of comparability of the various groups of subjects studied. For example, it may well be that girls who develop an eating disorder before they have had a first period, run a greater risk of longer term impairment of menstrual functioning, especially if the eating disorder runs a fairly protracted course during what is a critical period in terms of normal pubertal development. The return (or commencement) of normal menstrual functioning is often thought to be dependent on the ability to maintain a normal body weight, although it is true to say that the association is incompletely understood, and that there are plenty of exceptions to this rule. Some patients appear to resume menstruation while remaining underweight; in others, menses remain absent or irregular, despite normal weight.

Kreipe et al. (1989) found that 80% of their 49 adolescent females had a satisfactory resumption of menses at follow-up. Similarly, Vilsvik and Vaglum (1990) reported that all but one of their 15 female subjects had overcome menstrual irregularities by the time of follow-up (mean four years). Sturzenberger et al. (1977) reported that menstrual outcome was good in 59–61% of their adolescent onset patients, intermediate in 9–24% and poor in 17–30%. Investigating younger onset patients, Bryant-Waugh et al. (1988) reported good menstrual outcome in 55%, intermediate in 14% and amenorrhoea in 31%. These findings are very similar to those of Walford and McCune (1991), who reported 50% good, 17% irregular and 33% poor. Hawley (1985) found regular menses in 60% of his series of 21 children, and irregular menses in 20%. By comparison, Hsu (1990) found that in older patients between 47–58% are reported as having regular menses, with 19–39% experiencing continuing amenorrhoea.

Mental State

A relatively small percentage of patients are generally found to be entirely symptom-free at follow-up (Rollins & Piazza, 1981; Sturzenberger et al., 1977). Again this is similar to the situation in older patients where around a third are reported to experience significant depressive symptoms, and generally high rates of affective symptoms and other psychopathological disturbances are often reported (Hsu, 1990). In early onset patients, the most commonly identified disorders at follow-up include depression, obsessive-compulsive behaviours, social phobias and eating disorders, although Walford and McCune, (1991) have commented that when a standardised psychiatric interview is used a somewhat lower than expected, but nevertheless significant, rate of psychological morbidity may be found. Using such an interview schedule, these authors found the mental state at follow-up to be good in 67% of their subjects, and poor in 33%.

These results are very similar to those of Bryant-Waugh et al. (1988), who report that outcome in terms of mental state was good in 62% of their series, but that the remaining 38% had a mild to moderate degree of psychiatric disturbance, with around a quarter requiring a further psychiatric admission. Hawley (1985) noted that 39% of his series had continued psychiatric disturbance at follow-up, and Vilsvik and Vaglum (1990) described a third of their patients as having "neurotic problems". Some authors have found much higher rates of psychiatric disturbance at follow-up: For example, Sturzenberger et al. (1977) reported that 70% of their series of 26 adolescents had moderate to marked clinical psychopathology. Again, it is likely that the patient groups included in these various studies are not directly comparable, and that different definitions of pathology are used.

Psychosexual Adjustment

Psychosexual adjustment is particularly difficult to assess in adolescents and is rarely commented upon in any detail in the early onset outcome literature. In older patients around 20–37% are reported as expressing fear or disgust in matters relating to sexual behaviour (Hsu, 1990). The numbers of early onset patients who in adolescence have "abnormal" sexual adjustment is simply not known, and would methodologically be practically impossible to determine.

Psychosocial Functioning

In general, social adjustment has been found to be relatively good, with many subjects leading a fairly normal life despite the fact that they may have continuing eating difficulties (Valanne et al., 1972). Goetz et al. (1977) have suggested that certain personality types, in particular "hysterical personalities", are most likely to make a good social adjustment, although this is an area of research that has been relatively limited in popularity. Kreipe et al. (1989) found that nearly all of their follow-up subjects had completed secondary education, and 40% had completed a university education, despite a third admitting that their continuing preoccupation with food and weight had significantly affected their ability to study. At the time of follow-up all 49 subjects were either in full-time work or education or at home caring for their own children. It seems that psychosocial adjustment may be slightly better in early onset patients assessed at intermediate follow-up periods (i.e. 4–8 years). Hsu (1990) has suggested that in older patients, around 68–78% are found to be in full-time employment, with very low unemployment figures, while rates in the early onset groups are generally higher for numbers in full-time education or schooling.

Assessments of the quality of personal relationships with family or friends are more difficult to make, but should be incorporated in assessments of psychosocial functioning. Using Morgan and Russell's (1975) psychosocial rating scale (adapted for use with a younger population), Bryant-Waugh et al. (1988) found outcome to be good in 59% of their series, while Hawley (1985) and Walford and McCune (1991) have reported good outcome in 72% and 80% respectively.

Growth and Physical Development

An episode of eating disorder in the critical period for growth and development of puberty has potential long-term adverse effects on height, physical appearance and fertility. In particular short stature and undeveloped breasts may result (Russell, 1983; 1985). Any outcome study of early onset patients should therefore include the documentation of the patient's height at follow-up, along with an assessment of physical development. In patients with a generally good outcome, significant improvements in stature have been noted, along with the late development of secondary sexual characteristics (Woodside, 1990). Thus it appears that catch-up growth and development is possible, even though this may have been completely suspended during the anorectic episode. The timing of this, however, is very important, and it appears that after the age of 17 catch-up growth and development is very unlikely even though normal weight may be maintained (Theander, 1988).

Higgs et al. (1989) found that only five of 23 (22%) early onset anorexia nervosa patients had follow-up heights less than two standard deviations from the norm for their age (mean age at onset 12 years, mean length of follow-up 5.2 years), while only one of these children was short at presentation. Walford and McCune (1991) reported that two of 15 (13%) patients were growth-retarded at follow-up and that this represented a cause for concern. However, these findings have not been replicated by the few other authors who mention height at follow-up. For example, Kreipe et al. (1989) reported that only one of their 49 patients was noted to be short, although the mean age of the subjects at the onset of the eating disorder was higher than in the two previously mentioned studies. There is clearly a need for more consistent documentation of follow-up heights before any picture can emerge about the longer term effect of an episode of eating disorder in this age group.

Global Measurements of Outcome

As mentioned earlier in this chapter, global measurements of outcome are of limited use because they obscure the tendency for patients to "recover" to different extents in different areas of functioning. Nevertheless, they are commonly reported and the results should be reflected here. Kreipe et al. (1989) conclude that the six-and-a-half-year outcome in their group of adolescent onset anorexia nervosa patients was "excellent" in 55% and "poor" in 14% (using their own Global Assessment Scale). Similarly, Sturzenberger et al. (1977) reported that 56% of their 26 adolescents fell into the good-outcome category of their own grouped global outcome measure. Martin (1985) reported that 76% of her series had an "excellent" outcome, 16% were "fair" or continuing in treatment and 8% had relapsed. Higgs et al. (1989), using Morgan and Russell's (1975) General Outcome Scale, reported a poor outcome (at five years) in eight of 16 girls (50%) with early onset anorexia nervosa, and in three of 15 (20%) girls with food avoidance emotional disorder (see chapter 2). In other early onset outcome studies the same scale has been used, and the results obtained suggest that general outcome is good in 47–58%, intermediate in 6–33% and poor in 17–26% (Bryant-Waugh et al., 1988; Hawley, 1985; Walford and McCune, 1991). In adults, using Morgan and Russell's General Outcome Scale, results are similar and range between 36%–58% good, 19–36% intermediate and 19–30% poor (Hsu, 1990).

PROGNOSTIC INDICATORS IN THE EARLY ONSET POPULATION

As with outcome, findings about factors associated with good or poor prognosis are varied. The following list is not exhaustive, but serves to illustrate the wide range of potential prognostic indicators identified.

Factors Associated with Good Outcome

Young age at hospitalisation and shorter duration of illness prior to treatment are both factors that have been associated with good outcome (Bassoe & Eskeland, 1982; Pierloot, Wellens, & Houben, 1975; Rowland, 1970). Both might be regarded as being associated with early onset, which in turn has been quoted as a favourable prognostic indicator by many authors (Bruch, 1973; Crisp, Kalucy, Lacey, & Harding, 1977; Halmi, Brodland, & Loney, 1973; Lucas et al., 1976; Russell, 1977). A view popular some years ago, but now waning, is that childhood onset anorexia nervosa is a less severe variant, and that outcome is therefore likely to be better than in older individuals (Lesser et al., 1960; Rowland, 1970). Sturzenberger et al. (1977) have suggested that early onset carries a better prognosis, not necessarily because the disorder is any less serious, but because in most children the duration of the disorder at the time they are included in a study is relatively short, often involving only one hospital admission. In addition, these authors claim that early onset patients tend to be relatively young at the time of follow-up, and may not be exposed to adult stresses. Minuchin et al. (1978) have stated that a young age at onset carries a more favourable prognosis because children are less likely to have been ill for a long period before treatment starts, they are less likely to have developed chronic patterns of behaviour, and they are less likely to have lost years of psychological and interpersonal development. Crisp (1980) has also implied that early onset improves the chances for recovery, but there is absolutely no evidence to support this as a general notion.

Remschmidt, Wienad, and Wewetzer (1991) have suggested that particular patterns of weight gain during in-patient treatment may be predictive of outcome, with in particular a slow, steady increase of weight appearing to be associated with a more favourable outcome. Being male has also been associated with a better prognosis, and Higgs et al. (1989) have suggested that males in the early onset group of eating-disorder patients may have a particularly favourable outcome. However, this has not been found in other studies (e.g. Bryant-Waugh et al., 1988; Hawley, 1985; Walford & McCune, 1991), although numbers of boys are typically very small so that statistically significant sex differences tend to be rarely observed. Follow-up studies of older onset patients also tend to conclude that the outcome is similar in both sexes (Hsu, 1990).

Vilsvik and Vaglum's (1990) follow-up study of 17 adolescent anorectics is described by the authors as "very positive" in its findings. They suggested that this is because their sample was characterised by stable family relationships and fairly good premorbid psychosocial functioning. They also claimed that the cluster of early age at onset, good ability to make verbal contact, good premorbid functioning and stable family background is associated with a subgroup of anorexia nervosa patients who have a particularly good prognosis.

Factors Associated with Poor Outcome

In contrast to the view mentioned above that early onset is associated with good outcome, some authors do not appear to attach any prognostic significance to age at onset (e.g. Hawley, 1985), while a few have expressed the view that younger patients (i.e. onset below the age of 14) carry a poorer prognosis (Dally, 1969). Commonly identified poor prognostic indicators in older patients include a longer duration of the illness prior to treatment, lower minimum weight, premorbid personality or social difficulties, disturbed family relationships and previous hospitalisations (Hsu, 1990). Some of these have also been identified in early onset outcome studies: Bryant-Waugh et al. (1988) identified young age at referral, lengthy or repeated hospital admissions, and anomalous family structure as poor prognostic indicators. Walford and McCune's (1991) follow-up findings support the suggestion that young age at onset and longer duration of hospital admission tend to be associated with poorer outcome in this group of patients. Depression accompanying the anorexia nervosa has also been found to be associated with poor outcome (Bryant-Waugh et al., 1988; Lesser et al., 1960), as has a history of eating disturbances in earlier childhood (Remschmidt et al., 1991).

CONCLUSION

The above findings would seem to support the opinion that the outcome of anorexia nervosa in children is as variable as in the older age group. This variability may be due to differences in the groups of subjects studied, to the treatment they have received, or to a whole range of as yet unidentified factors. Anorexia nervosa is a potentially fatal disorder with an apparently high potential for relapse. At present we still do not know which elements of treatment are essential, which patients require more intensive or different input, or which factors we should be aware of as predictors of poor prognosis (Martin, 1985). Patients should therefore be followed carefully so that we can improve our clinical practice to avoid unnecessary chronic physical and psychological impairment, and even death.

Swift (1982) has concluded that "even though clinicians may be correct in their report that early age of onset is associated with good outcome, there is insufficient evidence in the long-term literature to support this contention". He suggests that as more and better outcome research is conducted, it may emerge that early onset predicts a good outcome. However, over the decade following this statement, no such conclusion can be reached. Indeed, Theander (1988) has noted that when observed three years or so after treatment has ended, early onset cases tend to appear to be doing better than their older counterparts, but because of the potential for permanent physical handicap and the tendency for relapse, their longer term course may be less promising. Although we cannot say that the outcome of anorexia nervosa and related eating disorders is necessarily better in younger patients, it is likely that prognosis in this group is no worse than that for older individuals (Woodside, 1990).

REFERENCES

American Psychiatric Association (1987). *Diagnostic and statistical manual of mental disorders.* (3rd ed. rev.). Washington DC: American Psychiatric Association.

Bassoe, H.H. & Eskeland, I. (1982). A prospective study of 133 patients with anorexia nervosa. *Acta Psychiatrica Scandinavica, 65,* 127–133.

Blitzer, J.R., Rollins, N., & Blackwell, A. (1961). Children who starve themselves: Anorexia nervosa. *Psychosomatic Medicine, 23,* 369–383.

Bruch, H. (1973). *Eating disorders: Obesity, anorexia nervosa and the person within.* New York: Basic Books.

Bryant-Waugh, R., Knibbs, J., Fosson, A., Kaminski, Z., & Lask, B. (1988). Long-term follow-up of patients with early onset anorexia nervosa. *Archives of Disease in Childhood, 63,* 5–9.

Cantwell, D.P., Sturzenberger, S., Burroughs, J., Salkin, B., & Green, J. (1977). Anorexia nervosa: An affective disorder? *Archives of General Psychiatry, 34,* 1087–1093.

Crisp, A.H. (1980). *Anorexia nervosa: Let me be.* London: Academic Press.

Crisp, A.H., Kalucy, R.S., Lacey, J.H., & Harding, P. (1977). Anorexia nervosa: Some factors predictive of outcome. In R.A. Vigersky (Ed.), *Anorexia nervosa.* New York: Raven Press.

Crisp, A.H., Norton, K., Gowers, S., Halek, C., Bowyer, C., Yeldham, D., Levett, G., & Bhat, A. (1991). A controlled study of the effect of therapies aimed at adolescent and family psychopathology in anorexia nervosa. *British Journal of Psychiatry, 159,* 325–333.

Dally, P.J. (1969). *Anorexia nervosa.* London: Heinemann.

Goetz, P.L., Succop, R.A., Reinhart, J.B., & Miller, A. (1977). Anorexia nervosa in children: A follow-up study. *American Journal of Orthopsychiatry, 47,* 597–603.

Halmi, K.A., Brodland, G., & Loney, J. (1973). Prognosis in anorexia nervosa. *Annals of Internal Medicine, 78,* 907–909.

Hawley, R.M. (1985). The outcome of anorexia nervosa in younger subjects. *British Journal of Psychiatry, 146,* 657–660.

Higgs, J.F., Goodyer, I.M., & Birch, J. (1989). Anorexia nervosa and food avoidance emotional disorder. *Archives of Disease in Childhood, 64,* 346–351.

Hsu, L.K.G. (1980). Outcome of anorexia nervosa: A review of the literature (1954–1978). *Archives of General Psychiatry, 37,* 1041–1046.

Hsu, L.K.G. (1990). *Eating disorders.* New York: Guilford Press.

Kreipe, R., Churchill, B., & Strauss, J. (1989). Long-term outcome of adolescents with anorexia nervosa. *American Journal of Diseases in Children, 143,* 1322–1327.

Lesser, L.I., Ashenden, B.J., Delruskey, M., & Eisenberg, L. (1960). Anorexia nervosa in children. *American Journal of Orthopsychiatry, 30,* 572–580.

Lucas, A., Duncan, J.W., & Piens, V. (1976). The treatment of anorexia nervosa. *American Journal of Psychiatry, 133,* 1034–1038.

Maloney, M.J. & Klykylo, W.M. (1983). An overview of anorexia nervosa. bulimia nervosa, bulimia, and obesity in children and adolescents. *Journal of the American Academy of Child Psychiatry, 22,* 99–107.

Martin, F.E. (1985). The treatment and outcome of anorexia nervosa in adolescents: A prospective study and five year follow-up. *Journal of Psychiatric Research, 19,* 509–514.

Minuchin, S., Rosman, B., & Baker, L. (1978). *Psychosomatic families: Anorexia nervosa in context.* Cambridge, Massachusetts: Harvard University Press.

Morgan, H.G. & Russell, G.F.M. (1975). Value of family background and clinical features as predictors of long-term outcome in anorexia nervosa: Four year follow-up study of 41 patients. *Psychological Medicine, 5,* 355–371.

Patton, G. (1988). Mortality in eating disorders. *Psychological Medicine, 18,* 947–951.

Pierloot, R.A., Wellens, W., & Houben, M.B. (1975). Elements of resistance to a combined medical and psychotherapeutic program in anorexia nervosa. *Psychotherapy and Psychosomatics, 26,* 101–117.

Remschmidt, H., Wienand, F., & Wewetzer, C. (1991). *The long-term course of anorexia nervosa.* Paper presented at the European Society for Child and Adolescent Psychiatry 9th Congress, London, 11–14 September 1991.

Rollins, N. & Piazza, E. (1981). Anorexia nervosa: A quantitative approach to follow-up. *Journal of the American Academy of Child Psychiatry, 20,* 167–183.

Rowland, C.V. (1970). Anorexia nervosa: A survey of the literature and review of 30 cases. In *Anorexia nervosa and obesity. International Psychiatry Clinics.* Vol. 7. Boston: Little, Brown.

Russell, G.F.M. (1970). Anorexia nervosa: Its identity as an illness and its treatment. In J.M. Price (Ed.), *Modern trends in psychological medicine.* London: Butterworth.

Russell, G.F.M. (1977). General management of anorexia nervosa and difficulties in assessing the efficacy of treatment. In R.A. Vigersky (Ed.), *Anorexia Nervosa.* New York: Raven Press.

Russell, G.F.M. (1983). Delayed puberty due to anorexia nervosa to early onset. In P.J. Darby, P.E. Garfinkel, D.M. Garner, & D.V. Coscina (Eds.), *Anorexia nervosa: Recent developments in research.* New York: Alan R. Liss Inc.

Russell, G.F.M. (1985). Premenarcheal anorexia nervosa and its sequelae. *Journal of Psychiatric Research, 19,* 363–369.

Russell, G.F.M., Szmukler, G., Dare, C., & Eisler, I. (1987). An evaluation of family therapy in anorexia nervosa and bulimia nervosa. *Archives of General Psychiatry, 44,* 1047–1056.

Steinhausen, H.-C. & Glanville, K. (1983). Follow-up studies of anorexia nervosa: A review of research findings. *Psychological Medicine, 13,* 239–249.

Sturzenberger, S., Cantwell, D.P., Burroughs, J., Salkin, B., & Green, J.K. (1977). A follow-up study of adolescent psychiatric patients with anorexia nervosa: The assessment of outcome. *Journal of the American Academy of Child Psychiatry, 16,* 703–715.

Swift, W.J. (1982). The long-term outcome of early onset anorexia nervosa. *Journal of the American Academy of Child Psychiatry, 21,* 38–46.

Tanner, J.M., Whitehouse, R.H., & Takaishi, M. (1966). Standards from birth to maturity for height, weight, height velocity and weight velocity: British children 1965. Parts 1 and 2. *Archives of Disease in Childhood, 41,* 454–471.

Theander, S. (1970). Anorexia nervosa: A psychiatric investigation of 94 female patients. *Acta Psychiatrica Scandinavica,* Supp. 214.

Theander, S. (1985). Outcome and prognosis in anorexia nervosa and bulimia: Some results of previous investigations compared with those of a Swedish long-term study. *Journal of Psychiatric Research, 19,* 493–508.

Theander, S. (1988). Outcome and prognosis in anorexia nervosa with an early age of onset. In D. Hardoff & E. Chigier (Eds.), *Eating disorders in adolescents and young adults: An international perspective.* London: Freund Publishing House.

Valanne, E.H., Taipale, V., Larkio-Mittinen, A.-K., Moren, R., & Aukee, M. (1972). Anorexia nervosa: A follow-up study. *Psychiatrica Fennica,* 265–269.

Vandereycken, W. & Vanderlinden, J. (1983). Denial of illness and the use of self-reporting measures in anorexia nervosa patients. *International Journal of Eating Disorders, 24,* 101–107.

Vilsvik, S.O. & Vaglum, P. (1990). Teenage anorexia nervosa: A 1-to-9-year follow-up after psychodynamic treatment. *Nordisk Psykiatrisk Tidsskrift, 44,* 249–255.

Walford, G. & McCune, N. (1991). Long-term outcome in early onset anorexia nervosa. *British Journal of Psychiatry, 159,* 383–389.

Warren, W. (1968). A Study of anorexia nervosa in young girls. *Journal of Child Psychology and Psychiatry, 9,* 27–40.

Wing, J., Cooper, J., & Sartorius, N. (1974). *Present state examination.* Cambridge: Cambridge University Press.

Woodside, D.B. (1990). Anorexia nervosa and bulimia nervosa. *Current Opinion in Psychiatry, 3,* 453–456.

CHAPTER SEVEN

Assessment

Marianne Tranter

INTRODUCTION

Clinical assessment of children referred to the Department of Psychological Medicine at Great Ormond Street for investigation and diagnosis of an eating disorder commences with information being supplied in writing by the referrer. This may be a general practitioner, paediatrician, or child psychiatrist, who has some knowledge of the child and her symptomatology following primary assessment. Because of the Hospital's role in providing tertiary diagnostic and treatment services, many children will already have been evaluated elsewhere and some will have received a period of in-patient and out-patient care in other paediatric or psychiatric settings. Sometimes a request is made for a second-opinion assessment and sometimes for alternative or complementary treatment where progress has been slow or management of the child's condition has proved unusually difficult.

The age of children referred to the Department is generally between 8–14 years, although younger and older children have in unusual circumstances also been seen. The assessment process may be divided as follows:

1. Meeting with the child in her family context.
2. Individual assessment interview (with the child).
3. Physical state examination.

The key features to be sought at physical state examination are described in chapter 3, and this chapter is devoted to the assessment of the child's psychological state and the family.

INITIAL ASSESSMENT INTERVIEW

Initially the whole family, including the identified patient, are asked to attend for interview in the Department of Psychological Medicine. A Case Manager from the multi-disciplinary clinical team will have been appointed to manage the case and to be responsible for co-ordinating various aspects of the assessment procedure. Overall clinical responsibility is taken by the Consultant Psychiatrist.

The interview generally commences with the interviewer seeking from the family their view of the reason for referral to a specialist setting and their expectations of the referral. Their definition of the problem is therefore established early on and a careful history is taken of the onset, form and duration of the illness. Each family member might be asked to contribute their view about this, including the effect each thinks it has had both on the patient and on family life. Questions such as, "Who do you think is most worried about Susan's illness?" together with eliciting an accurate account of mealtime behaviours often gives a picture of the family's response to the problem. While a general question directed at the identified patient will seek to elicit her view of her illness, a more detailed assessment of this area will be made during her individual assessment interview.

The ill child will be weighed and measured routinely and the results will be fed back in the assessment interview to form the basis of discussion about the duration and severity of illness. The interviewer will observe and record both the information *reported* by family members and patterns of interaction as *viewed* during the interview.

SEARCH FOR CAUSATIVE FACTORS

It is useful to gain an initial impression from the family about how each member defines the current problem in respect of the eating difficulties and to take a careful history of its onset. Typically a child may have been ill for several months and been treated elsewhere before referral to the hospital. Information is sought about the early presentation of the illness, such as the development of "faddy" eating patterns and the preoccupation with weight resulting in noticeably different eating habits and loss of weight. Family members may also have noticed a change in the affect of the ill child and comment on her apparent sadness or withdrawal from family or social life. It is important to establish the context around the time of the onset of symptoms, asking questions about whether at that time there were any particular stresses in the family such as loss, bereavement, separation; whether there were particular financial worries or stresses within the marital relationship, etc. In respect of the child, questions are asked about school, including whether there was a change of school around that time, or difficulties in maintaining academic performance. It is interesting that a number of anorectic girls are described as "high achievers"; they set themselves high standards and, at times of struggling to maintain these, may become despondent and lacking in self-confidence. They may find themselves seeking some consolation in taking an unusual degree of control in respect of their eating. Alternatively, they may have experienced difficulties in peer relationships at school or with teachers and been unable to find alternative ways of resolving these difficulties.

HISTORY OF ILLNESS

Having noted factors which may have been associated with the onset of illness, it is important to obtain a careful history of its duration, including the length of time over which the child has been ill; the times of improvements or deterioration and whether there are any factors that might be associated with these trends.

PARENTS' MANAGEMENT OF ILLNESS

It is important to establish a history of parents' attempts to manage the illness and to note the similarities and differences in their response to this. This may reveal that the parents have worked quite well together, supporting one another and the child throughout her illness; conversely it may reveal that the parents themselves have been divided in their management. This has resulted in mixed messages being conveyed to the child, particularly regarding expectations around mealtimes.

THE SEVERITY OF ILLNESS

The severity may be determined by:

1. Length of duration of the illness and proportion of weight loss.
2. Extent of refusal to eat (including the presence of supplementary feeding).
3. Presence of other significant psychological or psychiatric factors in the child or family.

4. Differential perceptions of family members of the severity of the illness.
5. Response of the illness to earlier management.

Depending on the extent of severity of the illness, consideration will need to be given to whether or not the child can continue to be managed on an out-patient basis with regular monitoring of weight and height together with ongoing therapeutic help, or whether hospitalisation is required if not already being provided. This is highly likely to be recommended in cases where out-patient management has not been successful and where the eating disorder appears to be intractable.

PERSONAL HISTORY

A careful history is taken of the mother's pregnancy, the child's birth and achievement of developmental milestones, such as eating, sleeping, talking and walking. Questions about the child's temperament as an infant, together with a description of her early attachment relationships to significant parental figures, is also elicited. Note is taken of any significant losses or separations and of the child's response to starting nursery school. A detailed history of her health is also obtained, noting any significant illnesses or developmental problems. In younger children about whom concern may have been raised regarding possible anorexia nervosa it is very important to obtain a detailed history of their eating patterns, as early food refusal and the development of eating problems may at times be confused with the presentation of secondary eating disorders such as anorexia nervosa.

FAMILY HISTORY

Both parents are asked about whether either of them has had an eating disorder or suffers from any other psychosomatic disorder, such as migraine, and whether anyone in their extended families has had similar problems. General questions will be asked about the marital relationship to establish whether or not there have been particular difficulties or periods of stress caused by separation, prolonged absences due to long hours spent working or travelling abroad, etc. The parents will also be asked about their families of origin and their health, and about their family relationships.

ASSESSMENT OF FAMILY INTERACTIONS

The interviewer will both elicit and observe the patterns of family interaction. Not only will each family member be asked to contribute his or her view of family life, and in particular their response to the identified patient's illness, but the following areas of family functioning will be observed and recorded.

1. Alliances

Note will be taken of where the family members choose to sit in the room and of their closeness/distance from one another. Sometimes the child with an eating disorder might take a central position in the family, suggestive of her perhaps having a significant amount of control of family life or of being the centre of concerned attention. Alternatively, she may sit on the edge of the family circle, her body posture may be hunched up and withdrawn and she may present and be viewed as somewhat peripheral. Similar observations can be made of all family members, together with an assessment of the amount and quality of their interaction with one another. Sometimes one might observe a very close relationship between the ill child and her mother; this may reflect a sympathetic, concerned attitude by the mother towards her which is appropriate to the circumstances; alternatively there may be a degree of despair or anger/hostility in that relationship. Sometimes in her attempt to support her child the mother may have developed a somewhat over-close or collusive relationship with her, tending to trivialise the severity of the illness. Alternatively, the girl may have responded consciously or unconsciously to a perceived need in her mother for comfort or support, perhaps because of the difficulty in the marital relationship, for example, which leads the mother to turn to her daughter for emotional support.

Note should be taken of the relationship between the father and the identified patient to see whether there is evidence of warmth and support in an appropriate way; or whether there is an atmosphere of hostility or criticism. There may be an air of impatience or bewilderment in knowing how best to help his daughter. Alternatively, an over-close relationship might be noted here, perhaps including a good deal of physical interaction, and this may appear relatively welcomed or unwelcomed by the child.

Relationships between the ill child and her siblings should also be noted, including close alliances and less-close or overly hostile ones. Similarly, alliances between the siblings should also be noted.

2. Family Boundaries

Observations of style of interaction can be noted, for example, whether or not family members are encouraged to speak for themselves rather than be spoken for; whether there are appropriate boundaries respecting the need for closeness, but also whether the need for individual space and privacy are observed. Sometimes inappropriate degrees of intrusiveness may be noted, for example, a father talking about the details of his daughter's personal hygiene or coping with menstruation in front of everyone, or a mother describing the private contents of her daughter's diary. There may have been a failure in the family to observe the child's requirement for privacy: Parents may still expect to enter her bedroom or bathroom while she is undressed without respecting her wish for privacy. Alternatively, a father, for example, may still expect a degree of physical closeness or affection with his teenage daughter as was more appropriate when she was a much younger child, encouraging her still to sit on his lap or engage in a "rough and tumble" form of play. The young adolescent girl might find this disquieting, but be unsure of how to deal with the situation without hurting her father's feelings.

Sometimes there may have been a far more serious transgression of a boundary between, for example, physical and sexual affection, resulting in inappropriate dialogue, touching or more serious forms of sexual contact between a father and daughter where the incest boundary or taboo has clearly been broken. This is unlikely to be addressed in a family interview, but sometimes inappropriate somewhat sexualised forms of interactions can be observed or alternatively a degree of "freezing" and a deliberate distancing of herself from her father may be noted on behalf of the girl.

3. Family Atmosphere

Note is taken of the degree of warmth versus an atmosphere of hostility; whether or not it appears safe for family members to express their views and be respected rather than humiliated or ignored; whether a difference of opinion can be voiced with the possibility of resolving it. This may contrast sharply with family patterns which are characterised by avoidance of conflict where differences or the expression of anger or loss of temper are not tolerated and therefore family members might feel under pressure to suppress their feelings and have no outlet for the ordinary expression of them. The somatisation of such feelings can lead to psychosomatic illness of various forms, including eating disorders. Minuchin, Rosman, and Baker (1978) have described some families where there is a poor ability to resolve conflicts, particularly perhaps in the marital relationship, and these may get channelled through one particular child who thus becomes triangulated within her parents relationship. (See the case example later in this chapter.)

Alternatively, the family may be one characterised by a rather chaotic structure in which conflict is easily and overtly expressed and arguments and disagreements are frequent. While most members of the family may cope quite well with this, it may be the case that one child, for example, the ill child, may feel overwhelmed or ill-equipped to deal with this amount of expressed hostility, have difficulty in competing for attention within the family or in exerting control on its relationships and finds an alternative means of trying to gain control through her eating behaviour.

4. Executive System

It is important to note whether or not there are clearly stated generational boundaries within the family with the parents forming an executive system taking charge of family rules and decision-making and the children recognising their authority and feeling appropriately contained and guided by it. In some families we may see distortions such as lack of agreement between parents about their roles, one parent, perhaps the father, assuming responsibility to help his sick daughter get better but finding that his wife is unwilling or unable to co-operate with him fully. She may be torn between her allegiance to him and her allegiance to her child whom she may wish to protect from what she may perceive as a rather authoritarian approach to her eating as exemplified by her husband. In some families we observe a degree of enmeshment in the relationship between the mother and the ill child, almost as though in a sense they constitute the marital pair and exclude the father who may be a somewhat peripheral member of the family. Sometimes girls caught in this position are fearful of growing up and separating from their mothers or leaving home for fear of how the mother will occupy herself when that point is reached, doubting the support she may receive from within the marriage. By being ill and dependent on her mother and eschewing the task of growing up, a girl may unconsciously be attempting to provide her mother with a task for life in terms of her role as primary caretaker.

5. Family's Affective Responses

General assessment should be made of the affective status of each member of the family to ascertain whether they may be feeling despondent or depressed, frustrated or angry or indifferent to their daughter's (or sister's) illness. Asking questions about past psychiatric history is important, as well as asking questions such as: "Mrs X, what effect do you think Susan's illness has had upon your husband?" and similarly "Mr X, what effect do you think it has had upon your wife?" Seeking information about how family members recognise and can respond to each other's emotional needs may be elicited by asking questions such as: "Who in the family is usually the first to know when Mum/Dad is feeling upset?", "Who is the best worrier in your family?", "Who does that person most take after?", "Who is best at shouting in your family?", "Who is best at getting their own way or getting angry?" And to the parents: "Which of the children is best at winding you up/causing you sleepless nights?"

Asking future-orientated questions may also be important in gauging the family's capacity to cope with chronic illness and emotional stress. "If Susan's illness continues, what do you think will happen?" The family's hitherto unspoken fears that she may die (for example) need to be discussed and this also gives the therapist an opportunity to mention the life-threatening qualities of anorexia nervosa and hence to emphasise the seriousness of her condition. "If Susan died who would be most upset?", "Who would miss her most?", "Who would blame themselves most?", "Who would feel most guilty?"

Alternatively, questions about her recovery should also be asked: "How would things be different if Susan was well again?" "Who would be most relieved?" "Do you think Dad would need to be around so much at mealtimes?" "Would Susan be able to go out more with her friends?" "What would Mum do if she did not have to look after her any more?"

Thus some exploration may be made of both the development of the illness, its significance within the family and whether it may be serving some function within the family and therefore unwittingly being maintained.

Given the fact that anorexia nervosa is considered a multi-factorial disorder with a complex aetiology, it is often only possible at the assessment stage to begin to assess the differential significance of the various aetiological factors and form the beginning of an understanding of their unique presentation in this particular child and her family.

INDIVIDUAL PSYCHOPATHOLOGY

Aspects of individual assessment of the child include:

1. Physical examination, including pelvic ultrasound scan.
2. Mental state examination.

3. School and/or psychological reports.
4. Overall assessment interview.

These various sources of information will be co-ordinated by the case manager who will liaise directly with colleagues involved in the assessment procedure, as well as with primary health-care colleagues, school teachers, psychologists, etc. A standardised questionnaire (Rutter, 1967) will be sent to the child's school (with the parents' consent) seeking information about the child's academic performance, estimate range of ability, emotional behavioural state in school and relationship with peers and teachers. This may well provide some useful baseline information from which to pursue other areas in more detail. A psychologist's report might well be indicated or available in cases where, for example, a child is under-achieving at school according to his or her estimated ability and a more objective assessment is required. Emotional problems, lack of self-esteem, difficulty in concentrating, and specific learning or cognitive problems might emerge in this and again will form part of the overall assessment of the child's functioning. Similarly, anxieties about peer relationships, bullying, feeling socially withdrawn or isolated may also be revealed and a general assessment be made of self-esteem and overall cognitive functioning.

INDIVIDUAL ASSESSMENT INTERVIEW

Following the child's initial visit to the Department of Psychological Medicine with her family she is seen (with her parents' consent) by a member of the clinical team for assessment. In this interview the child's own views and feelings are explored:

(a) Perception of Illness.   It is important to establish whether there is any common perception between the child and her family concerning the nature and severity of her illness. Girls may be reluctant to acknowledge having an eating disorder, but may be prepared to accept that they are ill in a general sense. They may be more able to talk about the effects of their illness, such as hospitalisation, absence from school, stress within the family, loss of outside activities and friends, rather than the *form* of their illness as being directly related to their reluctance or refusal to eat. In fact, they may often be very defensive about their eating behaviour, saying that they *do* eat, but other people do not recognise this or believe them. As far as they are concerned they eat adequate amounts and they cannot see why parents and others take a different view of this, encouraging them to eat more. The little amount they do eat is usually rationalised or justified as an attempt to control fatness, although in addition they may claim not to like certain foods. There is rarely an accurate perception of the severity or seriousness of their illness or of its likely consequences unless properly treated, such as death through starvation. Some girls do register some concern if they are amenorrhoeic, but most disregard this or trivialise it.

Some girls will acknowledge feeling depressed or sad at times and some on exploration will acknowledge some suicidal ideation or a generalised feeling of not really caring whether they continue to live or not. Some girls (as has already been mentioned in previous chapters) also have other psychiatric problems, such as refusing to walk or talk or care for themselves. Others may appear frozen and unresponsive to attempts to help them articulate their fears, anxieties or worries.

(b) Body Image.   A characteristic of girls with anorexia nervosa is their distorted perception of their bodies as being unusually fat and /or unpleasant/unsatisfactory. They may be preoccupied with their body image to the point of constantly looking in the mirror, seeing themselves as grossly overweight. Others, in addition to not eating, may continually exercise, running or jumping up and down on the spot, to try to reduce their weight still further. It is important to ask a girl how she currently feels about her size and shape and what her desired size would be: whether she thinks she is about "right" or whether she thinks she is somewhat on the thin side or somewhat on the fat side. Even girls in a state of emaciation may protest that they need to lose "at least a stone" before they will feel content with their weight.

(c) Perception of Self in Relation to Family.   Exploration will be made with the child about how she feels she gets along with other members of her family; to whom she feels closest/least close, in whom she can confide, etc. She will be asked who she thinks is most worried about her since becoming ill and what effect her illness has had on the family as far as she can see. Her view about each family member in relation to herself, and each other, including her view of her parents' relationship, is important as is her feeling about major life changes or crises within the family. A girl may have a previously undisclosed worry about her mother being ill or her father spending long periods outside the home or some difficulty in her relationship with a parent or sibling.

(d) School.   It is important to know what the young person's attitude to school is, including whether or not they feel they are coping reasonably well with academic work, or whether they are not managing to achieve in the way they used to. Illness can provide a "legitimate" reason for not attending school and so escaping pressures that may have

built up there. There may be problems in relationships either with a teacher or teachers in general and these need to be explored together with the child's own view of her difficulty in dealing with them. She may have been the victim of bullying or aggressive behaviour by other pupils or through lack of confidence have felt socially isolated within her peer group.

(e) Interests and Activities. It is helpful to find out what the girl used to like to do before she was ill, her interests in school and outside school and whether she may have become rather preoccupied or fixated upon a particular activity, such as horseriding, ballet, or gymnastics. Exploring her feelings about losing her energy or motivation to participate in activities which she previously enjoyed can help to focus on the negative effects of her illness and be used to try to encourage her to get well in the future. Feelings of sadness and loss often accompany a sense of social isolation and often the girl will have become quite withdrawn and feel unable to participate in peer-group activities.

(f) Anxieties. We usually ask if someone has anything on their mind which has worried or upset them and this may be to do with home, school, friends, relations, etc. A girl may be able to talk about worries about a parent or her relationship with them or worry that she has fallen behind in her schoolwork and is feeling particularly despondent about that.

(g) Attitude towards Puberty/Growing-up/Sexuality. General discussion of the physical and emotional changes of adolescence and establishing the girl's feelings about these can give some useful insight about any fears or anxieties she may have here. Sometimes girls will find it extraordinarily difficult to talk about menstruation and are often quite relieved that they have either not commenced menstruation or that it has ceased, so that they can avoid the most obvious signs of puberty. They may express distaste for their changing bodies and quite often their style of dress in loose, baggy clothes serves to conceal their changing shape. Some may be uncomfortable about their own nakedness and wear several layers of clothing, even at night.

Discussion about growing up and thinking about making close relationships with boyfriends, for example, may be viewed as a taboo subject almost too painful to contemplate. Even girls of 14 or 15 years old, who may acknowledge that other girls in their class at school are beginning to be interested in boyfriends, may demonstrate an avoidant or ostentatious disregard or distaste for such matters themselves. Alternatively, some girls may acknowledge having had a boyfriend but may have had some off-putting or confusing sexual experience which has resulted in them perhaps attempting to retreat into a pre-adolescent stage of development in order to avoid such encounters again.

(h) Exploring Adverse Sexual Experiences.   Given the various studies both clinical and non-clinical (Calam & Slade, 1989; Palmer et al., 1990) showing the significant numbers of adult women with eating disorders who report adverse sexual experiences in childhood, we have felt it important to pay attention to this possibility in the context of our individual assessment interviews with children with anorexia nervosa.

In talking to a girl about what she understands about pubertal development and the onset of menstruation, we will usually explore the extent of her sexual knowledge in respect of conception and birth, etc. Most children have received some form of sex education at school and we will generally ask whether this is the case and proceed from there. Some children may appear to be very reluctant or ill-at-ease in discussing such matters. If so, we will ask them whether there is any particular reason that they find this a difficult area to talk about, while reassuring them that we generally include some discussion about these matters within our hospital setting with girls of their age. We will then ask in context whether or not they have ever had any experience of being spoken to or touched in a sexual way which might have made them feel confused or uncomfortable. Some may report something in relation to a boyfriend; others may disclose having been touched, fondled or even penetrated within their immediate or extended family or social network. Some girls may look very distressed or uncomfortable (far more so than other girls of their age discussing such matters) but not disclose inappropriate sexual contact or experience. The interviewer may be left with a question mark as to whether or not something inappropriate may have happened which the young person is unwilling or unable to divulge at this point in time. Some girls have disclosed sexual abuse after a period of time working with a member of staff and others have not disclosed while being treated at our Unit, but have done so on re-referral back to their local unit. Some girls may make a partial disclosure of something sexual having happened to them, but are unable to elaborate any further. Again in consultation with a colleague from the multi-disciplinary team, a decision may be made to do some ongoing work with that girl to see whether over time she may be able to confide further.

It should be noted that some girls are able to be quite clear that they have not had any unwelcome sexual experiences and their verbal and affective responses are often very different in quality to those of an abused child. It must be remembered that by no means all children with eating disorders have developed such illnesses in response to having been sexually abused.

CASE STUDY 1

Out-Patient

Neeta, aged 14, was referred to the out-patient team at the age of 12. She had a history of anorexia nervosa for approximately one year with one previous admission to a paediatric ward for management.

Neeta was accompanied for her first assessment interview to the Department of Psychological Medicine by her parents Mr and Mrs F and her sister Fatima. The family is of Asian origin with all members of the extended family living on the Asian subcontinent. The family follows the Muslim religion.

At interview there was a striking difference in the perception of Neeta's illness between her parents. Her father expressed distress and very real concern about his daughter's illness; her mother appeared not to understand or accept the seriousness of it. There was no clear agreement between the parents in respect of the management of eating; the father tended to be rather strict and authoritarian and became angry at Neeta at the table. Her mother stuck up for her and tried to persuade her husband that Neeta had eaten a reasonable amount. It was established that Neeta's calorific intake was extremely low and her weight was approximately 76% for height. She was admitted to an in-patient paediatric setting for a few weeks to stabilise her medical condition and improve her weight until it was thought safe to discharge her home to the care of her parents. Out-patient family work continued and several major themes emerged.

1. Neeta herself appeared quite depressed. She reported difficulty in sleeping, lack of motivation, lethargy, lack of interest in outside activities, etc. She was often tearful at interview and her appetite remained extremely poor. After some months of work with her, it was decided to try her on a course of anti-depressants. These appeared to have helped to improve her mood and her appetite to some extent.
2. Considerable conflicts were observed in the marital relationship with almost complete disagreement between husband and wife about the management of Neeta's illness. Attempts by therapists to encourage them to try to work together and support one another were in vain.
3. The parents argued in their native language: The father acknowledged that he and his wife had many major disagreements; he felt that she did not respect or love him; his wife denied that this was the case although in an individual meeting with the therapist she was able to explain that in her

culture a wife should not disagree with her husband. Thus
there was some denial on her part of the extent of the conflict
in her relationship with her husband.

4. The parents had had an arranged marriage and appeared to
"accept" their lot rather grudgingly.

5. In family meetings a major alliance was noted between Neeta
and her mother who would mediate between the girl and her
father. While the father was speaking the therapist often
noticed the mother making knowing eye contact with her
daughter, as though saying "Here he goes again".

6. Father reported mother treating Neeta like a baby, helping her
dress for school, combing her hair and running around after
her when she came home from school. By contrast Neeta's
younger sister Fatima, was a much more independent girl who
dressed, ate and took care of herself quite independently. There
were no problems reported in respect of her at school and she
pursued quite an active social life with her friends.

7. Attempts to encourage the parents to follow a fairly strict
feeding programme in respect of Neeta proved extremely
difficult as the mother would tend to collude with Neeta's
refusal to eat the required amounts. This would often provoke
an argument between her mother and father which Neeta
found very upsetting.

8. Neeta felt her father preferred her sister and was over-critical
of her. She was very sensitive to his shouting at her or her
mother and would cry easily about this.

9. Attempts by the therapist to help the parents reconcile their
obvious disagreements and conflicts by working with them as
a couple on some occasions appeared to meet with no success
so that their relationship remained largely unchanged.

10. Neeta's illness has continued although she has very slowly
gained weight to the point where she is not dangerously ill,
although she is still only 90% weight/height and 85%
height/age.

Comment

It is important to understand and be sensitive to issues surrounding
ethnicity and religion when working with any family in a therapeutic
setting.

Our analysis of the aetiology and function of Neeta's illness was that
it seemed that in some ways Neeta had become triangulated in her
parents' difficult marital relationship. Her mother had formed a

collusive and enmeshed relationship with her, turning to her for the emotional support and comfort she appeared unable to obtain from her husband. Neeta occupied a great deal of her mother's time, not only because each meal took approximately one and a half hours and her mother would sit with her, but also because she behaved in a very regressed way ensuring that her mother had a continuing role as the caretaker of a dependent child. When asked what she thought her mother would do when she, Neeta, and her sister Fatima were grown up, Neeta replied in a rather matter-of-fact way, "I guess she will spend more time with her friends." In reality Neeta's mother was discouraged by her father from participating in social relationships outside the family and attempts to encourage Mrs F to attend English classes were in effect vetoed by her husband. Nevertheless he claimed to be attempting to behave as a liberal Muslim father and did allow his daughters to go to the cinema and to participate in some social events with friends.

Attempts to help the parents develop more functional ways of resolving their own difficulties proved impossible and although Neeta was considerably subdued in her father's presence and asked whether she could be seen at the clinic only with her mother, his presence was found to be extremely important in that he was much more co-operative in following advice about Neeta's eating and management.

School

Neeta continues to do reasonably well; her physical condition is satisfactory, she has commenced menstruation and therefore did not require an ovarian scan. Various members of the clinical team have collaborated in her management, and treatment and advice has also been sought from Asian colleagues about particular aspects of the family's culture and religion.

Neeta and her family are still in treatment.

CASE STUDY 2

Sometimes, aspects of assessment may continue beyond the commencement of treatment especially when the girl herself gives some indication that she has more information to share. Also, in cases where a patient's recovery is extremely slow, and she appears to have a "secret", it may be very important to explore sensitive issues further.

In-Patient

Deirdre, aged 12 at the time of referral, had been anorectic for approximately one year and had been treated and managed in a paediatric setting. Onset had, according to her parents, coincided with her recent transfer to secondary school where she had had problems settling in. School and psychologist reports indicated that she was girl of above average ability, among the top five in her class.

Prior to her illness Deirdre had had a wide range of outside interests including horseriding, ballet, and gymnastics. On admission she was in an emaciated and dehydrated state, having lost almost 50% of her body weight. She refused anything by mouth and was fed by nasogastric tube. In addition to her primary anorexia nervosa, she refused to walk, to talk, to bathe herself, comb her hair, or see to herself in the toilet. She was only mobile if pushed by wheelchair and the nursing staff had to look after her physical needs as though she were a very young child.

Although she did not talk except in grunts initially, Deirdre would spend long periods of time screaming. She appeared like a frightened animal, imprisoned in a world of her own and being unable or unwilling to communicate the reasons for her obvious distress.

Her family consisted of mother and father, both in their mid-thirties, one older sister aged 13, and one younger brother aged 11. Both these children enjoyed good health, but both were noted to have significant emotional and behavioural problems at school.

Management of Deirdre's illness on the ward consisted in encouraging her gradually to take a little fluid by mouth; physiotherapy to improve the muscle functioning in her legs and to gradually encourage her to take a few steps and commence walking again; and encouraging her to take some responsibility for her personal and intimate care. She received weekly sessions with the child psychotherapist who began to form an impression of her feelings about herself, her family and others, and of group therapy on the in-patient Unit where she was encouraged to try to talk to other children and staff.

After several months there was some gradual improvement in her condition and one day Deirdre told her special nurse that she had a secret that nobody except her toy bunny knew about. Some sessions were arranged for her with a member of the Out-patient Clinical Team who has experience of working with both anorectic girls and with girls who have been sexually abused or traumatised. Over a course of approximately six sessions Deirdre was able to disclose the content of her secret which was that she had been sexually abused and tortured, including being bound and gagged. Her abuser threatened that if she divulged this he would kill her mother and this had proved a very effective silencer. Deirdre was unable to reveal the identity of her abuser, although she told her therapists on one occasion that she had dreamed about him and that he had had the face of her father.

Within a short time after her disclosure of serious sexual abuse, Deirdre began to make an accelerated recovery. She resumed eating, was able to talk about her experiences further and continued to make progress with her psychotherapy. Her screaming stopped. Having at times expressed suicidal ideation, a few weeks before her discharge from hospital, she announced to her therapist that she no longer wished to be dead but had decided she was going to live.

Deirdre was discharged to the care of two very experienced foster parents. Two years after her discharge from hospital, she is continuing to make excellent progress and has recently returned to the care of her parents.

CONCLUSION

While as much information as possible is elicited during the initial assessment phase, it should be remembered that this is also an ongoing process. Care needs to be taken to ensure good communication between patient and staff and among relevant members of the staff teams, as well as with parents and other family members.

Understanding the aetiology of an individual's eating disorder requires time, patience and the establishment of trust between family, child and professionals. Treatment begins as soon as possible after the diagnosis is made.

REFERENCES

Calam, R.M. & Slade, P.D. (1989). Sexual experiences and eating problems in female undergraduates. *International Journal of Eating Disorders, 8,* 391–397.

Minuchin, S., Rosman, B., & Baker, L. (1978). *Psychomatic families: Anorexia nervosa in context.* Cambridge, Mass.: Harvard University Press.

Palmer, R.L., Oppenheimer, R., Dignon, A., Chaloner, D.A., & Howells, K. (1990). Childhood sexual experiences with adults reported by women with eating disorders: An extended series. *British Journal of Psychiatry, 156,* 699–703.

Rutter, M. (1967). A children's behavioural questionnaire for completion by teachers—preliminary findings. *Journal of Child Psychology & Psychiatry, 8,* 1–11.

CHAPTER EIGHT

Management Overview

Bryan Lask

INTRODUCTION

Eating disorders in children can lead to severe physical complications (see chapter 3), and are often associated with a high incidence of continuing morbidity (see chapter 6). A few children die from anorexia nervosa or its complications. Clearly for such serious disorders a rapidly initiated, intensive and comprehensive treatment programme is indicated. The rest of this book is devoted to a detailed description of the treatments used.

The essentials of such a programme include:

1. The provision of information and education for the parents and other family members.
2. Ensuring that the adults are in charge.
3. Making a decision about the need for hospitalisation.
4. Calculation of a target weight range.
5. Physical treatments including re-feeding.
6. Behaviour therapy.
7. Cognitive therapy.
8. Psychotherapy.
9. Family therapy.
10. Group therapy.
11. Schooling.

PROVISION OF INFORMATION AND EDUCATION

Explanation and education form an essential part of the management of eating disorders. Parents and child need a clear statement about the diagnosis, its perpetuating factors, the treatment, and prognosis. Parents are often very eager to discuss the cause of their child's illness, but this rarely proves fruitful. It seems more useful to focus on those factors that appear to be maintaining the problem and to find a means of overcoming them.

Parents are often unaware of the seriousness of their child's problem. We have found it helpful to adopt a ritual-like method of conveying the severity of the situation. Having completed the initial assessment we make a statement such as:

As you are probably aware your daughter has anorexia nervosa. Although this is uncommon in children, we see a large number in this clinic. It is a difficult illness to overcome and can be very serious. Indeed, less than half make a full recovery. It can delay growth and puberty, and possibly have an adverse effect on fertility. Some children become desperately ill, and a very few die. Fortunately we do know some of the factors that contribute to recovery. The children who do well are those whose parents are able to work *together*, and are able to work *with us*, to ensure their child's health. It is often a long, hard struggle, because people with anorexia nervosa are so desperate to avoid gaining weight that they often resort to a wide range of other means to stay dangerously thin. It will be necessary for a while for you to take control of your daughter's health-care, including what she eats. However, if you as her parents can resolve to work together, and with us, to ensure her health, then there is every reason to believe she will be able to recover.

The words of this statement can be altered as necessary to fit the circumstances, and using the child's name rather than "your daughter" probably has a greater impact. At this point questions and discussion should be actively encouraged. We have also found it useful at the end of the first meeting to provide a fact-sheet, which the parents can study at home.

Most parents seem to find this approach very helpful, and thank us for being so clear and direct. They often state that they have not previously been given any clear explanation of what is wrong. They also seem to value the opportunity to share the responsibility for their child's care.

At the next meeting it is important to put time aside to answer further questions and discuss areas of concern or uncertainty. In our experience it is essential to provide this information and allow opportunity for questions and concerns to be raised early in our contact with families, for otherwise unresolved anxieties can interfere with the process of treatment. Once the parents have had a chance to ask any questions and raise points for discussion, it is essential to tackle the issue of control.

ENSURING THAT ADULTS ARE IN CHARGE

Three important aspects of childhood onset anorexia nervosa are : (a) its life-threatening nature; (b) the patient's lack of insight; and (c) battles around control. These interact in that the child may be seriously ill, but have little insight into her condition, and she fights to retain control over what she eats. Such children often feel they have little or no control in their lives, and that two areas in which they can have control are their food intake and their weight. An understandable reaction is to over-control food intake, with a resultant sense of achievement. This ability to control food intake and body shape and size is so satisfying that it develops an addictive quality. However, its health- and life-threatening nature demands intervention.

For this reason it is vital that the adults responsible for the child's welfare take charge. Almost always this will be against the child's expressed wishes. It is not at all unusual for the parents to have colluded with their daughter's weight avoidance either by not having noticed how much weight she had lost, or by not intervening firmly enough once the weight loss had become obvious. Understandably, parents may consider that such weight loss is due to physical ill-health and seek alternative explanations to self-starvation. Also, even when avoidance of weight gain becomes apparent, parents are loath to take a firm approach for fear of further upsetting their daughter.

It should be obvious, therefore, that a key feature of management is that the adults responsible for the child's welfare take firm control. A clear statement to this effect should be made to the parents early in the contact. For example:

> You can see that Alison is very ill, having lost a third of her body weight. You can also see that she does not accept that she is ill. If this is allowed to go on unchecked, she could get worse or even die. Therefore as from this moment it is not appropriate for Alison to continue taking responsibility for her health and diet. She has shown you that she cannot do it safely. You must make a decision as to how you want to proceed from here, but it would be unwise to be influenced by Alison's protests.

At this stage it is likely that Alison will indeed be protesting, but if not she will most certainly start to once the discussion turns to her required food intake, for this is likely to be at least three times greater than current intake. The child may challenge the right of the professional to dictate such terms, or the right of the parents to take control, or she may start crying or screaming. Whatever the topic of discussion at the time the protest commences, it is important to demonstrate the battle for control to the parents, and to help them recognise the need for them to win.

This does not mean that the parents should take control over *all* areas of their daughter's life, but specifically those concerning her health and welfare. It is important that she retains control in other areas of less immediate importance, such as choice of clothing, hobbies, or friends.

This is a useful time to reiterate the importance of the parents working together, offering mutual support, and agreeing a consistent plan of management. It is not at all unusual for parents to be in conflict over various issues, but particularly in relation to how to handle the eating disorder. One parent may feel unsupported, or that the other is too strict or too lax. Frequently the child is sided with one parent against the other. Clearly the parents cannot be in charge as long as they are not in agreement.

Issues over which the parents may well disagree, and therefore need help to resolve, include how to help their daughter to eat, whether or not they wish to accept treatment, and whether or not their child should be admitted to hospital. The professional's role here is not to take sides but rather to offer advice, and to help the parents to reach agreement, preferably without being adversely influenced by their daughter's protests.

It is sometimes difficult to feel sympathetic towards a child who has what initially appears to be a self-inflicted problem, who denies she is ill, and angrily rejects all attempts to help. Nonetheless it is important to acknowledge her distress, and a statement along the following lines may be helpful:

> Alison, I know that just now you are feeling very angry with me because of what I have said to your parents, and angry with them for listening. You may not believe me but I do understand not only how angry you are, but also how worried you are about your weight, and whether everything will get completely out of control. If your parents want me to I will help them to help you get well again. We're not going to let you die and nor will we let you get overweight. Now if you have any questions I'll do my best to answer them.

Often at this point the child renews her protests or turns to her parents for support. It is helpful to note at this point whether the parents have been able to adopt a firmer and more united stance.

It is important to emphasise that not all children with eating disorders will need such a vigorous approach. Selective eaters, for example, (see chapter 2) are rarely physically ill and in such cases the parents may need help to allay their anxieties and to accept that their child is not ill. Children with food-avoidance emotional disorder do not usually lose dramatic amounts of weight, and treatment can focus quite quickly on the underlying emotional problems. This is in contrast with anorexia nervosa in which the child cannot focus on underlying problems until some weight has been restored.

THE NEED FOR HOSPITALISATION

An early and important decision that needs to be made involves whether or not the child should be hospitalised. A range of factors need to be considered in making this decision, including the parents' wishes, the availability of appropriate resources, and the child's physical and mental state. In general we give serious consideration to the possibility of hospitalisation under any of the following circumstances:

1. The child's weight is less than 80% weight for height by age (Tanner Whitehouse Standards: Tanner, Whitehouse, & Takaishi, 1966).
2. The child is dehydrated.
3. There are signs of circulatory failure such as low blood pressure, slow pulse or poor peripheral circulation.
4. Persistent vomiting or vomiting blood.
5. Marked depression or other major psychiatric disturbance.

Our task is to advise the parents so that they can make an informed decision. However, it is also necessary to consider what resources are available. For urgent medical treatment such as rehydration or electrolyte replacement, admission to a paediatric unit is clearly appropriate. However, for the more long-term treatment of underlying emotional problems the emphasis in such a unit on immediate and physical care makes admission less appropriate. The ideal is possibly to have the choice between a short admission to a paediatric unit for medical emergencies, with intensive psychiatric help being offered on an out-patient basis, or admission to a psychiatric unit that can offer both the immediate medical care plus the more lengthy psychiatric treatment. Day-care programmes for children in Britain have yet to be described, presumably because of the lack of resources, but given their efficacy for adults (Freeman, 1991), they warrant investigation.

Whatever programme is being considered, it *must* be remembered that such children will need highly skilled psychiatric treatment over and above any medical care.

TARGET WEIGHTS AND RANGES

Unlike children with other eating disorders, those with anorexia nervosa are unduly preoccupied with their weight. The temptation therefore is to try to distract them from this theme. However, such ploys are unlikely to work and it seems more helpful to discuss with the child what weight she wants to be, and compare this with what is actually a safe weight. We prefer to use a weight-range rather than a specific weight, and we refer to this as the target range.

Various factors need to be taken into account in determining the target range. First, no children with anorexia nervosa will want to be of even average weight, let alone above it. Second, whatever lowest figure is agreed the child will aim below it. Third, menstruation is unlikely to occur at less than 94% weight for height (Lask et al., in press). For these reasons it is wise to set a target range of 95–100%. This may need to be

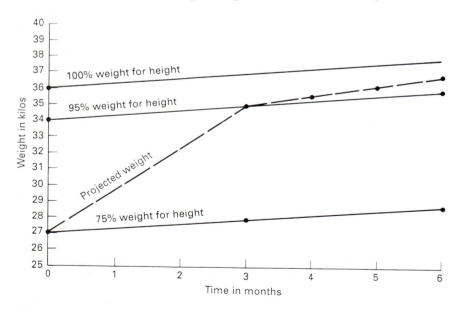

FIG. 8.1. A sample growth chart.

adjusted upwards if menstruation fails to occur, and the child and parents should be reminded that as the child gets older, and hopefully grows, so the actual weights that represent 95–100% will increase.

It can be helpful to plot out on a graph the anticipated weights on a monthly basis. This is illustrated in Fig. 8.1 which shows that the current weight is 75% weight for height and the current range should be between 34 and 36 kgs. As weight recovery takes time and can be anticipated to occur at about 2.0–2.5 kgs. per month the projected weight after one month is about 29.5 kgs., after two months 32.3 kgs., and after three months 35 kgs. Thereafter the projected weight will be between the two lines representing 95% and 100% weight for height.

A COMPREHENSIVE APPROACH

There is far more to the treatment of eating disorders than weight restoration. Indeed in most eating disorders weight is not a major concern either for the child or others, and in anorexia nervosa the preoccupation with weight is usually the surface presentation of underlying difficulties. The sooner such issues can be focused on the better. For these reasons it is essential to adopt a comprehensive approach to management.

A comprehensive approach involves paying due attention to physical, social and psychological factors (Lask & Fosson, 1989). This includes the role of the family, school, and peer group, as well as the physical aspects. Access to a multi-disciplinary team is essential. While many of the tasks can be carried out by staff from a range of disciplines, paediatricians may well be required to advise on medical issues such as dehydration or electrolyte imbalance, and psychiatrists to assist with the assessment of mental state and the use of psychotropic medication. Dieticians have particular expertise on the composition of a satisfactory diet, and psychologists can advise on behavioural and cognitive treatments (see chapters 11 and 12) and carry out psychometric assessments, often necessary when there are concerns about school performance. Teachers should be consulted in the same circumstances and are essential on an in-patient programme (see chapter 16).

Social workers are able to provide a broader perspective to assessment and management. Their expertise and statutory powers are necessary when abuse is suspected, or on the rare occasions when the parents decline treatment for their sick child. In such conditions the social worker can advise on the need for, and if necessary organise, a professional's meeting or case conference. It is important to share information and exchange views in such worrying circumstances before making definite decisions about management.

STAGES OF RECOVERY

In children with anorexia nervosa particularly, but also in those with food avoidance emotional disorder and indeed most emotional disorders, we have noted specific patterns of behaviour which predominate at certain times. These are illustrated in Fig. 8.2 and are usefully categorised as three stages. The first is that of the presenting problem, when the eating disorder is the predominant feature. The child is preoccupied with her weight and food intake almost to the exclusion of all other considerations. With the possible exception of schoolwork the child shows no interest in anything else. She is unable to recognise that she has any problem other than that "stupid grown-ups are trying to make me eat far more than I need to".

Once treatment is initiated, and usually within a few weeks, there is a slow improvement in the presenting problem, and on average after about six months it has almost resolved. However, as this stage one behaviour diminishes it is replaced by an increasing assertiveness. This stage two behaviour is characterised by excessive expression of negative feelings, with an apparent absence of concern for the feelings of others.

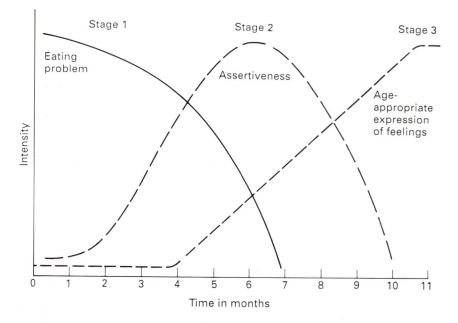

FIG. 8.2. Stages of illness and recovery.

The child behaves in a manner that is totally uncharacteristic, and causes great distress to her parents. Indeed, they often blame us for turning their child "into a monster". This stage has now become so familiar to us as a necessary step to recovery that we not only predict it but positively welcome it. We advise the parents in advance along the following lines:

> If your child is to make a full recovery she will go through a phase of utter obnoxiousness: she will be horrible to you and probably us as well. You will be very angry with us, and feel that we have made her worse. However, we will be pleased because this means that she is getting better. It is as if she has been unable to express these feelings and they have built up inside her almost to the point where she cannot eat. Once treatment starts, however, these feelings will come pouring out, almost like a volcano exploding. We will of course do our best to support you during this stage and it will come to an end.

As stage two behaviour diminishes it is gradually replaced by a more age-appropriate expression of feelings. For example, she might express her anger directly at the person concerned, but within a few minutes is able to discuss it in a relatively calm and rational manner. Once this behaviour predominates over eating difficulties and obnoxiousness, stage three has been achieved and the child is well on the path to recovery.

There is considerable overlap between these stages, leading to some confusion. However Fig. 8.2 demonstrates that the overlap is part of the sequence. It is helpful to know where the child is in this sequence, for to some extent the staging will guide treatment approaches.

The various available treatments are discussed in more detail in the succeeding chapters. They are by no means mutually exclusive; indeed our experience indicates that for the more severely ill children with eating disorders, an integrated programme of combined treatments is necessary. We have not found that one particular treatment interferes or invalidates another, providing the therapists liaise well.

REFERENCES

Freeman, C. (1991). Day patient treatment for anorexia nervosa. *British Review of Bulimia and Anorexia Nervosa, 6,* 3–8.

Lask, B. & Fosson, A. (1989). *Childhood illness: The psychosomatic approach.* Chichester: J. Wiley.

Lask, B., de Bruyn, R., Bryant-Waugh, R., Kroll, L., Hankins, M., & Sheddon, J. (in press). *Use of pelvic ultrasound in early onset anorexia nervosa.* Paper presented at 6th International Conference on Eating Disorders, New York, 1992.

Tanner, J., Whitehouse, R., & Takaishi, M. (1966). Standards from birth to maturity for height, weight, height velocity and weight velocity: British children 1965. *Archives of Disease in Childhood, 41,* 454.

CHAPTER NINE

Nursing Management

Laura Glendinning and Michelle Phillips

INTRODUCTION

This chapter is based on our work with children admitted to the Mildred Creak Unit, an eight-bedded child psychiatry in-patient ward within the Hospital for Sick Children, Great Ormond Street. The Unit accepts referrals of children between the ages of eight and 15 from all over the country. It is a five-day unit open Monday to Friday which means that children must travel to and from their local area for the weekend. The Unit's nursing team consists of registered psychiatric nurses, registered sick children's nurses and child care workers. There is also a full-time teacher based in the Unit. Staff from other disciplines attached to the Unit on a part-time basis include three psychiatrists, a psychotherapist, a social worker and a psychologist.

A large portion of children admitted to the Unit have eating disorders. At least half the admissions annually are children who have anorexia nervosa or related eating disorders. Children are also admitted with severe behavioural problems, depression, psychosis and obsessive compulsive disorders.

ADMISSION OF A CHILD WITH ANOREXIA NERVOSA

Admitting a child to a psychiatric ward is a traumatic event for both the child and her family. The main indications for admitting a child with an eating disorder to the Mildred Creak Unit include:

1. The child is emaciated—below 80% weight for height (see chapter 3.)
2. The child is dehydrated.
3. The eating disorder is accompanied by severe depression, suicidal behaviour or other psychiatric illness.

Admission enables staff to work with the whole family in more depth than is possible on an out-patient basis. The parents of children with eating disorders often feel desperate. This desperation is easily projected on to professionals, resulting in premature admission. Our team policy is to see the family at least twice prior to admission to assess motivation and commitment to the proposed treatment. When parents are unable to accept our way of working, for whatever reason, we recommend referral to their local hospital instead. We have learned from bitter experience that admitting children to the Mildred Creak Unit when their parents are not in agreement leads to almost certain failure.

In addition to making a formal assessment in the hospital, a home visit is carried out where the family can be observed in their own surroundings. As part of gathering information and making links with the child's home setting, a school visit is also made. If a local hospital is involved, nurses also visit there.

The Child's First Week

On admission each child has a thorough medical examination. Some children may not have eaten anything for a while, sometimes for many weeks. Other children are consuming small amounts of low calorie food. Whatever the child's eating habits, the first priority is to prevent any further physical deterioration in the form of weight-loss. If necessary, naso-gastric tube-feeding is initiated (see page 144).

The second priority is to establish that adults are in charge. All decisions regarding health and safety will be taken by parents or staff, thus removing responsibility from the child for her own health and well-being. Often families need help and advice on how to assume control and to implement appropriate rules and boundaries, as they may have become very caught up with their child's anorectic behaviour.

When Anita arrived on the Unit she was severely emaciated but insisted on jogging up three flights of stairs holding her luggage, with her parents following. They were all aware that there was a lift.

All children admitted to the Mildred Creak Unit are allocated a key nurse, a support nurse, and a case manager. This "mini-team" is responsible for the child's management throughout the admission.

In the first week the child is expected to come to every meal and to attempt to consume some food and drink. Nursing staff are supportive and responsive to the child's efforts but not directive in any way. No pressure is placed upon the child to eat or drink. Nursing staff ensure that the rules that apply to meal times are explained (see pages 144–147).

There are a number of general considerations to be made for any child admitted. The following points need to be considered in allocating a room for a child with anorexia nervosa: Does the room have a basin in which she might vomit? Should the child share the room with another child who has an eating disorder (as this may result in excessive conversation about weight, food and exercise)? Will she receive enough privacy in a certain bedroom?

> The result of Michelle and Judith sharing a bedroom was that they constantly compared notes and fuelled each other's determination not to gain weight. It accentuated their competitiveness and resulted in a prolonged period of time when neither gained weight

Weight

Every child with an eating disorder has a weight chart which is used as a guideline throughout admission to monitor her physical state. It also plays an important part in determining a plan of care. The weight chart is a graph (see Fig. 9.1) on which the child's weight losses and gains are plotted. Both the staff and the child have a copy of the weight chart.

The two main horizontal lines placed on the graph correspond to:

1. The child's "ideal" weight, calculated using Tanner-Whitehouse norms (see chapter 3.) taking age, height and sex into account. It is expressed in percentage terms with a 100% weight for height equivalent to ideal weight.
2. 80% weight for height below which the child is deemed to be in the wasting range.

Each child's weight and height measurements are recorded on admission. Thereafter all children are weighed twice a week in their underclothes after going to the toilet. Weighing takes place at the same time of day before and after weekend leave. Children are not weighed during the week, even on request, as this places an undue focus on weight.

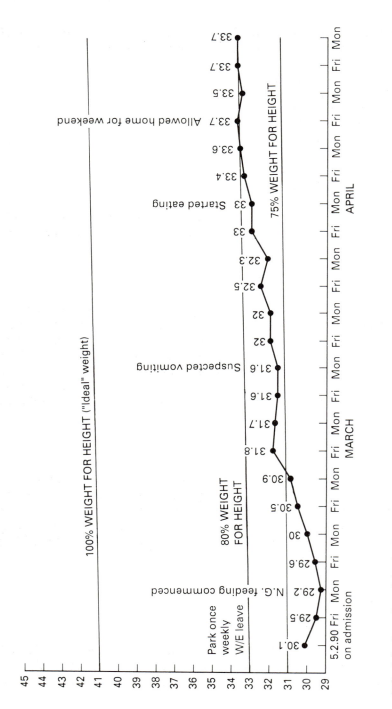

FIG. 9.1. Sample weight chart.

Figure 9.1 illustrates a weight chart for a 13-year-old girl (date of birth 17.7.76) who is admitted to the Mildred Creak Unit on 5/2/90.

Her weight on admission is 30.1 kg.
Her height on admission is 145.3 cms.
Calculated percentages:
Weight for height = 73%
Weight for age = 61%
Height for age = 91.8%
"Ideal" weight (100%) = 41 kg.
"Ideal" height = 157.5 cms.

These figures alter each month due to predicted normal growth curves which result in an incline on the chart (the "ideal" weight curve).

Predicted "ideal" weight in 3 months = 41.8 kg.
Predicted "ideal" height in 3 months = 158 cms.

It is our aim to normalise the child's lifestyle and distract from continuous thought about weight. Anorectic children are often very anxious that they will gain excessive weight quickly and are used to weighing themselves frequently. This fear is explored with the child during individual sessions with her key nurse. We believe it is very important that these children are given the opportunity to learn to trust the nursing staff regarding their weight. For this reason it is vital that the nurses are available to discuss weight-related issues.

DIET

Food is a central issue when working with children who have anorexia nervosa. On admission the child's percentage weight for height is calculated, and the degree of emaciation estimated. Her capacity to eat is assessed and a diet regime planned, with the help of a dietician. The child is encouraged to participate in the planning of her diet. By making choices and stating preferences she is helped to feel involved and is not forced to eat foods she dislikes.

Bridie flatly refused to eat butter, but with negotiation would accept toast with peanut butter.

Obviously there are some limits to the choice available if a balanced diet is to be implemented. Members of staff are aware of minimum, non-negotiable requirements. Anorectic children often show a keen interest in planning a diet sheet, responding enthusiastically to being given choice. Many take great pride in designing diet sheets on large sheets of paper, demonstrating their artistic talents.

Figure 9.2 shows a diet sheet for a child of ten years, who, on admission, demonstrated that she was able to consume approximately half of an age-appropriate meal.

Yellowlees, Roe, Walker, and Ben-Tovim (1988) have shown that anorectics may have a distorted perception of food quantities, and that

---

Breakfast
1   Slice of buttered toast with spread
1   Egg
½   Bowl of cereal with milk

Mid-morning
½   Glass fruit squash
1   Biscuit

Lunch	*Some Examples*
½ Glass water	Rice, potatoes, chips, pasta, cheese, fish,
½ Portion carbohydrate	meat, pulses, peas, carrots, salad.
½ Portion protein	
½ Portion vegetable	
½ Portion dessert	A chosen dessert cannot be a piece of fruit. However, as fruit is part of a healthy diet, it can be an optional extra.

Afternoon Drinks
½   Glass fruit squash
1   Biscuit

Supper
Soup
1   Slice of bread with butter
Main meal: as lunch

Evening Drinks	*Some Examples*
½ Mug milk-based drink	Milk shake, cocoa, Ovaltine.

FIG. 9.2. Sample diet sheet.

it is less disturbing for a child to see a smaller portion of food on her plate than she may be able to eat, than a large portion which may heighten her anxiety and lead to failure. For this reason a child is given portions dependent on how much the staff feel she can realistically eat. Portions can initially be small, increasing in relation to progress until the child is able to consume complete age-appropriate meals.

Every child is required to choose one portion of food high in carbohydrate, one high in protein, and a portion of vegetables at both lunch and supper. In our experience, it is not valuable to indulge in conversation about calorific values because this is not a feature of normal daily life. People do not normally scrutinise everything they eat. We emphasise the need for variety and do not encourage high carbohydrate food as a weight-gaining strategy. This can produce panic in the child, and is not a reflection of what could be described as a "normal healthy diet". Many young children quite naturally like sweet foods and children with anorexia nervosa are no exception to this, while at the same time fearing the high calorie content.

The diet regime enables staff to set limits with the child's eating habits. It is often reassuring for the child to know that the staff will not allow any extreme form of unhealthy eating. When the diet plan is completed, it is placed on the wall in the dining-room area. This display enables the child, her parents and staff to know what the child is expected to eat at each meal.

Anorectics constantly compare their diet sheets and they often compete to have the smallest portions. Although progress can be taking place in a variety of areas, the transition from ¼–½ portions or ½–¾ portions can be a terrifying step for an anorectic and she may be resistant to this change. These problems are not easily resolved and are somewhat inevitable. However, we strive to help each child to concentrate on her individual goals.

Different hospitals have different arrangements for the provision of food. On the Mildred Creak Unit there is a choice available at most meals and snacks. For example, at mid-morning there are different drinks available and a selection of biscuits. At lunch and supper, there are at least two options available of each food type. If a child has a particular dislike of potatoes, which usually represents a fear of the calorific content, there will be an option of rice or pasta. The nursing staff are responsible for ordering the types and quantity of food required at each meal for all children on the Unit. Ordering is completed one day in advance. With experience, nursing staff are able to ensure that their orders are, to some extent, reflective of the children's likes. Children are not consulted when the ordering takes place. Apart from the difficulty of trying to get them to agree on two main dishes, children with anorexia nervosa have a tendency to choose the same food continually, usually of low calorific value. Changing the food options available prevents this rigid and unhealthy process.

Naso-gastric Feeding (N.G. Feeding)

Our team is always reluctant to decide upon naso-gastric feeding as a management strategy. However, if a child is severely emaciated or dehydrated and unable to consume adequate amounts of food, it is considered vital in restoring the child's weight to a safe level. The dietician decides how much milk-based feed is required to ensure gradual weight gain in the child.

Children are often frightened by the thought of naso-gastric feeding and the fear of sudden weight gain.

Ruth was so anxious about having naso-gastric feeds that on two occasions half her feed disappeared from the fridge. She thought the night staff would not notice (we never did find the feed!).

On another occasion Michelle discarded 12 packets of feed through a window. Unfortunately for her they landed on a passing paediatrician who promptly returned them.

Although children may be receiving naso-gastric feeds, the aim is to help them return to normal feeding. However, they can be even more reluctant to eat because they are being artificially fed and do not wish to gain any further weight.

Ellen refused to eat when naso-gastric feeding commenced for fear of gaining too much weight too quickly. It was not until a programme was devised where if she ate, her feed would be reduced accordingly, that Ellen started eating again.

The children's naso-gastric feeding takes place overnight to prevent interference with daytime activities. Night staff are responsible for administering feeds. Communication about each child needs to be detailed to prevent splitting between day and night staff.

MEAL TIMES

Children with anorexia nervosa can be viewed as communicating their distress by not eating. Meal times are always difficult. It is a time when the child can show the staff and her family whether or not she is ready to move on from her rigid position of self-starvation. To be able to progress she needs the staff to acknowledge her feelings, and to know that even if she gains weight, they will still remain aware of her distress. Anorectic children often fluctuate in what they want: Sometimes they can see their difficulties with peers and families clearly and, at other times, deny them totally. They are often anxious, requiring reassurance that staff will remain constant in their approach and will continue to recognise their concerns, irrespective of eating improvements.

Anita found it helpful to meet with a nurse prior to meals to discuss her concerns and carry out some relaxation exercises. This reduced her anxiety at the meal table.

Preferably one nurse should sit with a child throughout the meal, providing support and encouragement. Tasks are negotiated with the members of staff according to the child's ability, with the aim of slowly helping the child eat more. If the child has not eaten for some time, tasks may start with touching cutlery, brushing lips with food, then moving on to taking mouthfuls. We can, however, only accept these small tasks if the child's physical health is not in immediate jeopardy. It is important that the staff give clear instructions and are firm in their approach so that every child knows what is expected from her from the beginning of the meal. It is necessary, before each meal, for nurses to consider their own expectations of the child and to assess how realistic they are in relation to the child's progress. Achievements are more likely to be met if expectations are realistic and fair. Team communication is particularly important to ensure expectations are the same among various members of staff.

Bridie was popular among staff and peers. Most mornings she would leave a spoonful of egg in its shell hoping the nurses would not notice. It was tempting not to confront this as it would inevitably end in an argument. It caused division among the nurses, some feeling it was petty to insist and others believing it was important to maintain their expectations. After much discussion the nurses were able to unite in their approach and Bridie was able to finish her egg!

Patience, and the ability to gauge a child's potential accurately, help the meal-time relationship, and let the child know that the staff are prepared to work at her pace. The result is that a child, often for the first time, feels that her real concerns are being acknowledged, and that adults are able to understand the link between her not being able to eat and her distress.

A child's refusal to eat an adequate diet can often seem unchangeable and so the use of compromise is an important strategy. Negotiation and flexibility are both encouraged.

> Before admission Gary's father told him he would make him sit at the table until he finished his meal. They sat there for 18 hours before his father gave in.

Compromises lead away from the rigid battle situation where everyone loses out.

> Denise was totally unable to drink any of her milk at mid-morning drinks, having previously agreed to drink half. In discussion a compromise was reached requiring her to take ten sips.

It is important that a child's opinion is taken into consideration even though adults stay in charge. If a child is unwilling to discuss tasks, it is necessary for staff to think about what it is that makes the child want to remain in the "sick" position. Is it that if she eats, everyone will think she is better? Will other demands be made of her? Will things get out of control regarding her weight? Will she be sent home immediately, into an environment which may have contributed to her illness? Is this the only way she can let people know when she is angry or upset? It is essential to try to appreciate what the child is feeling and the difficulties she is experiencing. She may mention a particular fear during the meal or a nurse may be aware of a pertinent issue. In such cases, it is important that there is full acknowledgement of the concerns. It is only then that a child can set aside these worries and continue with her efforts to eat.

Meals need a beginning, a focus and an end. It is useful to have a time limit for each course. Once the task or tasks are performed a child should be allowed to relax. It is tempting to encourage more achievements if the tasks have been performed with relative ease. However, this would contradict previous agreements. Time limits may be set for a child to perform each task: for example, five minutes to pick up cutlery. It is important for a child to have time and space to try and achieve a goal. If this is not possible, staff are there to help with her feelings of failure. Whether tasks are performed or not, the meal must end on time.

Throughout the meal, staff should verbally encourage and empathise with the child, but negative feelings can also be shown. It can be extremely irritating if a child who has been previously eating and performing tasks well, suddenly refuses to do anything. This frustration can be put to a child in a constructive way. "I feel irritated that you are not eating anything, as you have been doing well. I would like you to try and help me understand what is stopping you." There may also be times when a nurse feels intensely frustrated and, on reflection, thinks that it may be a projection from the child. This can be put back to the child by saying: "I'm sitting here feeling pretty awful. I wonder if this is also how you are feeling?"

These techniques help to establish an openness within the relationship and encourage talk about feelings. A child needs to know the links between her emotional state and physical actions, and the consequence of these. It is up to the nurses to pre-empt these situations so that nurse and child do not end up both demoralised and in conflict. A nurse can help a child to think of more appropriate ways in which to express herself when she is angry, or hurt, rather than compromise her health.

Nurses eat all meals with the children, as modelling appropriate eating habits can be beneficial. Staff must be able to support each other at meal times and work together, as we expect parents to do. When serving a child at meal times, it is helpful if a nurse checks the amount with another nurse before it is given to a child. If a child is upset or angry at what she has been given to eat, two nurses having been in agreement can give the one serving the child the confidence to remain firm.

After meals, children continue with the normal ward routine, as determined by their weight. If despite eating adequately and/or being naso-gastrically fed, a child does not gain weight, it is likely that she is vomiting or purging. The necessary steps are then taken to supervise her during toileting and bathing. This action is intrusive, but privacy can only be restored when weight gain commences.

Ruth had been losing weight, and vomit was smelt in her bedroom but on thorough search nothing was found. Further examination found her pot plants had been recently watered. A simple litmus paper test showed that the plants had not only been watered. After this discovery the key nurse was able to take the necessary steps to prevent Ruth from vomiting.

THE ACTIVITY PROGRAMME

Children arrive on the Unit in varying states of emaciation. At home a child may have been allowed to exert herself, sometimes to the point of exhaustion. Family members collude with the child, and there is often a general denial that she is physically ill. Although there may be a realisation of the links between her not eating and the necessity for rest, it is rare to find parents who have acted on this awareness. It is a common occurrence to find a child with anorexia nervosa exercising continuously.

Michelle, while sitting down, would continually "jig" her legs in an attempt to lose weight, while Anita developed bed sores on her back following repeated wriggling in bed.

On the ward, all activities are restricted and rest is implemented, because of the child's poor physical state. If very underweight, she is initially denied access to the normal ward routine, but as she gains weight, her participation gradually increases. This is not a reward, but a statement that her physical health has improved slightly, and as a result, she has more energy to participate in activities.

Every child with an eating disorder has an activity programme which corresponds to her weight. Attendance in groups, at the Unit school and in other activities, is all based on the child's physical health. An important part of the programme is to encourage peer contact. Many children have become withdrawn and depressed. It would be easy to perpetuate this by keeping a child isolated from group work and on prolonged periods of bed rest. We believe it is essential that she shares her experiences with other children so they can help each other. Our activity programme outlined below is constructed as a guideline, but is modified for individual needs.

Ward Activity Programme for Children with Eating Disorders

1. Every child will attend meals in the dining room, and attend all groups. Physical exertion may be restricted, depending on weight.
2. Activities when *below 75%* weight for height:
   (a) Morning school only.
   (b) Bed rest 12–3pm, up for lunch.
   (c) Attend all therapy groups but remain physically inactive in groups, such as drama and social skills.
   (d) Individual sessions in bedroom only, except for once-weekly when a walk to the playroom is permitted.
   (e) Bed rest from 5.30 till bedtime, up for supper.
   (f) Specific sedentary activities like watching television are allowed.
   (g) No weekend leave.
3. Activities when *75%–80%* weight for height:
   As above, but weekend leave is determined by how confident parents and staff are that the child can maintain her weight at home.

4. Activities when *80%* weight for height and above:
   (a) Weekend leave as in 3.
   (b) Physical activities will gradually be introduced.
   (c) Individual sessions can be held in the playroom.
   (d) Outings will be reintroduced and eventually swimming and more strenuous exercise will be permitted.

Our activity programme is to some extent flexible, and the planning often involves much discussion between the key nurse and case manager, and other members of the multi-disciplinary team. When introducing new activities into the programme we take into consideration the child and family's interests and way of life. Although the staff discuss possible targets, only two at a time are negotiated with the child and are placed on her chart (see Fig. 9.1). This helps cut out lengthy discussion, and allays anxiety by focusing on the present, rather than the future. It is quite acceptable for the child and family to ask for certain activities, for example, a haircut or a visit to a friend. Such requests are discussed by the nursing staff and the decision is always based on the child's physical health, not on whether parents or the nursing staff feel she deserves it.

The nursing staff explain the necessity for rest in relation to physical health, and try to encourage each child to gain weight, however small the amount. If a child refuses to comply with restrictions, the staff decide on an appropriate way to enforce the management. It is important that she can experience adults making necessary decisions and enforcing them.

NURSE–CHILD RELATIONSHIPS

Key Nurses

A key nurse is intensely involved with a child throughout admission. The relationship develops at many different levels and there is often a great sadness felt between nurse and child at discharge. It is the key nurse's task to ensure that the child's planned nursing management is adhered to by all staff, and to provide an environment where the child feels safe enough both to express her feelings and to gain insight into her behaviour so that she can find other means of expressing distress than avoidance of weight gain. It can seem confusing for a child that a nurse is her confidante at some times yet at others may be firmly setting boundaries on her behaviour. However, we believe it is helpful for a child to experience a normal adult/child relationship characterised by consistency, clear communication, firmness, caring and responsiveness.

The close involvement between nurse and child results in the nurse receiving powerful projections from the child. Nurses frequently complain that they feel miserable and impotent in helping the child, who is probably feeling the same. Regular supervision for nurses is essential so that the feelings evoked can be identified and explored in an attempt to understand the child's feelings. Nurses often feel very frustrated, particularly at times when change is not occurring. Excitement and relief are often felt when a child starts to make progress. The key nurse is often in the strongest position to appreciate and acknowledge the child's achievements and understands how difficult it has been for her.

In addition to a key nurse, each child is also allocated a support nurse, whose relationship may differ because of different personalities. Sometimes a child relates to one nurse as the totally "good" person, with whom she develops a very positive relationship, while the other becomes the recipient of all her negative feelings. Skilled supervision and careful handling is necessary to prevent splitting. The nurses need to help the child value and depend upon both of them for their expertise.

> Ellen complained bitterly to her support nurse about her key nurse when she was required to eat more. Both nurses met together with her to acknowledge her irritation and to show that the change in her diet had been a joint decision.

This process of splitting may replicate what happens in the family with one member seen as the bad person (see chapter 14).

Individual Work

The key nurse meets with the child every day for what is referred to as an "individual session" or "individual work". This usually lasts for about half an hour. The time is structured in different ways depending on the child's age, her particular difficulties and in some instances her preferences. The sessions will take place in the form of counselling, play, cognitive therapy, or art therapy. These meetings are usually held in the playroom, unless the child's weight dictates she should stay in bed.

Some sessions may be used to explore the child's inner world through non-directive play. This allows a child to act out fantasies without being judged or criticised. It helps a child to accept herself and to feel more confident instead of being frightened by the aggressive parts of her inner world. The child is allowed to explore the playroom, playing with whatever toys are available. It may be beneficial to have more directive sessions where themes relevant to the child are focused upon. A nurse might explore the child's patterns of behaviour in an attempt to help the child discover new ways of "being" and relating to others. A child may need to learn practical skills in communication, such as how to express herself appropriately when angry or sad. She can then be set tasks to practise while with relatives or peers. Progress can be discussed in future meetings. As well as learning to explore and express her feelings appropriately, it is important that she can learn coping strategies such as containing her anxieties between sessions.

> Judith labelled a small box her "worry box". Whenever she had a worry she was encouraged to write it down and post it in the box. This helped her to cope better with her anxieties.

Other areas of individual work include discussion of the child's mistrust of staff who are perceived as wanting to control rather than help. Children with eating disorders are dependent on feedback from others to maintain their self-esteem, making them particularly vulnerable to the influences of their family and peers. Much of the individual work is spent enhancing a child's self-esteem. Anorectics tend towards perfectionism and have a high level of competitiveness with peers. They may have an all-or-nothing attitude which relates not only to eating but to exercising, relationships and many other areas. Perhaps the hardest part of individual work is helping a child with anorexia nervosa to accept both the positive and negative parts of herself; for example, sometimes being the most popular child on the ward and at other times being feared or ignored.

Unit Milieu

The milieu is of great value in helping children with eating disorders along the difficult road to recovery. They have an opportunity to meet other people and experience new ways of relating, different boundaries and expectations, all within the contained environment of the Unit. Although the dynamics are often complex there is always a great sense of unity among the children, who often identify with each other's struggles. The nursing staff help to develop this cohesiveness so that each child has the opportunity to achieve her full potential. The fruits of this lengthy and complex process are both exemplified and formulated when the child is discharged.

> Prior to admission Bridie was shy and isolated from peers at school. During her admission she was able to develop closer relationships with peers. Other children supported her attempt to make friends. She was

able to use the experience positively, making links at home with children with the confirmed belief that she was a valuable friend.

PARENTS AND THEIR INVOLVEMENT

Although there is no proof that family dysfunction can create an eating disorder, the family certainly have a vital part to play in helping their child recover. At the time the child is admitted the family is almost always "stuck". Sometimes families feel so relieved by the admission that they wish to opt out. From the very beginning our aim is to include the parents in the management of their child. We encourage them to take responsibility for regaining appropriate control in relation to their child.

This is exemplified by our policy of ensuring that the parents make the final decision as to whether or not their child is admitted, and that they agree not only to participate in formal family-therapy sessions, but also in management on the Unit.

At meal times Jane would make her nose bleed to avoid eating. Her father was obviously frustrated by this but was unable to insist that she keep eating. When the key nurse encouraged the parents to continue helping her to eat, her father became verbally abusive to the nurse. It was only with great patience and sensitivity to the family's feelings that the nurses were able to help the family cope with their frustration, and help Jane to eat.

Themes that often become apparent from the child's therapies and the family therapy can be worked on with parents in the ward setting. For instance, it may become clear that a child fears menstruation. This issue may be addressed with the child and her mother. Such work is often referred to as "growing-up work". This is a time when the mother can help her daughter with issues pertinent to her adolescence, including, when necessary, sex education.

Any behavioural programme implemented involves the parents to some degree. A programme may be devised to help a child with peer relationships. Although not necessarily directly involved at all times, the parents are helped to show interest and encourage their child. At a later date the programme may be continued at home if necessary. Dysfunctional patterns of relating can also be tackled. If, for example, a mother is particularly intrusive towards her daughter, not allowing any privacy, staff help the child discuss this with her mother and negotiate some boundaries.

One of the main areas of work with parents is to help them make their child eat. All parents are asked to attend for supper once a week. This is a hectic and exhausting occasion but has many advantages. It allows staff to observe the family in a less formal setting. It gives families a chance to meet each other and it encourages parents to feel part of the working ward. Most importantly, for families where a child has an eating disorder, it is a time for them to learn to feed their child. Many parents have become exasperated because they cannot get their child to eat. This is a time when parents and staff can work together. With staff support they can learn to understand their child's behaviour and start to confront the eating issue. Our aim is to teach the parents an appropriate way of managing meal times. They will serve their child optimal portions of food, making decisions together and supporting each other, so that splitting does not occur between parents. At meal times they will have to set tasks and help the child perform them if she is not able to do them alone. They learn to lower their expectations and to praise their child for small achievements, realising that such a serious condition can only change slowly.

A member of staff, usually one of the key nurses, is allocated to each family after the meal. The nurse advises the parents on how to help the child, acting as a facilitator. However, situations can occur where, because the parents feel blamed, they join or protect their child against the staff.

> Anita's parents were quite protective of her. On one occasion her father was observed eating his daughter's snack, to avoid the frustration of failing to get her to eat.

It is important to remember that children eat at different rates, often corresponding to how work is progressing in family and individual therapy. Parents may also learn at different rates and this too can depend on how family therapy is progressing. It may be that when the child is first admitted, the parents work very separately and have opposing views on the child's behaviour. It can take many weeks before they can even agree on the goals of each meal. However, as they learn co-operation and consistency, so they are more likely to help their child to start eating healthily.

WEEKEND MANAGEMENT

The majority of children are initially admitted from local hospitals and may return there for weekend care. The staff are usually sympathetic but often lack experience in relation to the physical and emotional aspects of eating disorders. Consequently they may find it difficult to implement our regime. Paediatric wards are usually busy with very sick children requiring complex medical or surgical treatment, placing their staff under immense pressure. This can result in a lack of appreciation of the severity of the disorder, when often the only clear presenting feature is a refusal to eat. The weekend staff often express their frustration and confusion as to why the child continues to starve herself out of choice. Alternatively, some weekend nurses ally with the child's resentment towards our firm approach.

With these differences in approach, families can become confused and irritated. A coalition can occur between the family and the weekend staff against us. They are both under similar pressure to adhere to our difficult regime, and gain comfort from joining together. It is essential, for this reason, that liaison takes place at least twice a week, and that regular meetings occur. We telephone the hospital on a Monday for a verbal handover and write our report in letter form on a Friday, including all care plans. We also telephone on a Friday to talk through the regime with the nursing staff on duty over the weekend.

Whereas the parents attend meal times and family-therapy sessions to learn new ways, the weekend staff have to learn everything over the telephone and through letter contact. As a result, weekend staff often complain of feeling unsupported, especially when a child refuses to comply with a regime the nursing staff are expected to enforce. Sometimes, because they feel controlled and unsupported, they are unable or unwilling to impose the regime with a consequent weight loss over the weekend.

We encourage nurses from the local hospital to visit the Unit for a day, to give them a chance to view our way of working and experience the ward milieu. It also helps to show the child and family that we are all working together, despite being in different hospitals.

We feel that any child whose weight is below 80% weight for height (wasting) should not go home for weekends as her health is at risk. It is imperative that an arrangement is made before admission, with the local hospital, to have the child at weekends for an indefinite period. This part of the regime is perhaps one of the most difficult for the family to accept.

When the child is out of the wasting range, plans for the weekend are considered. If it seems that parents are able to take control and work together, weekend leave can commence. It is quite common for children to lose weight at weekends and gain during the week while on the Unit. Although this slows down their overall weight gain, it is useful to show the family that the child's weight gain is dependent upon parental unity and firmness, as well as the resolution of underlying problems. The nursing staff make sure the parents are fully aware of their child's present management, ensuring they have dietary instructions, and know how much activity is allowed.

When the child returns from weekend leave, after being weighed, the nurse, child and accompanying parent meet to discuss the weekend. It is important that the nurse knows which areas to explore with the family and she hears about the positive as well as the difficult aspects of the weekend. Gradually parents begin to trust the staff and discuss weekends more openly. Soon they become able to predict whether or not their child has gained weight. As they become able to ask staff for help in specific areas, so their child's recovery continues.

DISCHARGE

Once the child is eating healthily and has reached a satisfactory weight range, a graded discharge is commenced. Initially weekends are increased to three days, later four, with an accompanying re-entry to school. As much support as possible is offered during this period, including, if possible, home and school visits.

Preparation for leaving takes place long before discharge, being explored within the different therapies and the milieu. The final part of the leaving process takes the form of the leaving tea. This involves the children and nurses planning and making a personalised cake. Everybody attends the tea. The leaver makes a speech and the nurse makes a speech about the child and her progress. Often the child has been on the Unit for a long time and as a result of the relationships developed it can be an intensely emotional occasion, but one that is beneficial for children who have learned about the expression of feelings and can acknowledge their sadness at leaving.

CONCLUSION

It is essential that nurses understand the full complexity of the illness when caring for children with eating disorders and their families. Just as much time should be spent focusing on a child's interpersonal and family relationships as on her eating difficulties and low weight. These children and their families are among the most difficult to work with and can be emotionally draining for the whole team. An essential component in helping these families is a well-functioning multi-disciplinary team with each person's contribution being valued and respected.

REFERENCES

Yellowlees, P.M., Roe, M., Walker, M.K., & Ben-Tovim, D.I. (1988). Abnormal perception of food size in anorexia nervosa. *British Medical Journal, 296,* 1689–1690.

CHAPTER TEN

Physical Treatments

Bryan Lask and Abe Fosson

AIMS

The basic aims of physical treatment are: (a) rehydration; (b) reversal of electrolyte imbalance; (c) remedying nutritional deficiency; (d) weight-gain; and (e) restoration of psychological well-being. While these are clearly interrelated there is also an order of priority. Dehydration and electrolyte imbalance are life-threatening and require immediate attention, whereas the other components do not have the same degree of urgency. Nonetheless, each responds to re-feeding and it is this that is the mainstay of the physical approach to treatment.

RE-FEEDING

Re-feeding may be achieved by oral, naso-gastric, or intravenous feeds. The decision on how to proceed is made on the urgency of the situation. When a child is severely dehydrated or has an electrolyte imbalance, a delay of more than a few hours can be dangerous. In consequence it is reasonable to spend some time encouraging and helping the child to eat and drink, but if there is no immediate success, further delay in instituting artificial feeding should not be countenanced. Fortunately, the majority of children do not require artificial feeds and respond over time to encouragement to resume a normal eating pattern. Whether this is best achieved by a graded re-feeding programme, or trying to impose a normal diet immediately is arguable. In general, children whose weight loss is not too severe, whose illness is of recent onset, and who are being treated on an out-patient basis should be encouraged to resume a normal diet as quickly as possible. For children whose weight-loss is substantial or long-lasting it may be easier for them to resume normal eating if offered a graded re-feeding programme.

Graded Re-feeding

The full details of such a programme are discussed in chapter 9. It is useful to seek the advice of a dietician in determining the required daily intake, which is likely to be between 2000 and 3000 calories, and how this may be constituted. The child can be party to such discussions but should not be allowed to dictate what she eats. One should aim to start with relatively small portions, so avoiding frightening the child, and gradually building up the amounts. A useful rule of thumb might be that a small portion served on a large plate is more likely to be consumed than a large portion served on a small plate! It is important to try to include foods that are attractive to the child and are appealingly presented, a sometimes difficult task if in hospital. For the first week, portions can be one quarter of normal size, and increase to half after a week or so, with equivalent weekly increments until a normal intake is resumed. Full details of such a programme are described in chapter 9.

Naso-gastric Feeding

When the child's physical state demands immediate re-feeding, naso-gastric feeding should be implemented. Such a programme should be carefully co-ordinated with liaison between the nursing staff, a dietician, paediatrician and child psychiatrist. The aim should be to ensure that the child is receiving an adequate diet and preferably in the region of 2000–3000 calories daily. It is usually helpful to tell the child exactly what the planned intake will be, and to say that any amount taken by mouth will be deducted from the 24-hour total naso-gastric feed. (See chapter 9 for further details.)

Naso-gastric feeding of children with eating disorders does cause some concern with regard to the infringement of children's rights and the mistaken view that this is force-feeding. If a child has a life-threatening illness and is unable to consume sufficient nutrition there is general agreement that artificial feeding by naso-gastric tube is perfectly acceptable, and no-one would consider such action as infringing the child's rights. However, because eating disorders present with the child *refusing* to eat sufficiently, anxieties then arise about overruling the child's wishes. Such views are based on an underlying misunderstanding of the psychopathology, which renders the child just as unable to eat adequate amounts as a child with any illness that impairs the appetite. If the child's life or long-term health is put at risk by the diminished intake, then whatever the underlying illness, remedial action has to be taken.

The intended course of action should always be discussed with the child, and her agreement sought. Surprisingly, it is very rare for a child to refuse. It seems that most children in these circumstances are relieved that the responsibility for eating is taken away from them, at least temporarily. If a child does strongly object to naso-gastric feeding, she can be offered the alternative of intravenous feeds (see below).

There is some debate as to whether or not naso-gastric feeds should be administered at night. The advantage of night feeding is purported to be that the child can lead as normal a life as possible during the day without being perceived as being different from others. This potential advantage could be outweighed by the possibility of her interfering with the feeds during the night. Further, whether or not the repeated passing of the tube each evening is useful is unclear. Some children find it aversive, and quickly opt to eat adequate amounts by mouth, while others very quickly adapt to it and even pass their own tubes! There is now some evidence that regular feeds over 24 hours are more likely to hasten a normal eating pattern than is overnight feeding.

Notwithstanding this uncertainty, there is no doubt that some children become quite dependent on the tube and make no effort to eat normally. For example, Judith, aged 12, was admitted to hospital having lost 55% of her body weight over a 12-month period. Her physical state was such that artificial feeding was essential and she continued to refuse to eat or drink anything by mouth for a further 18 months. All efforts to withdraw naso-gastric feeding failed. Eventually she only started normal eating after living with a foster family for six months. Such circumstances are unusual and possible related more to Judith's fear of returning to her family than to dependency. There is no evidence that long-term dependency on tube-feeding does occur. In general, however, naso-gastric feeding should be seen as a life-saving measure, preferably to be used for time-limited periods.

Intravenous Feeding

Intravenous feeding, in which the gastro-intestinal tract is bypassed, may be used as an alternative to naso-gastric feeds. All necessary nutrients are fed directly into a vein via an in-dwelling needle or catheter. Its usefulness is limited by two factors: (a) because highly concentrated solutions cannot be tolerated, a dilute solution has to be administered on a continuous basis, thus severely restricting the child's mobility; and (b) there are only limited sites available for insertion of needles; as needles have frequently to be replaced it is difficult to maintain intravenous feeding for lengthy periods. However short-term favourable responses have been reported in anorexia nervosa (Croner, Larsson, Schildt, & Symreng, 1985).

The use of intravenous feeding is best reserved for the rare times when immediate fluid or electrolyte replacement is vital, or the child can neither eat or tolerate naso-gastric feeding. It should always be carried out under the supervision of a paediatrician with the assistance of a dietician, and electrolytes should be monitored every two days. It should only be seen as a short-term measure.

MEDICATION

Medication has but a small part to play in the management of eating disorders. Those preparations that have been considered include appetite stimulants, neuroleptics, anti-depressants, vitamins, iron, zinc, and other forms of mineral supplementation.

So-called appetite stimulants have never been shown to be helpful, but this need not be surprising given that in anorexia nervosa there is often no loss of appetite, and that there are no truly effective appetite stimulants. In consequence, there is no place for the use of this range of medication in childhood eating disorders.

Neuroleptics also have little value despite the fact that anxiety, phobias, and obsessionality are all common concomitants of eating disorders. There is no evidence in children that such medication alters the course of the illness, or for that matter has a substantial impact upon any of the symptoms. Their use is best reserved for children who are suffering from extreme anxiety, and, as with all forms of psychotropic medication, should be supervised by a child psychiatrist. The newer forms of neuroleptic medication, including dopamine antagonists such as pimozide and sulpiride, may eventually prove to be of some value, but as yet the results are not very encouraging (Vandereycken, 1984; Vandereycken & Pierloot, 1992).

Anti-depressants do have a slightly more useful role in childhood eating disorders than any other form of medication. When a child is depressed with psychomotor retardation, feelings of guilt and worthlessness, and biological changes such as poor sleep and diurnal mood variation, tricyclics such as amitryptiline are of value. Providing normal cardiovascular functioning has been documented on an electrocardiogram, a reasonable starting dose is 25–50 mgs. depending upon weight. This can be increased at weekly intervals until the therapeutic range is achieved. Medication is best given as one dose at night, and its effectiveness cannot be truly evaluated for two to three weeks after the implementation of a therapeutic dose. If effective, tricyclics should not be discontinued less than four months after improvement has been noted.

Vitamin and mineral supplementation are popular but of no proven value. Such deficiencies are usually rapidly remedied after the implementation of a normal diet, and what little evidence exists suggests that supplementation is no more effective than a re-feeding programme in overcoming the deficiencies (e.g. Lask, Fosson, Thomas, & Rolfe, 1993).

Finally it is worth cautioning against the use of laxatives when constipation, common in anorexia nervosa, is troublesome. Such children are only too eager to learn new techniques of weight control, and the constipation is best overcome by dietary means.

CONCLUSIONS

The physical treatments that are of most value are the artificial feeding programmes such as naso-gastric feeding. Anti-depressants are of value when a biological depression complicates the clinical picture, but as yet there is no evidence for the effectiveness of other forms of medication.

REFERENCES

Croner, S., Larsson, J., Schildt, B., & Symreng, T. (1985). Severe anorexia nervosa treated with total parenteral nutrition. *Acta Paediatrica Scandinavica, 74,* 230–236.

Lask, B., Fosson, A., Thomas, S., & Rolfe, U. (1993). Zinc deficiency and childhood onset anorexia nervosa. *Journal of Clinical Psychiatry.*

Vandereycken, W. (1984). Neuroleptics in the short-term treatment of anorexia nervosa. *British Journal of Psychiatry, 144,* 288–292.

Vandereycken, W. & Pierloot, R. (1992). Pimozide combined with behaviour therapy in the short-term treatment of anorexia nervosa. *Acta Psychiatrica Scandinavica, 66,* 445–450.

CHAPTER ELEVEN

Behaviour Therapy

Jacky Knibbs

INTRODUCTION

There is a large amount of literature from the 1960s and early 1970s on the application of behavioural techniques to the management of anorexia nervosa and related eating disorders. These accounts are characterised by minimal follow-up information and relatively little assessment detail. There is a clear requirement for significant changes in eating behaviour and weight gain to be incorporated into any treatment package, and in recent years more attention has been focused on developing multi-modal behavioural-assessment techniques in an attempt to address the complexity of the disorder. There remains a need for better standardisation of instruments for child and adolescent populations and longer term follow-up evaluation of interventions.

ASSESSMENT

A prerequisite to any behavioural intervention is a thorough behavioural analysis. Here information is gathered about behaviour, its antecedents and consequences. This information is used to provide a formulation of the problem, identify dysfunctional behaviours, measure outcome and evaluate different methods of intervention. In a very useful overview of behavioural-assessment techniques for eating disorders in adults, Williamson (1990) covers three major groups of measures which may contribute to systematic behavioural analysis. These assess: 1) Eating disturbance; 2) Body image disturbance; and 3) Secondary psychopathology. These areas will be covered here with particular reference to anorexia nervosa and related eating disorders in children.

1. Eating Disturbance

(a) Measurement of Weight. The assessment of current and ideal weight is particularly important in goal-setting. Typically an individual's current weight is compared to his or her ideal weight taken from a set of normative height and weight tables. There can be considerable debate about the proper estimates of ideal weight for an individual. Useful weight-to-height ratios for children can be derived from the Tanner-Whitehouse Standards (Tanner, Whitehouse, & Takaishi, 1966).

(b) Structured Interview. This involves a systematic gathering of information which then yields itself to psychometric evaluation. There are a range of structured interviews currently being developed for use with adults with eating disorders (Cooper & Fairburn, 1987; Palmer et al., 1987; Williamson, 1990). Although there are no published reports of structured interviews devised specifically for use with children and adolescents with eating disorders, there is certainly scope for the adaptation of techniques for use with a young population (Gross, 1984; Murphy, Hudson, King, & Remenyi, 1985), particularly where questions may be used with family members in a separate interview (Williamson, 1990).

(c) Eating Disorders. Observation and measurement of eating behaviour under controlled conditions is the optimal form of behavioural assessment. A video recording of family or individual meals may prove a useful way of gathering baseline information (Williamson, 1990). Specific features of eating behaviour such as the rate of eating and the range of foods eaten may be recorded.

Particularly for in-patients, staff-rated checklists of eating behaviour are a useful part of assessment. These observations then serve as a supplementary measure to weight gain for assessing treatment efficacy.

To some extent anorexia nervosa may be construed as an anxiety disorder in which the avoidance of eating or purging serves to relieve anxiety associated with food consumption (Ollendick, 1979). Here it is useful to establish a hierarchy of foods from the most to the least acceptable. Anxiety may be further evaluated by exposing the individual to the anxiety-producing object, i.e. high calorie food under standardised conditions, and then measuring both food consumption and self-reported anxiety (Williamson, 1990).

(d) Self-report Measures.   The Eating Attitudes Test (EAT) described by Garner and Garfinkel (1979) was standardised on a group of adults (mean age of illness onset for the group was 18.4 years). It is a 40-item self-rating scale and gives a general index of anorectic characteristics, such as restrictive eating patterns and fear of weight gain.

The Eating Disorder Inventory (EDI) developed by Garner and Olmstead (1984) is designed for use by individuals aged 12 years and upwards. It is a 64-item forced-choice questionnaire which aims to measure the cognitive and behavioural characteristics of anorexia nervosa and bulimia. It differs from the EAT in that it is less specific to the symptoms of anorexia nervosa, focusing on eight different areas for evaluation. These include the drive for thinness, bulimia, body dissatisfaction, ineffectiveness, perfectionism, interpersonal distrust, awareness of own emotions and maturity fears.

The use of self-report inventories with anorectic populations has been questioned because of the significant denial associated with the disorder (Kalucy, Crisp, & Harding, 1977). However, young people with anorexia nervosa may initially be more comfortable with paper and pencil exercises than interviews, and useful supplementary pre-and-post measures of outcome may be obtained. Instruments are required which are standardised on lower age groups and are thus suitable for the pre-pubertal anorectic population.

(e) Self-monitoring.   This is one of the most widely used procedures in behavioural assessment of eating disorders in adults (Williamson, 1990). Self-monitoring data can be helpful for diagnosis, functional analysis (Gelfand & Hartmann, 1975) and evaluation of the efficacy of treatment procedures. There are several aspects of self-monitoring information that are useful for examining treatment outcome. The information can be easily quantified and can then be depicted in tabular form to help in clearly documenting baseline parameters. The situational and emotional antecedents and consequences of eating can be clarified and targeted during treatment.

In children and young people the usefulness of self-monitoring is more variable. This is particularly so in anorexia nervosa and will be influenced by the child's developmental stage, the level of motivation and resistance and parental reinforcement. Ollendick and Cerny (1981) discuss the problems of self-monitoring with poorly motivated children and recommend direct training in self-assessment procedures. Further research is clearly required to establish the usefulness of self-monitoring in a young anorectic population.

2. Body-image Assessment

Williamson (1990) reviews the measurement techniques that have been developed to assess body-image dissatisfaction and distortion. These include (a) attitudinal measures; (b) distorting image techniques; (c) body-part size estimation; and (d) silhouettes of differing body sizes.

(a) Attitudinal Measures. Questionnaires may be used to measure dissatisfaction with body size—particularly the body-dissatisfaction scale of the EDI (Garner & Olmstead, 1984). Johnson et al. (1984) studied body-size dissatisfaction in a female high-school population, while Leon et al. (1985) focused on sexual and body-image attitudes in anorexia nervosa, using a semantic differential image.

(b) Distorting Image Techniques. Here individuals estimate their overall body size using images of their own bodies in a mirror or camera. Williamson (1990) suggests that while these techniques have proved useful for showing body-image distortion in bulimia nervosa, the results are less consistent in anorexia nervosa. In addition the techniques are not useful as a measure of therapeutic outcome as they appear to be insensitive to variations in body image over time.

(c) Body-part Size Estimation. Slade & Russell (1973) applied visual-size estimation to anorectic populations. Individuals use a pulley to adjust two lights on a horizontal bar to estimate the width or depth of specific body regions. Again, results using this technique have been inconsistent and Williamson (1990) suggests that further validation is required before being usefully applied as an assessment technique.

(d) Silhouettes. With this technique individuals are presented with a series of silhouettes of gradually increasing body size and are asked to select both their actual size and their ideal size (Count & Adams, 1985; Williamson, Davis, Goreczny, & Blouin, 1989). Although to date there are no published accounts or norms for the application of this technique to children and adolescents, it is a very simple assessment task to administer and is a potentially useful addition to any behavioural assessment battery.

3. Secondary Psychopathology

Williamson (1990) discusses the range of other problems found to be associated with eating disorders and points to the importance of properly evaluating secondary problems and incorporating them into a behavioural-treatment plan. Touyz et al. (1984) and Fundudis (1986) advocate the use of a multi-modal behaviour-therapy approach (Keat, 1979). A key feature of this is specificity—namely, a clear delineation of the various important components of the problems. Some of the more relevant psychometric instruments available for use with children and adolescents will be high-lighted here:

(a) Depression. Depression is frequently associated with anorexia nervosa and related disorders. Fosson, Knibbs, Bryant-Waugh, and Lask (1987) found that 56% of their sample of children with early onset anorexia were clinically depressed. There are a number of self-report scales for assessing depression in children and adolescents reviewed by Kazdin (1990). One of the more useful is the Birleson Scale validated for children aged 8–14 years (Birleson, Hudson, Gray, & Wolff, 1987).

(b) Obsessive-compulsive Behaviour. This behaviour is common in anorexia nervosa (Holden, 1990): 29% of the 48 children described by Fosson et al. (1987) displayed obsessions or compulsions. The Leyton Inventory for Children (Berg, Rapoport, & Flament, 1986) provides a standardised measure of the severity and content of obsessive-compulsive behaviour for 12–16-year-olds.

(c) Social Skills. Young people with anorexia nervosa are frequently socially isolated (Pillay & Crisp, 1981) and it is important to establish the extent to which social anxiety or poor social skills contribute to this. La Greca et al. (1988) have recently described the development of a social-anxiety scale for children, yet to be applied to an anorectic population.

Although there are no norms available, the social skills assessment battery devised by Spence (1983) for 10–17-year-olds may provide an additional useful framework for examining areas of difficulty to incorporate into a treatment programme.

(d) Family Problems. The importance of family variables in the development of anorexia nervosa has been well-documented (Minuchin, Rosman, & Baker, 1978). The Bene-Anthony Family Relations Test (Bene & Anthony, 1985) provides a useful structured way of gathering information about young peoples' (7–17 years) views of their family.

Williamson (1990) recommends the use of the Family Environment Scale (Moos & Moos, 1986) for a general profile of family characteristics, although there is some debate about its reliability (Roosa & Beals, 1990). Harding and Lachenmeyer (1986) have used the Structural Family Interaction Scale (Perosa, Hansen, & Perosa, 1981) to examine family interaction patterns in anorectic populations, although no significant differences were found from a control group on this measure.

(e) Locus of Control. Several studies have assessed the locus of control in anorexia nervosa in an attempt to validate Bruch's (1974) arguments that anorexia nervosa involves the individual attempting to secure a sense of self-identity or personal control. Harding & Lachenmeyer (1986) and Hood, Moore, & Garner (1982) found that anorectics scored higher on internal locus of control in comparison to norms for non-patients of the same age. Strober (1982) reported that anorectics scored in a more internal direction than other adolescent psychiatric patients. In both studies those anorectics who scored in a more external direction on the particular locus of control measure used, were more likely to engage in vomiting. These authors used a modified version of Rotter's (1966) scale—the I–E scale (Reid & Ware, 1974). An alternative locus of control scale for children has been described by Nowicki and Strickland (1973) (age range 18–17).

(f) Stress. Pressures from examinations are reported to be harmful stressors which may influence the age of onset or course of the disorder (Mills, 1973). Other events which have been identified as preceding the onset of eating disorders include change of home or school, separation from a friend or the serious illness of a family member (Gomez & Dally, 1980). Williamson (1990) points to the importance of assessing common daily stressors, such as family arguments, because of their predictive relationship to psychological and somatic symptoms (Delongis et al., 1982). He recommends the use of either the Hassles Scale (Kanner, Coyne, Schaefer, & Lazarus, 1981) or the Daily Stress Inventory (Brantley, Waggoner, Jones, & Rappaport, 1987) identifying the latter particularly as allowing for a detailed analysis of the relationship between stress and eating behaviour.

INTERVENTION

Published accounts of the use of behavioural techniques with individuals with eating disorders may be grouped as follows: 1. reports following an operant model where the use of reinforcement contingencies are central; 2. those formulating eating disorders in terms of anxious, phobic or compulsive behaviour and on the application of techniques consistent with this; 3. behavioural techniques as part of combined approaches—within in-patient regimes or in single case reports. Most of these accounts relate to work carried out with older eating disorder patients.

1. Use of Reinforcement

A number of studies in the 1960s and early 1970s focused predominantly on the application of operant conditioning techniques to the treatment of anorexia nervosa (Bhanji & Thompson, 1974; Leitenberg, Agras, & Thomson, 1968; Scrignar, 1971). Briefly, this involves the systematic manipulation of reinforcement. Contingencies widely used are physical or social activity and material or visiting privileges contingent on weight gain. Some regimes include reinforcement deprivation to increase the range of available rewards, e.g. removal of key possessions. It is clearly important to carry out a detailed individual behavioural analysis before instituting any reinforcement programme of this kind: The use of social activity as a reinforcer would not be indicated for an already withdrawn and isolated anorectic. In one of the few controlled behavioural studies, Agras et al. (1974) used systematic analysis to suggest that informational feedback about weight and caloric intake may be a particularly important variable. The authors found that without such feedback, positive reinforcement appeared to be relatively ineffective. The timing of reinforcement is important; Halmi (1987) suggests that adolescents require at least daily reinforcement for weight increases. Schedules of reinforcement should, however, be sensitive to the goal of restoring normal eating patterns, i.e. encouraging steady weight gain. Some of the early attempts to increase weight gain quickly were likely to have inadvertently reinforced bingeing (Agras & Werne, 1977).

Negative reinforcement is also a powerful operant technique, although it has not been systematically evaluated in the management of eating disorders. This involves attempting to increase behaviour by having it prevent aversive consequences. Programmes where hospitalisation or tube-feeding accompany weight loss or failure to gain weight may negatively reinforce eating behaviour (Kellerman, 1977).

Bruch (1974) has criticised operant management techniques. She suggests that they are resented by patients and that this may impede subsequent psychotherapy, a criticism perhaps particularly pertinent to adolescent management. Touyz et al. (1984) have attempted to address this by comparing "strict" and "lenient" operant conditioning techniques in the management of anorexia nervosa (age range 13–35 years). The strict regime included a bed-rest programme with an individualised schedule of reinforcers for each 0.5 kg. of weight gain. The lenient and flexible behavioural programme involved a week of bed-rest followed by a contract with each patient to gain a minimum of 1.5 kg. per week. Compliance with this was enforced by requiring a week of bed-rest if the weight gain was not achieved. No significant differences were found in the rate of weight gain between the two treatments. The lenient programme was recommended as the treatment of choice both in terms of its practicality and acceptability, although follow-up data were not available. In general, the more rigid practices described by the authors of the 1960s and 1970s are now considered largely outdated, and do not form a treatment of choice for children with anorexia nervosa.

2. Management of Anxious, Phobic and Compulsive Behaviour

Behavioural analysis may suggest that anxiety related to eating should be the key focus for intervention (Hallsten, 1965; Ollendick, 1979; Schnurer, Rubin, & Roy, 1973). Here the intervention of choice would be systematic desensitisation as described by Hallsten (1965). A 12-year-old girl who developed a fear of gaining weight and becoming fat was taught to relax and then instructed to visualise herself being called to the table, at the table, eating, eating specifically fattening foods, enjoying them, having eaten, and then going to stand before a mirror in her mother's bedroom and perceiving that she was gaining weight. Schnurer et al. (1973) also used systematic desensitisation with a young woman who "was afraid that if I started to gain weight again, I would blow up like a balloon and never be able to stop". Hierarchies related to the anxiety associated with progressive weight gain and changes in appearances were formulated.

Neither of these studies presents follow-up data for more than one year. Ollendick (1979) suggests that cognitive restructuring may have to be included to maintain treatment effects. (See chapter 12 on cognitive approaches.)

Mavissakalian (1982) recommends direct behavioural treatment of phobic compulsive behaviour in anorexia.

Two 17-year-olds were treated with response prevention of compulsive exercising and prolonged exposure to phobic stimuli. This was in addition to an operant programme of weight gain and unfortunately both young women become overweight as a consequence—a finding not readily explicable by the study. Although behavioural analysis may suggest that these techniques be incorporated into a treatment plan, there are clear phenomenological differences between phobic obsessive compulsive disorders and eating disorders (Cooper, 1985).

3. Combined Approaches

Most published descriptions of child and in-patient regimes incorporate a range of treatment approaches (Jenkins, 1987; Lask & Bryant-Waugh, 1986; Russell, 1985; Steinberg, 1983). Establishing a contract for treatment with the parents of young persons under 16 is an important part of the work (Steinberg, 1983). Agras (1987) argues that only a medical emergency should lead to immediate hospitalisation and it may take many weeks for some families and young people to agree the need for hospital care and the basic treatment contract. Behavioural techniques featuring widely in in-patient regimes include individualised treatment contracts (Touyz et al., 1984) and clear goals for weight gain (Russell, 1985). Weight gain may be negatively reinforced by decreased supervision or avoidance of bed-rest, contingent on weight gain (Jenkins, 1987), and positively reinforced by allowing participation in games and hobbies contingent on appropriate eating behaviour (Steinberg, 1983).

Comparison studies of behavioural regimes with other forms of management have generally failed to establish significant differences between results using operant techniques and those using other forms of treatment including nursing care (Eckert et al., 1979; Garfinkel, Moldofsky, & Garner, 1977). However Agras and Kraemar (1983) argue that behaviour therapy is more efficient than medically or psychotherapeutically oriented therapy because the length of stay in hospital may be significantly shorter.

Clearly the major test of the behavioural approach is in its ability to achieve long-term results and to address the broad spectrum of presenting problems. Touyz et al. (1984) and Fundudis (1986) suggest that the multi-modal behavioural approach (Keat, 1979) presents a significant advance because it attempts to deal with the complexity of the disorder. The major advantage of this approach is operational precision where there is a clear description of the components and procedures of treatment. Fundudis (1986) presents a very useful multi-modal profile of an 11-year-old girl with anorexia nervosa (see Table 11.1).

Environmental stimulus control was aimed at encouraging adaptive behaviour to compete with maladaptive, food refusal and social withdrawal. This included encouragement of social activities such as clubs and societies which did not involve excessive physical activity but which addressed feelings of social isolation. Systematic desensitisation was aimed at reducing both school-related anxiety and that associated with food intake.

Carr, McDonnell, and Afnan (1989) describe the treatment of a 14-year-old anorectic boy with combined behavioural and family therapy. The behavioural treatment included a contract specifying how

TABLE 11.1

Multi-modal profile of 11-year-old girl with anorexia nervosa

MODALITY	(A) PRESENTING PROBLEMS	(B) PROPOSED FORMS OF TREATMENT
Behaviour	Resistance of eating (refuses food).	Stimulus control.
	Excessive physical activity (athletics, team sports, jogging).	Systematic desensitisation.
Affect	Feels "miserable". Is easily upset/overly senstitive to comments from parents, teachers. Highly "nervous", (anxious) around exam times and when asked questions by teachers in classroom situation. Feels "upset/angry inside".	Cognitive restructuring. Relaxation training. Systematic desensitisation. Family therapy and dyadic therapy.
Sensation	"Tight-feeling" in stomach. "Sick in stomach". "Full feeling". "Butterflies" in stomach (when anxious).	Systematic desensitisation.
Imagery	"I'm not a very nice person". "I'm hateful" (bad opinion of self). Sees self as "tomboyish" and as	Cognitive restructuring. Social reinforcement.
Cognition	"different from other girls". (Query sexual identification problems.)	
Interpersonal	Wants to be accepted into peer groups, but usually remains on periphery, often finds that she is "left out" by others. Parents and grandparents are "always on at me". Reluctance to being away from home. Bottles up feelings.	Environmental stimulus control.
Drugs/biology	Markedly underweight (below 3rd centile for age). Very thin in appearance.	

From: Fundudis, T. (1986). Anorexia nervosa in pre-adolescent girls: A multi-modal behaviour therapy approach. *Journal of Child Psychology and Psychiatry, 27,* 261–273.

privileges may be obtained by achieving eating and weight targets. A useful aspect of the description of this programme is coverage of some of the problems encountered during the behaviour programme, such as attempts by the boy to inflate his weight artificially.

CONCLUSION

In conclusion, the behavioural approach to anorexia nervosa has moved on from the narrow regimes criticised by Bruch (1974) to recognise the importance of multi-modal analysis and intervention. This incorporates use of baseline measures by which therapeutic progress may be monitored and there are clear advantages to the stringency and operational precision of behavioural analysis. A combination of treatment approaches where behavioural techniques may be supplemented by cognitive interventions, family therapy and individual/group psychotherapy as required seems to be the most useful way forward.

REFERENCES

Agras, W.S. (1987). *Eating disorders: Management of obesity, bulimia and anorexia nervosa.* New York: Pergamon Press.

Agras, W.S., Barlow, D., Chapin, H., Abel, G., & Leitenberg, H. (1974). Behavioural modification of anorexia nervosa. *Archives of General Psychiatry, 30,* 279–286.

Agras, W.S. & Kraemar, H.C. (1983). The treatment of anorexia nervosa: Do different treatments have different outcomes? In A.J. Stunkard and E. Stellor (Eds.), *Eating and its disorders.* (pp. 286–302). New York: Raven Press.

Agras, W.S. & Werne, J. (1977). Behaviour and modification in anorexia nervosa: Research foundations. In R.A. Vigersky (Ed.), *Anorexia nervosa.* New York: Raven Press.

Bene, E. & Anthony, J. (1985). *Bene-Anthony family relations test: Childrens version.* Windsor: NFER-Nelson.

Berg, C.J., Rapoport, N.L., & Flament, M. (1986). The Leyton obsessional inventory child version. *Journal of American Academy of Child Psychiatry, 25,* 84–91.

Bhanji, S. & Thompson, J. (1974). Operant conditioning in the treatment of anorexia nervosa: A review and retrospective study of 11 cases. *British Journal of Psychiatry, 124,* 166–72.

Birleson, P., Hudson, I., Gray, J., & Wolff, S. (1987). Clinical evaluation of a self-relating scale for depressive disorder in childhood. *Journal of Child Psychology and Psychiatry, 28,* 43–60.

Brantley, P.J., Waggoner, C.D., Jones, G.N., & Rappaport, N.B. (1987) A daily stress inventory: Development, reliability and validity. *Journal of Behavioural Medicine, 10,* 64–71.

Bruch, H. (1974). Perils of behaviour modification in treatment of anorexia nervosa. *Journal of the American Medical Association, 230,* 1419–1422.

Carr, A., McDonnell, D., & Afnan, S. (1989). Anorexia nervosa: The treatment of a male case with combined behavioural and family therapy. *Journal of Family Therapy, 11,* 335–352.

Cooper, P.J. (1985). Eating disorders. In F. Watts (Ed.), *New developments in clinical psychology.* (pp. 1–15). Chichester: Wiley.

Cooper, P.J. & Fairburn, C.G. (1987). The eating disorder examination: A semi-structured interview for the assessment of the specific psychopathology of eating disorders. *International Journal of Eating Disorders, 6,* 1–8.

Count, C.R. & Adams, H.C. (1985). Body image in bulimia, dieting and normal females. *Journal of Psychopathology and Behavioural Assessment, 7,* 289–301.

Delongis, A., Coyne, J.C., Dakof, G., Folkman, S., & Lazarus, R.S. (1982). Relationship of daily hassles, uplifts and major life events to health status. *Health Psychology, 1,* 119–136.

Eckert, E.D., Goldberg, S.C., Halmi, K.A., Casper, R.C., & Davis, J.M. (1979). Behaviour therapy in anorexia nervosa. *British Journal of Psychiatry, 134,* 55–59.

Fosson, A., Knibbs, J., Bryant-Waugh, R., & Lask, B. (1987). Early onset anorexia. *Archives of Disease in Childhood, 62,* 114–118.

Fundudis, T. (1986). Anorexia nervosa in pre-adolescent girls: A multi-modal behaviour therapy approach. *Journal of Child Psychology and Psychiatry, 27,* 261–273.

Garfinkel, P.E., Moldofsky, H., & Garner, D.M. (1977). The outcome of anorexia nervosa: Significance of clinical features, body image and behaviour modification. In R.A. Vigersky (Ed.), *Anorexia nervosa* (pp. 315–330). New York: Raven Press.

Garner, D.M., & Garfinkel, P.E. (1979). The eating attitudes test: An index of the symptoms of anorexia nervosa. *Psychological Medicine, 9,* 273–279.

Garner, D.M., Garfinkel, P.E., & Bemis, K. (1982). A multidimensional psychotherapy of anorexia nervosa. *International Journal of Eating Disorders, 1,* 3–46.

Garner, D.M. & Olmstead, M.P. (1984). *Manual for the Eating Disorders Inventory. (EDI).* Windsor: NFER: Nelson.

Gelfand, D.M. & Hartmann, D.P. (1975). *Child behaviour analysis and therapy.* Oxford: Pergamon.

Gomez, J. & Dally, P. (1980). Psychometric rating in the assessment of progress in anorexia nervosa. *British Journal of Psychiatry, 136,* 290–296.

Gross, A.M. (1984). Behavioural interviewing. In T.H. Ollendick & M. Hersen (Eds.), *Child behavioural assessment, principles and procedures.* New York: Pergamon.

Hallsten, E.A. (1965). Adolescent anorexia treated by desensitisation. *Behaviour Research and Therapy, 3,* 87–91.

Halmi, K.A. (1987). Anorexia nervosa and bulimia. In V.B. Van Hasselt & M. Hersen (Eds.), *Handbook of adolescent psychology.* (ch. 15). New York: Pergamon.

Harding, T.P. & Lachenmeyer, J.R. (1986). Family interaction patterns and locus of control as predictors of the presence and severity of anorexia nervosa. *Journal of Clinical Psychology, 157,* 440–448.

Holden, N.L. (1990). Is anorexia nervosa an obsessive compulsive disorder? *British Journal of Psychiatry, 157,* 1–5.

Hood, J., Moore, T.E., & Garner, D.M. (1982). Locus of control as a measure of ineffectiveness in anorexia nervosa. *Journal of Consulting and Clinical Psychology, 50,* 3–13.

Jenkins, M.E. (1987). An outcome study of anorexia nervosa in an adolescent unit. *Journal of Adolescence, 10,* 71–81.

Johnson, C., Lewis, C., Love, S., Lewis, L., & Stuckey, M. (1984). Incidence and correlates of bulimic behaviour in a female high-school population. *Journal of Youth & Adolescence, 13,* 15–26.

Kalucy, R.S., Crisp, A.H., & Harding, B. (1977). A study of 56 families with anorexia nervosa. *British Journal of Medical Psychology, 50,* 381–395.

Kanner, A.D., Coyne, J.C., Schaefer, C., & Lazarus, R.S. (1981). Comparison of 2 modes of stress measurement: Daily hassles and uplifts vs major life events. *Journal of Behavioural Medicine, 4*, 1–39.

Kazdin, A.E. (1990). Childhood depression. *Journal of Childhood Psychology and Psychiatry, 31.*

Keat, D.B. (1979). *Multimodal therapy with children.* New York: Pergamon.

Kellerman, J. (1977). Anorexia nervosa: The efficacy of behaviour therapy. *Journal of Behaviour Therapy and Experimental Psychiatry, 8*, 387–390.

La Greca, A.M., Dandes, S.K., Wick, P., Shaw, K., & Stone, W.L. (1988). Development of the social anxiety scale for children: Reliability and concurrent validity. *Journal of Clinical Child Psychology, 17*, 84–91.

Lask, B. & Bryant-Waugh, R. (1986). Childhood onset of anorexia nervosa. In R. Meadows (Ed.), *Recent Advances in Paediatrics, 8.*

Leitenberg, H., Agras, W.S., & Thomson, L.E. (1968). A sequential analysis of the effect of selective positive reinforcement in modifying anorexia nervosa. *Behaviour Research and Therapy, 6*, 211–218.

Leon, G.R., Lucas, A.R., Colligan, R.C., Ferdinande, R.J., & Kamp, J. (1985). Sexual, body image and personality attitudes in anorexia nervosa. *Journal of Abnormal Child Psychology, 13*, 245–258.

Mavissakalian, M. (1982). Anorexia nervosa treated with response prevention and prolonged exposure. *Behaviour Research and Therapy, 20*, 27–31.

Mills, I.H. (1973). Endocrine and special factors in self-starvation and amenorrhoea. In A.T. Proudfoot & R.F. Robertson (Eds.), *Anorexia nervosa and obesity* (pp. 31–43). Edinburgh: The Royal College of Physicians.

Minuchin, S., Rosman, B.L., & Baker, L. (1978). *Psychosomatic families: Anorexia nervosa in context.* Cambridge MA: Harvard University Press.

Moos, D. & Moos, B.S. (1986). *Family environment scale* (2nd ed.). Palo Alto: Consulting Psychologists Press.

Murphy, G.C., Hudson, A.M., King, N.J., & Remenyi, A. (1985). An interview schedule for use in the behavioural assessment of children's problems. *Behaviour Change, 2*, 6–12.

Nowicki, S. & Strickland, B.R. (1973). A locus of control scale for children. *Journal of Consulting and Clinical Psychology, 4*, 148–154.

Ollendick, T.H. (1979). Behavioural treatment of anorexia nervosa. *Behaviour Modification, 3*, 124–135.

Ollendick, T.H. & Cerny, J.A. (1981). *Clinical behaviour therapy with children.* New York and London: Plenum.

Palmer, R., Christie, M., Cordle, C., Davis, D., & Kendrick, J. (1987). The clinical eating disorder rating instrument (EDRI): A preliminary description. *International Journal of Eating Disorders, 6*, 9–16.

Perosa, L., Hansen, J., & Perosa, S. (1981). Development of the structural family interaction scale. *Family Therapy, 8*, 77–90.

Pillay, M. & Crisp, A.H. (1974). The impact of social skills training within an established in-patient treatment programme for anorexia nervosa. *British Journal of Psychiatry, 139*, 533–539.

Reid, D.W. & Ware, E.E. (1974). Multidimensionality of internal vs external control. *Journal of Behavioural Science, 6*, 131–142.

Roosa, M.W. & Beals, J. (1990). Measurement issues in family assessment: The case of the family environment scale. *Family Process, 29*, 191–198.

Rotter, J.B. (1966). Generalised expectancies for internal vs external control of reinforcements. *Psychology Monographs, 80.*

Russell, G.F.M. (1985). Anorexia and bulimia nervosa. In M. Rutter & L. Hersov (Eds.), *Child and adolescent psychiatry.* (2nd ed). Oxford: Blackwell.

Schnurer, A.T., Rubin, R.R., & Roy, A. (1973). Desensitisation of anorexia nervosa seen as a weight phobia. *Journal of Behaviour Therapy and Experimental Psychiatry, 2,* 31–36.

Scrignar, C.B. (1971). Food as the reinforcer in the out-patient treatment of anorexia nervosa. *Journal of Behaviour Therapy and Experimental Psychiatry, 2,* 31–36.

Slade, P.D. & Russell, G.F.M. (1973). Awareness of body dimensions in anorexia nervosa: Cross-sectional and longitudinal studies. *Psychological Medicine, 3,* 188–199.

Spence, S. (1983). *Social skills training with children and adolescents.* Windsor: NFER-Nelson.

Steinberg, D. (1983). *The clinical psychiatry of adolescence.* Chichester: Wiley.

Strober, M. (1982). Locus of control, Psychopathology and weight gain in juvenile anorexia nervosa. *Journal of Abnormal Child Psychology, 10,* 97–106.

Tanner, J.M., Whitehouse, R.H., Takaishi, M. (1966). Standards from birth to maturity for height, weight, height velocity and weight velocity: British children, 1965, parts 1 & 2. *Archives of Disease in Childhood, 41,* 454–471; 613–635.

Touyz, S.W., Beumont, P.J.V., Glaund Phillips, T., & Cowie, I. (1984). A comparison of lenient and strict operant conditioning programmes in refeeding patients with anorexia nervosa. *British Journal of Psychiatry, 144,* 517–20.

Williamson, D.A. (1990). *Assessment of eating disorders: Obesity, anorexia and bulimia nervosa.* New York: Pergamon Press.

Williamson, D.A., Davis, C.J., Goreczny, A.J., & Blouin, D.C. (1989). Body image disturbances in bulimia nervosa: Influences of actual body size. *Journal of Abnormal Child Psychology, 98,* 97–99.

CHAPTER TWELVE

Cognitive Approaches

Jeremy Turk

It is not "things" themselves which disturb us but the view we take of them.
Epictetus

Je pense donc je suis.
Descartes

INTRODUCTION

What is Cognitive Therapy?

Cognitive therapy is a group of techniques which have developed from the basic notion that psychological change can be brought about by attention to, and attempts to alter, the thought processes (cognitions) of the individual. It is assumed that the underlying psychopathology relates to a deficiency or distortion of cognitive techniques which individuals use to appraise themselves and events occurring around them, and to generate expectations regarding future occurrences. These misinterpretations , or "maladaptive cognitions", result in the development of both inappropriate states of mind and detrimental behavioural patterns.

Cognitive principles aimed at altering these maladaptive cognitions are usually combined with behavioural techniques and referred to as "cognitive-behavioural therapy" (CBT). CBT deals with the present and is problem-orientated. Goals are clearly defined, and active exchanges are undertaken between therapist and client, in collaboration, as a means of working towards a consensus on what constitutes appropriate appraisals of situations and occurrences. Practical homework tasks may then be undertaken to test out the validity of these beliefs, which can be further adapted in the light of experience.

How Did Cognitive Therapy Develop?

A variety of schools of cognitive therapy have evolved including those based on personal construct theory (Bannister & Fransella, 1971) and rational-emotive principles (Ellis, 1962). The most popular and widely researched approach is that of cognitive-behaviour therapy (Beck, 1976; Hawton, Salkovskis, Kirk, & Clark, 1989). This technique developed from a growing awareness that therapeutic attempts aimed exclusively at the emotions or behaviour tended to be ineffective in producing change, highly vulnerable to relapse, or prone to a high prevalence of residual symptoms (Russell, 1981). A major factor appeared to be the individual's thought processes which often remained unaltered despite at least temporary behavioural improvement. More traditional analytic approaches, while sometimes improving the individual's sense of well-being, often did little to change the way they thought. In contrast, by altering the client's cognitions through a problem-orientated process of "collaborative empiricism" (Beck, 1976) therapists found themselves able to achieve genuine and enduring improvement not only in cognitive functioning but also in behaviour and emotional state.

The central assumption in cognitive approaches is that dysfunctional behaviours and emotions derive from distorted thinking. These cognitions should therefore be the primary focus for therapeutic intervention.

Applications

Initial efforts were focused on individual work with adults suffering with depression (Beck, Rush, Shaw, & Emery, 1979). Subsequently cognitive principles were applied to eating disorders in theory (Garner & Bemis, 1982) and in practice (Fairburn & Cooper, 1989; Hollin & Lewis, 1988), as well as to work with children and adolescents (Kazdin, 1985; Kendall, 1981; McAdam, 1986; Meyers & Craighead, 1984; Ronen, 1989). Cognitive-developmental models of personality development are well-established (Piaget & Inhelder, 1969), and this form of treatment has been applied beneficially to individuals irrespective of their intellectual level (Kuschlik, 1989).

BACKGROUND

It has long been acknowledged that thought processes determine directly the quality and intensity of emotional reactions (Lazarus, 1974). Such mechanisms also underlie coping activities which in turn shape the individual's emotional reaction (see Fig. 12.1). Thus a similar set of demands may be construed or appraised quite differently by two different people producing entirely opposite emotional reactions and behavioural responses. For example, a weight gain of one pound after a heavy meal usually produces a measured, calm awareness that this is likely to be a temporary increase. An individual with anorexia nervosa may interpret the same experience as catastrophic confirmation that their weight is out-of-control and prone to exponential increase. Intense anxiety and sense of loss of control then contribute to abnormal dieting behaviour with the reinforcement of beliefs that exceptionally punitive and self-destructive eating patterns are the only way to avoid extreme obesity.

Accordingly the meaning that an individual attributes to an event is as important as the event itself, and furthermore will inevitably colour

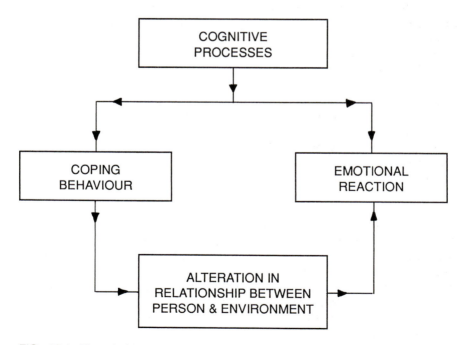

FIG. 12.1. The relationship between cognitions, behaviour, and emotions.

the prevailing emotional state and subsequent psychological adjustment. It is the discrepancy between objectivity and subjectivity which is important—not so much to what we react, but how we react (Tache & Selye, 1978). Because of the particularly unusual cognitions characteristic of anorexia nervosa, the bulk of this chapter deals specifically with this condition.

COGNITIONS IN ANOREXIA NERVOSA

Research suggests that people with anorexia nervosa differ from their peers in their thought processes, perceptions of social situations, and problem-solving skills (Garner & Garfinkel, 1980). The cause of anorexia nervosa is complex and multifactorial. However, irrational beliefs and attitudes play a major role in perpetuating the disorder, and precipitating relapse. The way a person thinks may even contribute to a predisposition to the disorder.

Maladaptive beliefs in anorexia nervosa can be grouped into three areas—the so-called cognitive triad (Beck, 1976) (see Table 12.1). Thus low self-esteem is a common finding in association with a negative view of the future ("I shall always be anorectic, nothing can help") and a negative view of people and happenings around one ("Everybody is well-meaning but they just don't understand"). Although some psychological features of anorexia nervosa may be due to starvation (for example, lethargy, slowing of thoughts, poor concentration, or depression), most are secondary to extreme attitudes and concerns, e.g. perfectionism, obsessional traits, or anxiety (Bemis & Fairburn, 1989). The enduring and overwhelming cognition in anorexia nervosa is persistent worry about body shape and weight, in association with preoccupying dysfunctional beliefs and values regarding food intake. Extreme dieting ensues, with associated behaviours aimed at marked weight loss.

Generally speaking, cognitions in anorexia nervosa tend to be self-defeating ("I have absolutely no self-control over food intake once I've started eating") and extreme ("I mustn't eat another crumb if I'm

TABLE 12.1
The Cognitive Triad

Self
Future
Environment

going to stay this weight") (O'Connor & Dowrick, 1987). Certain logical errors and inappropriate thought processes are particularly associated with eating disorders. These are listed with examples.

Magnification or Catastrophising.   Exaggerating the intensity, stressfulness or significance of events; embellishing situations with surplus meaning that is not supported by objective evidence. "I gained a pound in weight yesterday. That's it, I can't control my eating at all."

Personalisation or Self-reference.   Relating external events to oneself. "Two people laughed and whispered something to each other when I walked by—they were probably commenting on my appearance."

Superstitious Thinking.   Believing in cause-effect relationships between non-contingent events. "If I eat sugar it will be converted instantly into stomach fat."

Self-fulfilling Prophecy.   Making predictions about the outcome of events, and then acting in ways that ensure that prediction will occur. "This is my last chance—if I don't succeed this time, it's hopeless."

Dichotomous or All-or-nothing Thinking.   Thinking in extreme, absolute "black and white" terms. "Either you're thin or you're fat. There's no half way. You can't sit on the fence."
The therapist must also be on the look-out for other logical errors, particularly those commonly associated with depressive disorders, which need to be pointed out to the child and family and addressed, such as:

Arbitrary Inference.   The tendency to draw a negative conclusion on the basis of subjective impressions, even in the absence of concrete evidence to support these views. "People are only happy when they're thin and attractive—I need to lose more weight to be happy."

Selective Abstraction.   Repeatedly judging a situation on the basis of a fragment of the information available, focusing only on certain negative aspects and ignoring contradictory factors. "You say there are so many good reasons to gain weight. Well, if it weren't for my dieting I'd never have got that gymnastic medal. There you are, I'm right!"

Over-generalisation.   A general conclusion is drawn on the basis of a single incident, so that an isolated setback is interpreted as evidence of global lack of ability. "I gained a pound in weight two weeks ago. I can never control my weight. I need to diet more vigorously."

ASSESSMENT

Comprehensive evaluation of the client's presenting complaints, personal and developmental history, and the family structure and history are required. In addition information must be obtained regarding the individual's dieting history, methods of dietary restraint, real and perceived overcontrol or loss of control over food intake, and associated thoughts. Thorough initial evaluation is a prerequisite to successful therapy.

TREATMENT

Cognitive approaches are best combined with appropriate behavioural programmes (see Chapter 11). Direct efforts to alter eating behaviours are required as well as managements aimed at erroneous assumptions which need to be recognised, defined and abandoned. This unified approach allows for essential behavioural change in the first instance, and the necessary shifts in attitudes and perceptions required for the maintenance of improvement. In severely emaciated children it is wise to restore physical health to some extent, before commencing cognitive-behavioural therapy.

A major difficulty is the individual not perceiving her eating disorder as alien to her. Indeed, manifested behaviours may be condoned by cultural norms. Consequent problems in engaging anorectic patients is summed up by the quote "treating an anorectic is like throwing a life-preserver to a fish" (Bemis & Fairburn, 1989).

Who To Accept For Treatment

The major necessity is for the client to be able to consider alternative hypotheses, and to appreciate that these can be tested out practically. Earlier beliefs by professionals that such sophisticated thinking only develops just before adolescence has been superseded by awareness (developed through collaborative empiricism!) of just how young a child can be and still benefit from these techniques. Thus age and intellectual level are not exclusion criteria *per se*. Of more importance is the ability to entertain alternative possible explanations to the one currently held, and to be prepared to test out alternative hypotheses through practical exercises.

Therapist Variables

As with any form of therapy there are essential therapist attributes which are necessary for psychological change whatever the therapist's theoretical orientation. These "non-specific" therapeutic variables of unconditional positive regard, empathy, warmth and genuineness (Shapiro, 1969) facilitate rapport-building and therapeutic engagement before information-gathering and treatment. They also contribute directly to therapeutic change. Cognitive approaches, in addition, demand more active therapist intervention in asking questions, summarising, getting feedback and promoting alternative responses (McAdam, 1986). It is this combination of more universal therapist attributes with specific cognitive principles that make cognitive therapy so potentially useful.

Psycho-education

The sharing of information within a therapeutic relationship has dual functions. Knowledge gained assists in orientating the patient towards reality—it can be enlightening to realise that weight fluctuates up to four pounds per day in normal people because of hydration, humidity and bowel actions. Also, awareness of newly learned facts may have a direct impact on emotional state, and consequently on behaviour. Imparting information on symptoms, risks and the course of eating disorders allows the patient to attribute unwelcome symptoms to the syndrome and to recognise more clearly the potential benefits of change. Symptoms found to be unpleasant may vary considerably. One adolescent female was totally unfussed by prospects of sterility and life-long amenorrhoea. However, intense anxiety with behaviour change followed her awareness that brain shrinkage had occurred, as demonstrated on a CT scan, and might impair her intellectual performance. Forewarning of unpleasant but transient phenomena can also be shared, thereby anticipating them and minimising the chances of negative reactions such as initial upsetting of fat redistribution in the early stages of weight gain.

The goal of these techniques is the redefinition of the collection of ideas and behaviour as a syndrome rather than personal, immutable characteristics. Efforts can also be aimed at sensitising clients to ways in which attitudes are manipulated negatively by society, for example, in advertisement campaigns and magazine articles.

For children and adolescents with difficulties, education needs to be extended to family, friends and other significant people in the child's life. Parents will require support to deal with their own distress, which can be reduced by the clarification of important factual issues. This in turn will minimise destructive behaviours and attitudes ("She only does it to annoy, I won't have it") and facilitate constructive ones ("I know my daughter has a psychological problem, therefore there's no point in simply shouting at her and telling her to snap out of it"). Practical advice, for example the hiding of mirrors, may also be of direct help.

Altering Maladaptive Cognitions

People continually evaluate themselves in relation to their performances and to other people's opinion of them. These "automatic thoughts", if negative, will result in negative emotions. The conscious monitoring of cognitions, to enhance the person's awareness of them, is therefore a prerequisite to analysing and changing cognitions. Self-monitoring starts early in therapy. Clients are encouraged to keep diaries of beliefs they have and to trace them back to the underlying reasons. Diary entries should include:

1. Time.
2. Place.
3. Sensations e.g. hunger, craving, nausea, anger, resentment.
4. Food eaten.
5. Preceding events, thoughts and feelings.
6. Subsequent outcome, thoughts, feelings and behaviour.

Ponderous thoughts may pervade all themes (e.g. "I need to lose more weight"), requiring assistance in taking one thought at a time and following it through the series of logical assumptions back to the underlying core belief. Hypothetical questions can be useful, such as "If you were on a desert island ...", "If you could be average weight and feeling OK ...".

Rational evaluation of evidence for and against the holding of such beliefs can then commence. Cognitive analysis is approached in four stages by means of the following questions:

1. What is the evidence?
2. Are there any alternative explanations?
3. What are the implications if I am correct?
4. Is it functional?

Having applied these principles to the individual's automatic thoughts, the same process can be utilised to generate alternative ideas and to evaluate them objectively. Some beliefs will inevitably prove almost impossible to shift. These may be delusional, but more often are so culturally shared that proof against them may be difficult to find.

Parents, too, often require assistance to get in touch with the automatic thoughts contributing to the maintenance of their offspring's difficulties, and to treat these thoughts as a source of data rather than merely an irritating aspect of their child's disorder. People are generally not in the habit of examining their own cognitions; initially they may find it very difficult, particularly if they are suffering mood disturbance or other emotional disorder. Considerable therapist input may be required to help individual and family attend to and verbalise specific beliefs.

Cognitive Restructuring and Self-monitoring

Functional analysis of behaviours can be undertaken by examining common antecedents and consequences in order to clarify triggering and reinforcing events. This can be illustrated as an A→B→C format:

Antecedent ⟶ Behaviour ⟶ Consequence

A similar analysis of cognitions can be illustrated by the path:

Antecedent Event ⟶ Belief ⟶ Emotional and Behavioural
Consequence

The documenting of multiple examples, both in the therapy session, and as part of a homework exercise, helps to gain understanding of how particular beliefs are triggered and reinforced, and how these beliefs in turn can encourage either useful or maladaptive mood states and behaviours. Recognition of the significance of the choice of words can be a crucial turning point. The therapist can encourage the rephrasing of sentences to cut out the absolutes such as must, should, can't. Substituting "won't" may begin to re-establish a person's control over her own behaviour. It is also useful to encourage the client to view a situation through someone else's eyes in order to see that the distorted beliefs are not supported by real evidence. Depersonalising the discussion can reduce anxiety and allow for rational thought (e.g. "If a friend of yours were to be making himself very unwell but seemed to be unaware of what he was doing to himself, how might you feel? What would you want other people to do for your friend?")

Overall, therefore, the therapist does not act to persuade the child or family that their views are illogical or inconsistent with reality. The skill is to assist the child and family in discovering this for themselves.

Problem-solving

It is one thing to accept that certain beliefs or behaviours are detrimental to one's welfare and fulfilment. It is quite another to be able to do something about it. The mental steps required in problem-solving of any sort are self-evident to most people and don't even need consideration. For individuals caught in a trap of rigid, unhelpful beliefs, with associated depressed mood, this technique is far from obvious and may need to be taught, step-by-step, with practical exercises and a careful review of progress by the therapist. The experimental approach of collaborative empiricism is well suited to this testing of traditional versus irrational assumptions. Thinking can be put into practice to maintain and consolidate realistic and adaptive beliefs. Again, an ordered series of stages can be utilised:

1. *Identify the specific problem to be worked on.* The automatic tendency is usually to choose the most troublesome problem. However, such problems are also usually most resistant to change, presenting the risk of further failure and reinforcement of the sense of helplessness and low self-esteem. Encouragement is needed to help the client choose a problem likely to respond readily to treatment, thereby maximising the likelihood of a beneficial outcome, enhanced self-esteem, confidence in the technique, and subsequent successful attempts.
2. *Generate as many solutions as possible.*
3. *Weigh up advantages and disadvantages of each solution.* e.g. practicality, likelihood of success.
4. *Devise method for instituting chosen solution.*
5. *Try it out.*
6. *Review* (how did it go?), *evaluate* (how successful were you?), *reappraise* (how could you do it differently next time?).

Many individuals find it useful to carry a cue card on them listing these steps which can then be applied as and when required.

Problem-solving approaches rely on reality testing with real-life experiments. Within the therapy session occasions will frequently arise where client and therapist hold opposing and irreconcilable views. The construction of a mutually acceptable experiment which the client can undertake between sessions allows for these beliefs to be objectively evaluated.

Other Cognitive Techniques

Decentring.   Counteracting the tendency to beliefs that everything revolves around oneself (egocentricity). Assistance is needed to develop insight into the double standard whereby one judges oneself (or one's parents or children) more harshly than others.

Reattribution.   Reattribution is useful for body-image distortions. For example, one can assist cognitive change from "I have a need to be thin" to "I'm thin because I have anorexia".

DURATION OF TREATMENT

The number of sessions and their frequency varies considerably between patients. Even after initial improvement, follow-up appointments will be needed to ensure the maintenance of gains and the absence of relapse. Booster sessions may be held as long as six to twelve months after completion of the course to review the patient's progress and to reinforce techniques learned previously.

SOME SPECIFIC ISSUES RELATING TO WORK WITH CHILDREN

Cognitive Distortions vs Cognitive Deficiencies

Many of the techniques described above relate to distorted thought processes and inappropriate logical inferences. For children, however, the difficulty is often more one of a simple deficiency in cognitive skills. To an extent this is a developmental trait which will rectify over time. Nonetheless, steps can be taken to compensate for the child's lack of cognitive sophistication and facilitate more advanced thinking. Thus, educational issues, and prompts to consider aspects from experience, take priority over cognitive restructuring exercises. The problem-solving approach becomes particularly applicable.

The Need for Self-control

In anorexia nervosa the child can be perceived as needing to impose unrealistically strict limits on eating behaviour for fear of catastrophic "letting go". A gentler, more appropriate self-control technique can be taught. If necessary, this can commence with spoken instructions from parents under the therapist's supervision. The child can then progress to using his or her own overt speech and ultimately private internal commands to modulate and control desirable and undesirable behaviours. The use of a graded hierarchy breaks down an apparently insurmountable task into smaller, more manageable ones. It also helps the transfer of control over the child's behavioural problems from therapist through parents to the child his or herself, thereby enhancing independence and self-esteem.

The Use of Games

The child's co-operation, and application to important therapeutic tasks, is enhanced by presenting activities in the form of enjoyable games rather than arduous endeavours. Examples include the "I wonder what would happen if ..." game, which conveniently precedes the "Let's see what actually happens when ..." game. Using analogies from everyday life help, as in the "Stop and think" approach developed from road-crossing instructions every child is exposed to early in life (Kendall, 1989). The only limiting variable in this technique is the therapist's ingenuity in creating enjoyable games which also serve important therapeutic functions.

ILLUSTRATIVE CASE HISTORY

Anna, a 13-year-old single daughter of middle-aged parents, was referred to the eating disorders clinic because of her extreme reluctance to eat, with accompanying severe weight loss, emaciation and amenorrhoea. Over the preceding year she had developed extreme concerns over her appearance, believing that she was overweight. Progressively smaller food portions were consumed at meal times with careful avoidance of fatty and high carbohydrate items. Weight-reducing hobbies of gymnastics, dancing and netball occupied increasing amounts of time. Parental efforts to discuss her eating and weight met with verbally aggressive responses. Anna insisted she wanted to be underweight, and admitted to an intense fear of becoming fat, believing this would affect her hobbies and appearance catastrophically. School reports confirmed Anna to be industrious, with a high academic potential. However, socially she admitted to being a loner, desperate to do anything to gain some close friends.

During a six-month in-patient admission, Anna gained modest amounts of weight on a behaviour-modification programme based on incentives for weight increases and appropriate eating behaviours. Family therapy focusing on Anna's increasing need for independence from her parents, and the need to express and share important thoughts and feelings, was also undertaken.

Anna lost a kilogramme within a fortnight of discharge. On review she exclaimed angrily "Anybody can gain weight on an in-patient unit if that's the only way to get what you want and to go home. But you haven't changed me. I'm still the same person. I still think the same things." Direct questioning revealed that Anna also retained her marked fear of becoming fat, which was contributing significantly to her need to impose such strict controls on her eating.

Initially, Anna and her parents coped by developing a belief, mutually reinforced, that to be so underweight was in fact satisfactory for her. Ultrasound scans demonstrated just how shrunken her uterus and ovaries were. This information, together with the sharing of how high the risk of life-long sterility now was, unsettled the family and prompted the intensification of their efforts to help Anna to gain weight, and to adapt her view of the situation in order to avoid a further relapse.

A further six-week paediatric admission allowed for more educational input regarding the detrimental effects of emaciation and the positive results of healthy eating. Anna was tutored in a problem-solving approach to deal with her lack of friends, her difficulties in confronting her parents, and her under-developed repertoire of ways of showing anger and resentment. Her tendency to think in all-or-nothing terms ("If I'm not thin then I'm fat") was also tackled.

At one-year follow-up Anna remained below average weight for her age and height, but was clinically stable, and displayed a more realistic view of her problem and the need to keep up her weight.

CONCLUSIONS

Cognitive approaches to the management of anorexia nervosa in childhood form a powerful set of techniques which can be used in conjunction with a variety of other therapies, with either individuals, families or groups. By creating enduring changes in modes of thinking, and appraising situations and occurrences, the likelihood of relapse is reduced, and patients and their families are provided with a new set of techniques which can be applied to a wide variety of problems long after therapy has ended.

REFERENCES

Bannister, D. & Fransella, F. (1971). *Inquiring man: The psychology of personal constructs*. London: Croom Helm.

Beck, A.T. (1976). *Cognitive therapy and the emotional disorders*. New York: International Universities Press.

Beck, A.T., Rush, A.J.J., Shaw, B.F., & Emery, G. (1979). *Cognitive therapy of depression*. New York: John Wiley.

Bemis, K. & Fairburn, C. (1989). *Cognitive-behavioural therapy for anorexia nervosa and bulimia nervosa*. Oxford: World Congress of Cognitive Therapy, Abstracts.

Ellis, A. (1962). *Reason and emotion in psychotherapy*. New York: Lyle Stuart.

Fairburn, C. & Cooper, P. (1989). Eating disorders. In K. Hawton, P.M. Salkovsokis, J. Kirle, & D.M. Clarke (Eds.), *Cognitive behaviour therapy for psychiatric problems*. Oxford: Oxford University Press.

Garner, D.M. & Bemis, K.M. (1982). A cognitive-behavioural approach to anorexia nervosa. *Cognitive Therapy & Research, 6,* 123–150.

Garner, D.M. & Garfinkel, P.E. (1980). Socio-cultural factors in the development of anorexia nervosa. *Psychological Medicine, 10,* 647–656.

Hawton, K., Salkovskis, P.M., Kirk, J., & Clark, D.M. (1989). *Cognitive behaviour therapy for psychiatric problems*. Oxford: Oxford University Press.

Hollin, C. & Lewis, V. (1988). Cognitive-behavioural approaches to anorexia and bulimia. In D. Scott (Ed.), *Anorexia and bulimia nervosa: Practical approaches*. London: Croom Helm.

Kazdin, A.E., (1985). Cognitive therapy. In *The treatment of antisocial behaviour in children and adolescents*. Pacific Grove, California: Brooks-Cole.

Kendall, P.C. (1981). Cognitive-behavioural interventions with children. In B.B. Lahey & A.E. Kazdin (Eds.), *Advances in Clinical Child Psychology, 4*. New York: Plenum Press.

Kendall, P.C. (1989). *Stop and think workbook*. Pennsylvania: Temple University, Department of Psychology.

Kuschlik, A. (1989). *Helping caring adults to enjoy working directly with people with learning difficulties who also have severely challenging behaviours*. Oxford: World Congress of Cognitive Therapy, Abstracts.

Lazarus, R.S. (1974). Cognitive and coping processes in emotion. In B. Weiner (Ed.), *Cognitive views of human motivation* (pp. 21–32). New York, London: Academic Press.

McAdam, E.K. (1986). Cognitive behaviour therapy and its application with adolescents. *Journal of Adolescence, 9,* 1–15.

Meyers, A.W. & Craighead, W.E. (1984). *Cognitive-behaviour therapy with children*. New York: Plenum Press.

O'Connor, J. & Dowrick, P.W. (1987). Cognitions in normal weight, overweight, and previously overweight adults. Cognitive Therapy and Research, 11, 315–326.

Piaget, J. & Inhelder, B. (1969). *The psychology of the child*. London: Routledge & Kegan Paul.

Ronen, T. (1989). *Assessment and evaluation of a self-control intervention, package for imparting self-control skills to children and adolescents*. Oxford: World Congress of Cognitive Therapy, Abstracts.

Russell, G.F.M. (1981). The current treatment of anorexia nervosa. *British Journal of Psychiatry, 138,* 164–166.

Shapiro, A.D. (1969). Empathy, warmth and genuineness in psychotherapy. *British Journal of Social and Clinical Psychology, 8,* 350–361.

Tache, J. & Selye, H. (1978). On stress and coping mechanisms. In C.D. Spielberger & I.G. Sarason (Eds.), *Stress and anxiety, 5* (pp. 3–24). New York, London: John Wiley.

CHAPTER THIRTEEN

Individual Psychodynamic Psychotherapy

Jeanne Magagna

INTRODUCTION

"I was arguing with my mother. Afterwards I thought, 'Now I won't eat lunch. Then everything will be all right'." This is a puzzling statement made by an anorectic girl. Its possible meaning forms the basis of individual psychotherapy with a child having an eating difficulty. "Eating" does not simply refer to opening the mouth to take in food. It might simultaneously mean opening the mind to emotional experience. "I won't eat lunch" could mean closing the mind to conflicts or withdrawing from the nurturing emotional link with mother. My hypothesis is that the anorectic's "fear of fatness" includes the fear of intense sensations and feelings that overwhelm her to such an extent that they may threaten her personal identity, her perception of her body and her sanity.

Many anorectics have a distorted body image, perceiving the body to be much larger than it actually is. Distorted perceptions of body size can also occur fleetingly at moments of intense emotion. Dieting and thus attaining control of the "body shape" initially provides relief to the child, for she no longer feels a "helpless victim" but rather a potent and active agent. Accompanying this potent, active self is the use of massive denial of feelings: that is, "mental dieting", which restricts the awareness of threatening feelings and sensations.

Massive denial involves the obliteration of a large number of perceptions of reality to avoid mental pain. The anorectic uses this defence to break off contact with deeper emotional life. Denial displaces an effective inner psychic structure which normally functions like understanding parents.

This brittle defence was symbolised by one anorectic who drew a picture of how she felt (see Fig. 13.1). The drawing is of a tree without roots or leaves to absorb and digest light and water necessary for growth. Denial is used to break off contact with the roots of the self, with deeper, more infantile emotional life.

Individual psychotherapy for a child with eating difficulties is designed to enable her to tolerate emotional experiences rather than "closing her mind" to them. Once the anorectic learns to tolerate such emotional experiences she will no longer need to shut her mind and mouth. Palazzoli (1974) has suggested that the anorectic, through her symptom of starving, is trying to negotiate control and autonomy within her family.

FIG. 13.1. Tree without roots.

In my experience, the patient's emotional immaturity which accompanies the wish for control and autonomy necessitates a close examination of this desire for control. The anorectic's control is used as a defence against relationships with people. It should not be confused with the desire for autonomy of a child who has internalised good experiences with understanding parents, and has thus matured sufficiently to struggle for more autonomy and control over her own life. The more mature child gradually enters relationships outside the family.

The anorectic, on the other hand, is reliant on an internal "prison guard", a controlling force which restricts food intake, the experiencing of difficult feelings, pleasurable moments and intimate relationships. The "cruel prison guard" protects the child from becoming "too fat" through intense infantile feelings and anxieties aroused in intimate relationships with parents or peers. The control of "the prison guard" involves an identification with a kind of "superparent figure" (Box, 1981) who is a model of tough self-sufficiency who can obliterate human frustration or basic physical needs; the control is "omnipotent".

This chapter describes the way in which a child with an eating problem can be viewed as using "omnipotent control" (Rosenfeld, 1987) in lieu of identifying with parental figures looking after the infantile aspects of the self. The focus is on anorexia nervosa but the principles can be generalised to other eating disorders. A range of crucial therapeutic issues regarding individual psychotherapy are discussed. They include: providing an appropriate setting for treatment, assessing the severity of the child's underlying psychopathology and the aims of psychoanalytic psychotherapy. Typical problems for the therapist are also delineated. Particular emphasis is placed on the need to evaluate both internal psychic development and relationships with family, school and peers. The use of dreams as a focus for measuring psychic change is also illustrated.

THE TREATMENT FRAME

The context of individual assessment and therapy for children is crucial. Anyone treating an anorectic child must be closely allied with a physician, preferably a psychiatrist. A doctor should take medical responsibility during an initial consultation and for ongoing evaluation of the patient's physical condition. The psychotherapist needs to have a clear set of guidelines for the minimum weight and degree of physical ill-health that warrants hospitalisation.

It is likely that during very conflictual moments in therapy, and during the therapist's holidays, the anorectic child may wish to diet and discontinue therapy. This is part of the anorectic style of dealing with emotional conflict. For this reason, it is irresponsible for a therapist to embark on individual therapy without ascertaining that there is an effective therapeutic link between the parents and a colleague who will assist the parents at difficult times. It is not uncommon for a child to stop therapy, become more anorectic and have her parents deny that there is a problem. In view of this, it is essential to accompany individual therapy with some on-going work with the family or parents.

The most effective therapeutic frame I have encountered has involved:

1. At least two family assessments to ascertain strengths and weaknesses and the patterns of relating.
2. An individual assessment to ascertain the individual pathology underlying the eating disorder, bearing in mind that both anorexia nervosa and bulimia have typical behavioural patterns which conceal a wide range of emotional difficulties.
3. A medical practitioner to monitor weight changes regularly and to liaise with the parents and child regarding the child's physical health.
4. On-going parental or family work accompanying the individual therapy. This provides support for the child and enables the parents or family to find a safe context in which they can explore the problematic aspects of their relationships and develop their capacities.
5. Consideration of possible hospital provision in case the child's health deteriorates. This is particularly important for those children with severe difficulties, when they are faced with the initial holiday separations from the therapist.

DURATION OF TREATMENT

More than one anorectic child has expressed her fear, "When I look all right on the outside, I am afraid no one will now notice how bad I feel inside." In saying this the anorectic expresses her fear that she must continually display her "starvation" for fear that other people will do as she does: that is, deny inner emotional states and focus only on weight gain and sexual development. For this reason, the therapist needs to reassure the child that she will be able to receive therapy until it is no longer needed. A minimum of two years is generally required to assist a child to develop a stable psychic structure. For a child able to experience her feelings in a more mature way and remain emotionally linked in a helpful way to others, family therapy accompanied by a briefer period of individual counselling is appropriate.

ASSESSMENT FOR PSYCHOTHERAPY

As I approach an assessment interview, I bear in mind two patients: One is an anorectic adolescent who told me that she had never told the doctors or me, in two years of therapy, about repeated experiences of sexual abuse in her early childhood. When I asked why not, she said, "No one has ever asked about sexual abuse. I felt awkward in bringing it up myself." The second patient told me she had never told anyone about "her voices". When asked why this was, she said she was "afraid people would think that she was crazy" and anyway she "liked her voices because they kept her company". She said she was "afraid of losing them".

Beware of the "mask" of the anorectic or bulimic patient! An eating difficulty, whether it is bulimia or anorexia, involves the use of "omnipotent control" and projection of feelings. The pattern of eating difficulties may appear similar in many children while masking a variety of psychiatric symptoms. An anorectic child may be experiencing vivid auditory or visual hallucinations or ever-present "imaginary friends".

Because of the anorectic child's use of "omnipotent control" to feel and appear "normal" these pathological phenomena are frequently concealed. For this reason it is important to provide an individual assessment for each child with an eating disorder. Even if family therapy is the treatment of choice, each child with severe problems also deserves the right to a private space apart from the family to think about her life and those issues which initially may be difficult to share with the family.

In individual assessments I have found it helpful to have a preliminary meeting in which I ask the child to draw a picture of a person. Then I ask the child to tell me about the person and create a story for that person. Subsequently, with the assistance of the child, I try to find similarities and differences between the person in the story and the child I am meeting. The rest of the session is a space for the child to explore issues of her choice. Spontaneous play and drawings are used for the assessment of a younger child. When the child has difficulty in speaking about herself, I discuss her difficulty in meeting a stranger, her fear of my criticism and of me. I find it helpful to give her a small cloth family doll set and ask her to speak from the perspective of various family members, as I interview them regarding "their picture" of her life in the family.

I also encourage the child to tell me a dream, any recurring dreams and dreams from her past. In this way I gain access to the child's psychic structure. It is helpful to have at least one free-flowing assessment interview, in which the child is encouraged to use the opportunity to think about herself rather than supply information. Factual information can be gained in a subsequent interview and in other therapeutic settings.

Figure 13.2 illustrates how I consider the child's psychic structure. The key components are a maternal figure, a paternal figure, sibling figures and the infantile self. These paternal and maternal figures are typically used by children to represent the nurturing, procreating and regulating roles of each parent.

An examination of the maternal figures reveals the quality of nurturing and physical comfort and security provided, the capacity to receive distressed aspects of the infantile-self and the ability to modify pain.

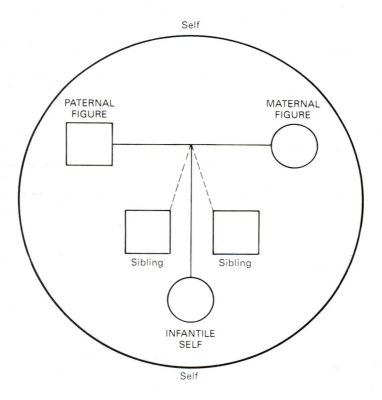

FIG. 13.2. Internal psychic structure.

Evaluation of the paternal figure includes noting the capacity to regulate emotion so that the feeling is not too intense or too restricted, evaluation of the capacity to differentiate good from bad and provide limits and a moral code out of concern for the self and others.

An assessment of the nature of the relationship with siblings and peers includes looking at the way in which conflicts between love, jealousy and anger are expressed in these relationships and also noting the capacity to acknowledge the existence and needs of these siblings. Evaluation of the relationship to the parents involves taking into consideration the relationship with emotional and intellectual nurturance and discipline by school figures.

My primary question is: What capacity does the child have, in identification with internal figures, for looking after her own infantile self? In empathically listening to a child, I hear the child's stories and tone of voice, as well as noting my emotional responses to the child's predominant attitudes to her experiences. I then develop a picture of the current relationships between the parental figures and infantile self present in the internal world of the child. I also consider the child's capacity to allow the internal parental figures to be together in various creative ways, including procreation and the care of siblings.

The nature of the internal parental figures will be influenced by the qualities of real parents and by the child's own feelings towards them. A stable sexual identity is based upon acknowledgement of one's gender, as well as identifying with both internalised parental figures performing their task of looking after the infantile self and joining together in creative ways. The child's experience of her own body is influenced by these identifications with the internal parents and reflected in a sense of physical security and physical movements, as well as in the themes of the child's play, dreams and stories.

Here are some remarks of Susan, an anorectic girl, which illustrates her internal configurations:

MOTHER
"My mother simply does not understand me. There is no point in talking to her."
FATHER
"My father vents all his anger on me, not on anyone else."
SIBLINGS
"My sister is a 'greedy cow'. She gets everything she wants."
PARENTS
"If I had to depend on my parents, I'd commit suicide."

The implication is that there are parental figures who cannot be depended upon, who do not understand. The child projects her own feelings into her angry father, greedy sister and non-understanding mother. The parental figure inside the child takes little responsibility for potentially overwhelming feelings such as greed, jealousy, anger and the incapacity to understand feelings in herself. The child-part of the personality feels so antagonistic to the parental figures that she would rather manage without them than face the frustrations of depending on them. Perhaps most striking is the inability of Susan to face the frustration of depending on her parents.

In the presence of such non-understanding internal figures, Susan is reliant on her own omnipotent methods of taking care of herself. This involves relying on concrete external things, such as dieting, calories and thinness, rather than on an inner capacity to tolerate her own feelings.

The psychotherapist needs to assess the severity of the child's omnipotent defence, represented by the child whose behaviour implied, "I can take care of myself through physical and emotional dieting or through bingeing." The stronger this omnipotent defence, the more likely that, in the initial part of therapy, there will be problems during separations and holidays. For this reason a supportive therapeutic team of parents and professionals is vital.

SUITABILITY FOR PSYCHOTHERAPY

Anyone is a suitable candidate for psychotherapy, as long as this person is willing to come regularly to the sessions and has an external network of professionals and parents who will support the treatment. The more crucial questions are:

1. Is the therapist suitably qualified with a compatible personality capable of and willing to tolerate the full brunt of this child's projections of mental pain? (Meltzer, 1967).
2. Does the therapist have the willingness and capacity to meet the needs of a child who has not yet transformed bodily experiences into emotions suitable for language to be used in the therapy: for example, the silent, negative or borderline psychotic child?
3. What supportive network can be provided to help a child who "closes her mind and mouth" to psychotherapy, transferring the anorectic or bulimic problems to the therapy?
4. Is in-patient treatment necessary initially to support the child in undertaking the burden of working through her difficulties?

Anyone with an eating disorder has a disturbed psychic functioning involving the denial of emotions. This denial impedes taking care of the infantile parts of the self and thus prevents the development of emotional maturity. For this reason individual therapy is suitable for all children with an eating disorder. In practice, because of the limited resources for individual treatment, and the efficacy of family therapy, individual therapy is often provided for children who, through family therapy, cannot develop their capacities for owning and containing their emotions, and for those who can afford it on a private basis.

AIMS AND THERAPEUTIC METHOD

A psychotherapist's task is in many ways similar to that of a parent. For this reason, psychotherapy is not a mode of treatment in which children must have good verbal capacity or intelligence. Psychotherapy is a place in which the therapist needs to be attuned to the emotional experience of being with the child, to give meaning to her communications. This is similar to a mother using her own emotional experience, coupled with her thinking, to make sense of the baby's projections of physical and emotional states. This is particularly important to remember for an anorectic child who often lacks integration of her physical experiences with her psychological experiences.

Because such lack of integration may be linked with a mismatch in communication in her primary experiences with her parents, an anorectic may need the therapist to consider her primitive experiences, including sensations and movements of the body, before she can put them into a symbolic form for communication. An integration of the body and psychological self can then occur. The therapeutic setting contains equivalents of the parent-child relationship such as a focus on the child's inner and outer experiences, consistency of care-specific and defined boundaries and acceptance of the child, even when she is destructive or rejective, and a reliable and regular framework of meetings to allow the patient to develop trust in the therapist.

Particularly at the beginning, the child often projects unbearable emotion and physical experiences on to the therapist before being able to feel, let alone verbalise, the experience. Therapists use their own physical and emotional experiences with children to understand these projections. The essential therapeutic task is to share the entire experience of the child, empathising with as much of the child's inner feelings as she will allow. Rather than intruding with questions or comments to the child, it is often appropriate for the therapist to speak "with the child's voice" suggesting that the child's non-verbal communication has been understood. For example:

Patricia, an adolescent girl, was silent. She looked at me and then down at her feet. I described the debate inside her: a debate about whether she talks with me or stays quietly alone. I also discussed how it seemed as if I were expecting something from her, and that she had told me she was too tired to talk with me. "Maybe," Patricia said in a dismissive way.

I said she spoke as though I really was a nuisance. I added, using a loud and angry intonation, as though I was speaking with Patricia's voice, "Things are all right. Let them be. Don't upset how I feel by talking seriously about something. It just causes problems."

Then Patricia, in a light, jokey mood, began talking about how the headmistress was cross with the girls. Only later was she able to admit being cross with me. I described how Patricia wished that I would simply listen to what she was saying and think about it. Then I commented on how she had experiences that she felt unable to put into words, and that she wished I could experience her depth of feeling without her having to put it all into words for me. Patricia responded, "Exactly."

Through the therapist's work of bearing feelings and giving them meaning, the child can be helped to experience being understood and accepted. This can be internalised to form a resilient mental structure for transforming unbearable sensations into feelings suitable for thoughts about them to emerge. The inner mental structure is designed to "hold in mind" intense and/or unbearable loving, hating and conflictual feelings. Only through the development of effective inner psychic structure, functioning as parents understanding the emotions of a child, can healthy psychological development be ensured.

DREAMS

Regardless of their underlying difficulties, children with eating disorders tend to progress through similar phases of emotional development in the course of therapy. This is well-illustrated by the dream-life of the child, "a kind of internal theatre with internal family figures entering into emotional relationships and conflicts with one another" (Meltzer, 1987).

The more stable developments in the personality structure are most reliably traced through assessing the child's dream structure and her emotional relationship to her dream experiences. At present, the study of psychic development as observed through the dream process is a poorly researched area, yet the dream and the child's relation to it potentially presents one of the clearest pictures of the child's developing emotional capacities.

There is a fluctuation in the phases of the psychic development of children in therapy suggested by the dream structure and the child's developing sense of emotional responsibility for the feelings expressed in the dreams. One can view the dreams as unconscious thinking, equivalent to the action and play of young children. As the child discusses her dream the therapist can focus on how the mind copes with emotional experiences, and how it deals with the distortions formed by the conscious self during the day. The focus of the therapist's interpretative work is to help the child look once again at her relationship with the parental figures as re-enacted in the relationship with the therapist. There is a gradual delineation of the infantile feelings of the child from the more mature parts of the child's personality.

The phases of the anorectic's dream-life reflecting psychic development seem to follow this sequence:

1. There is difficulty in remembering dreams and/or difficulty accepting that they are meaningful. There is a sense of a rigid barrier between rational thoughts and the spontaneous expression of feelings.

2. Dreams are described in which the child is overwhelmed with feelings that take over her sense of her self. Examples might be:

The child dreams that she is Mercedes racing. She has completely lost her own physical identity and becomes a racing car.

or

The child awakens as she disintegrates falling off a cliff.

3. Dreams are described in which the child uses "omnipotent control" as a means of caring for her distressed self. For example:

When the therapist is ill, the child dreams that she is in a hospital with the therapist's face appearing and then disappearing. The child is then left in a room in which big, fat cats and rats, black, furry monstrous creatures, are coming out from cages. She is terrified. She then pets a black creature and says: "Isn't it nice!" She has turned to a part of herself which gives her protection, but this is a false sense of safety, used to deny difficulties with separation from the nurturing therapist.

4. Dreams have more human figures in them, into which feelings are projected. Meanwhile, the self is experiencing a sense of hating, disowning and/or being frightened of these feelings in others. The child, in describing the dream, has not yet begun to acknowledge these disowned parts of herself. For example:

There is a teacher scolding all the other children in the class for being noisy and wanting too much attention.

5. Dreams are described in which the child projects her vulnerable feelings into others and, identifying with a parental figure, she takes care of her feelings located in others. At this point, the parental figure has developed the capacity for understanding and concern, but the child has not yet fully owned her dependent, vulnerable feelings located in "the others needing care". For example:

A child has a dream that a baby is falling off a cliff, but she has adequate life-saving equipment and is able to rescue the baby. This child had previously reported the dream of falling off the cliff.

6. The dreams suggest a more open acknowledgement of feelings in the self, but they are still uncontained and often seem to be on the verge of being enacted in the child's external life. For example:

The child dreams of getting into her parent's bed with a boy and then of having a huge feast prepared by her aunt. Here the child is confused between the wishes for comfort, sexual closeness and food. However, she has been able to dream, rather than act out these confusions as she had in the past.

7. The dreams suggest that not only is the child able to acknowledge more openly her own feelings and locate them in herself, but she is able to accept responsibility for her destructive feelings and show inklings of maternal concern for both herself and her siblings. The feelings seem more contained, as though there is the possibility of thinking before acting on the feelings. For example:

The child is shouting at her mother while her mother is talking to one of the younger children in the family. Then the girl decides she can join in the conversation too. She doesn't need to interrupt it by shouting. Later she is playing on the beach with her babysitter.

8. In the dreams there is a fluctuation between dependence on parental functions in herself and the therapist (representing understanding parental figures), and the use of omnipotent control. For example:

The child dreams that she is in a snowdrift. She is cold and being pushed down by the weight of the snow. She keeps going down, but then she sees a light and she struggles to reach it. In this dream there is a hint that turning towards insight, in herself and in her therapist, might help her with the depression which she feels as she acknowledges her loneliness.

9. In the dreams there is more frequent evidence of a developing capacity to acknowledge feelings, think about them and take moral responsibility for what they imply. There is a sense that the internal capacity to parent oneself, in identification with good parental figures, is being established. For example:

> The child cries in the dream, feeling sad when she quarrelled fiercely with her mother. When she awakens she says lately she has been feeling more kindly towards her mother and treating her with more consideration. As she talks about this dream she is able to show responsibility for the punitive way she handles arguments with her mother. She describes how she is trying to reach some resolution of the conflicts.

By the termination phase of therapy the child is able to move from the egocentric position of thinking only of her needs, to a position of concern for her "baby self" as well as her internal and external siblings and parental figures.

In this stage of therapy there is a continual struggle between loving feelings and angry, jealous ones. However, the loving feelings tend to dominate her relationships with others as well as her relationship with her "baby self". She no longer regularly treats her body or her feelings with "omnipotent control", but rather she attempts to take seriously her emotional and physical needs. She is able to truly "parent herself".

TREATMENT DIFFICULTIES

Eating disorders conceal a variety of underlying pathological states of mind. Despite this fact, a great majority of children with eating disorders present similar problems for the therapist. I shall highlight four ways in which the child challenges the therapy:

1. The child turns to food or starving as a defence against the emotions arising in the context of the relationship offered by the therapist. "Omnipotent control" is used in lieu of a dependent relationship on internal and external parental figures.
2. In a crisis, when there is a challenge to the child's use of omnipotent control, she shows extreme, uncontrolled emotional responses including suicidal threats.

3. Silence in the session requires an empathic response and interpretation.
4. Progress in the child's external relationships can obscure the lack of stability in her inner psychic structure. Guided by satisfaction with the external progress of the child, the therapist and treatment team may make premature emotional demands that threaten her with unbearable feelings.

Here is a clinical example to illustrate these common treatment dilemmas:

1. Addiction to Starving

An eight-year-old pre-pubertal anorectic boy, Peter, attempted to turn away from parental figures and had become addicted to starving and gymnastics, as a means of controlling his body and his emotions. He drew a picture of a child with a tiny body and giant-sized hands and feet. There was a suggestion that his impulses to strangle himself, break and throw objects, and run away from home threatened to overwhelm him. He frequently threatened to act out rather than contain his feelings. Near the same time he reported a dream in which people with lions' heads and hands were chasing after him to drown him.

Peter's starving seemed to coincide with those moments when he experienced his feelings as being bigger than himself. Starving seemed to be a method of gaining control over these overwhelming feelings. When he was most upset he became obsessed with talking about food issues, the quantity of food he ate, the timing of his meals, people's relationship to his eating, his pleasure in hoarding food and throwing it away.

In this situation, the therapist needs to acknowledge the child's need for protection against too much feeling, while at the same time not get drawn into colluding with repetitive discussions regarding food and weight. The awareness of food being more important than the therapeutic rapport can be frustrating for the therapist and can prompt an aggressive interpretation regarding the child's use of food as a defence.

2. Suicidal Threats

Minuchin's aim of helping parents work together (Minuchin, Rosman, & Baker, 1978) to provide firm boundaries and rules for the child may be suitable for some children with eating difficulties. However, the more vulnerably, helpless and disturbed child may feel intensely attached to "omnipotent control" as a protection and feel terrified by external threats to this defence. When behavioural procedures, including isolation, were prescribed, Peter responded by throwing tantrums, making suicidal gestures in front of his parents such as putting a rope round his neck, cutting his wrist with a knife and making attempts to jump from a top floor bedroom window.

Peter felt that his "omnipotent self" was being attacked and killed by external authoritarian controls. When this self felt attacked, it seemed to use death as its last weapon. Peter thought, "I don't need to live, death is the answer. Everything will be nice then." The destructive omnipotent self presented death not as a terror, but as a wonderful relief from the misery.

The suicidal attempts gave Peter a sense of power over his own life and a weapon to reduce his parents and therapist to helplessness. It was important not to enter into a power struggle with him, but necessary to point out his attempt to control and triumph over me with death. Rather than attempting to break Peter's omnipotent defences, my task as a therapist was to endure Peter's terror of death—the death of his sane self, the death of his omnipotent self (his only protection until he gained an inner psychical structure that was more helpful), the death of his physical and emotional self. This terror of death was a primitive anxiety, never sufficiently contained in Peter. He had tried to save himself from this terror through omnipotence, instead of through the painful process of containing his emotional experiences.

3. Silence

Because the child with eating difficulties has often internalised an impaired empathic link with the parents, therapists need to understand their fluctuating emotional responses to the silent child. During his silences, Peter mobilised various feelings in me: (a) boredom, when I felt useless and rejected by him: (b) intrusiveness, when my curiosity about what he was feeling became too intense; and (c) the desire to placate him when he was furious. This placation was linked with projection of my own anger into him.

Because such responses impeded Peter's progress, it was essential to probe the depth of my own emotional response before venturing to speak. If I did not monitor my own counter-transference experience, I was unwittingly scripted into a counter-therapeutic role. With Peter it was useful, during the silence, to ask myself: Who is Peter being? What am I feeling? What am I supposed to be feeling in the role in which Peter has cast me? What is this meaning of Peter's drama in which I am being invited to participate?

By using my counter-transference response, involving understanding Peter's feelings projected into me in the silence, I was able to give him the experience that unbearable feelings could be contained and thought about. Gradually he was able to give his own experiences a symbolic form, a name, and later he was able to consider them.

I was particularly aware of predominant states of mind which were communicated in Peter's silence.

(a) Don't Touch: Overcome by intense feelings Peter stopped speaking, as a way of protecting himself from these feelings which intensified as he described them. In a protective way, he was holding himself together through silence. He didn't trust me. When I talked about the need to protect himself from me, he would sometimes blurt out the problem, "I feel miserable at school" or "When I feel miserable, I just can't eat." In contrast, if I attempted to speak about his feelings when he was in this mood, he would shout, "Don't tell me what I feel."

(b) You're Useless: When he pursed his lips, going "tch", acting superior to me, I knew that Peter was into his omnipotent, combative self, aiming to silence me. I was made to feel small, unimportant and useless. This occurred around holiday separations and when the frequency of the sessions was diminished. Silent contempt was a way of communicating how he felt I treated him when I left him. By being identified with a contemptuous therapist he attempted to project into me the unpleasant emotional impact of the separations.

(c) I Want You to Understand Without my Having to Speak: At times Peter was visibly distressed, having argued with his sister or mother just before the session. When he was in an emotionally close posture, I felt I had permission to describe feelings. My understanding was often greeted with his wishes to talk with me or by appreciative pictures of animals mothering their young babies.

(d) Can You Allow Me to be Separate?   Peter and his mother had an enmeshed relationship. He needed to know that I could be different from her and tolerate not knowing what he felt. Plying him with too many questions would lead him to feel that he was having to speak in the sessions to please me. He needed to know that I could bear his existing independently, without my intruding into him, without my needing to be successful with him.

4. External Progress May Not Reflect Internal Psychic Development

When a child with eating difficulties re-establishes a normal pattern of eating, has regained normal weight for height and age, appears to have a good relationship with her family and friends, and is coping with school, the treatment team can easily be misled about the state of the child's internal development. These children have often seemed well before the development of the eating disorder, but for a long period they have been denying feelings and projecting them into others.

There are three steps frequently encountered in the process of recovery: (a) being able to talk about feelings, but not being sufficiently in touch with their emotional significance; (b) identifying with a caring figure while at the same time keeping needy or unpleasant aspects of the self projected into others; and (c) identifying with a figure who had a gradual increase of thoughtful, caring characteristics, while at the same time owning both destructive and loving feelings.

For example, Peter would vividly describe a terrible row he had with his mother, but he had little emotion as he spoke. It seemed that I had to experience the scene and how tormented he felt. When his weight approached normality he described how he was going to be a doctor, and do a better job of looking after the anorectics than the staff. Evident as he spoke was his sense of superiority both in relation to the staff and the feelings of anorectics. Much later Peter talked with sincerity about how he was struggling with his temper and jealousy which he felt interfered with developing a friendship with his older brother.

Peter gradually understood that although he might eat properly, there still remained the task of understanding his conflictual emotional experiences. We used his spontaneous communications, dreams and drawings to explore these. His dreams suggested his increasing capacity to explore feelings of love and hatred. At first he seemed to be an insecure child, a helpless victim of disasters such as floods and earthquakes. There seemed to be no physical security in the dreams and his terror was overwhelming. Later he visualised himself as having legs which enabled him to flee from attacking figures.

The most difficult aspect of the therapy was assisting Peter to acknowledge that some of the destructiveness in the dreams was his own. He was a model student, but still having severe examination anxieties, when he began discussing dreams about a feast in which he saw all the other children in a pot of sizzling oil. As he realised this depicted his own murderous competition with his siblings, Peter began to feel the pain of his destructiveness which had interfered with the lives of his family as well as with his own life.

In time, Peter's dreams held more benelovent scenes such as this: Peter was watching his mother sitting tenderly holding a small child in her lap. Another child was jealously looking on. He now had a feeling of a good maternal figure residing more permanently inside him. This caring maternal figure was connected with the paternal function of protecting the mother and baby, enabling the baby to remain alive. It provided the beginning of a base for healthy development to occur.

However, each frustration brought destruction of the parental figures. Dreams of the mother dying, but then recovering, formed the dream pattern for a later phase in the therapy. Peter's journey towards being a healthy adult involved moving from: "Everything is fine, I just can't eat", to developing a greater capacity for not simply eating and expressing his feelings, as well as being able to think about and take moral responsibility for the existence of the parental figures inside himself.

For those of us who are prone, as parents or clinicians, to rely on the child's comment: "My weight is right, now I should stop therapy," it is essential to remember that this is but the surface. We need to call on our understanding of the child's inner reality to ascertain his capacity to struggle with the destructive aspects of his personality and the frustrations in his relationships.

CONCLUSION

The professional team, parents and the child with an eating disorder face a similar problem: Having the patience and trust in a relationship between people to provide empathic nurturance and understanding, which will enable the child to feel understood and loved. In this way, the child with eating difficulties may find a way of developing sufficient concern for the internal parental figures, siblings, and the therapist, representing parental figures, to mitigate her rage about unmet needs. The development of a capacity for love and tolerance of the parents for their shortcomings enhances the capacity to bear separation from the parents in a mature way. Successful therapy involves the child taking responsibility for mothering herself, being concerned about the feelings of others and forgiving the parents.

REFERENCES

Box, S. (1981). *Psychotherapy with families*. London: Routledge.
Meltzer, D. (1967). *The psychoanalytic process*. London: Heinemann.
Meltzer, D. (1987). *Studies in extended metapsychology*. Scotland: Clunie Press.

Minuchin, S., Rosman, B., & Baker, L. (1978). *Psychosomatic families.* Cambridge, Mass.: Harvard University Press.

Palazzoli, M. (1974). *Self-starvation.* London: Jason Aronson.

Rosenfeld, H. (1987). *Impasse and interpretation.* London: Tavistock Publications.

CHAPTER FOURTEEN

Family Therapy and Parental Counselling

Bryan Lask

INTRODUCTION

Of all the therapeutic approaches to the treatment of eating disorders, family therapy is the only one to have been shown to be particularly effective in the younger age group (Russell, Szmukler, Dare, & Eisler, 1987). This study suggested that family therapy is more effective than individual therapy in the treatment of anorexia nervosa when the patient is below the age of 18 and has been unwell for less than three years. What is less clear from studies so far is which single component, if any, of the therapy is crucial. Authors of the many anecdotal reports claiming the effectiveness of family therapy (e.g. Minuchin, Rosman, & Baker, 1978; Palazzoli, 1978; Stierlin & Weber, 1989) seem to indicate that it is the therapy as a whole that is effective.

However, it is perfectly possible that it is the skill, experience or charisma of the therapist that effects the claimed success. The study by Russell et al., however, is unique because not only did it compare family therapy with individual therapy, but it also controlled for therapist variables. There is some evidence from that study that the crucial component may be that part of the therapy best described as parental counselling. The same authors are evaluating this further in another study. In this chapter, the application of family therapy to the treatment of early onset eating disorders is described in detail with particular attention being paid to parental counselling, in the context of structural considerations.

There are numerous different schools of family therapy and no one school can claim superiority over any other in the context of eating disorders. Choice of technique is a matter of individual therapist preference, and the style of therapy described in this chapter is one that seems to have proved useful for this group of children.

Understandable reactions to a major eating problem are considerable anxiety, anger, guilt and despair. Parents are frequently in disagreement over how to manage the problem: One parent often tends toward leniency, and the other adopts an opposite approach. Alternatively one parent, more often the father, may distance himself from the problem, while the other becomes over-involved. The child quickly learns to capitalise upon such splits. Further, there is often pre-existing marital conflict, in which the sick child is already caught up or "triangulated". Well siblings also find themselves taking sides. Clearly, therefore, the role of the parents is central to the management of eating disorders.

The essence of family therapy is the focus on the whole family rather than on an individual. Various aspects of family functioning warrant particular attention (see chapter 7) including (a) structural components such as the quality and effectiveness of the parenting, the quality of the marriage, the degree of closeness or distance between the children and their parents and the degree of protectiveness of the child with the eating disorder; (b) the patterns of communication; and (c) the history of the family and what contributions from the past are relevant to the current problem. There is considerable overlap between these and it is somewhat artificial to distinguish between them.

STRUCTURAL CONSIDERATIONS
INCLUDING PARENTAL COUNSELLING

The prime aim of family therapy and parental counselling should be to enhance the quality of the parenting, by helping the couple to start working together rather than against each another. The focus needs to be on their adopting a mutually agreed and co-operative approach, which they apply consistently, both between each other and over time. They will need to identify and acknowledge problems and conflicts and find a means of resolving them. This usually also involves the need to work on any dysfunctional communication patterns (see below).

It is advisable at the start of treatment to make a clear statement to the parents about what the therapy will involve, approximately how long it may last, and what will be the main aims. It is also useful to warn the parents that recovery can take a very long time, there will be many ups and downs, that it is possible and even likely that their child will become far more assertive as she starts getting better, and that there are bound to be times during the therapy when the parents start losing confidence in those looking after their child (see chapter 8). It is also important to acknowledge how hard they have already worked trying to help their child and how demoralising and frustrating the whole business is.

Similarly, it is helpful to point out that although issues of parenting are being considered, this does not mean that the more personal aspects of the marriage should be discussed. Without this reassurance many couples will resist exploring parenting issues. It is quite in order to make a statement along the lines:

> Almost certainly we will need to discuss how the two of you can work together to help your daughter to get better. This may show that at times there are differences between you but that doesn't mean that we need to do marriage counselling or anything like that. Rather, we will be discussing how you as parents can work better together as a team. Of course, if at any time you decide you would like to talk about matters such as your marriage, that's perfectly OK.

Sometimes it is very obvious that the parents are struggling with their own relationship, and it can be helpful to acknowledge this without forcing it on to the agenda. For example:

> I can see that things aren't as happy between you as perhaps you would wish. If you feel you would like to talk about this sometime, we could come back to it when your daughter is eating again.

It is perfectly in order to set the context as outlined above with all family members present, if so desired. Indeed, it is helpful for the children to know that the adults are taking charge of the situation and are going to be working together. At this point it is appropriate to agree the focus of work. One way of achieving this is to share with the family the therapist's observations and seek parental agreement to work on what the therapist believes to be the crucial issues. An alternative is to ask the family and particularly the parents what areas of family life they would like to work on. In this way therapists can be more certain that their aims and those of the family are congruent: an essential component of successful therapy.

Should the parents indicate that all they want is for their child to start eating properly again, and that they cannot conceptualise changes needed in the family as a unit, it can be useful to explore what happens at meal times, and to build up a picture of how the family functions around the eating disorder. Some therapists (e.g. Minuchin et al., 1978) have a family meal as a way of clarifying how the symptom becomes embedded in the family organisation. This session is used to create a crisis around eating by encouraging the parents to help their child to eat. Minuchin argues that the crisis quickly moves the identified patient away from her morbid intra-psychic obsessions, and helps the parents to see that they are dealing with a conflict between a difficult child and themselves (and perhaps between themselves) rather than with a mysterious disease. The dysfunctional organisation of the family rapidly becomes evident to everyone, and a time of crisis is often considered to be an optimal time for change. Clearly such techniques should only be used by experienced therapists who are confident of their ability to handle such fraught situations.

A similar but less formalised crisis can arise if a decision is made to admit a child to hospital. The child may protest loudly that she doesn't want to be in hospital and plead with her parents not to admit her, promising faithfully that she will eat normally as soon as they get home. If this entreaty fails, her protests may increase and then take the form of a wide range of threats such as: "I'll run away", "I'll never speak to you again" or "I'll kill myself." Such situations can be used in a similar way as the crisis engendered by the family meal.

The therapist's task here is not to make decisions for the parents but rather to help them reach agreement on how to proceed. They need to do this without being controlled by their child. Clinical experience and recent research findings (Bryant-Waugh, Lask, Fosson, & D'Angelo, in press) indicate that the majority of children whose parents are unable to work together, and unable to adopt a mutually agreed and consistent approach, are less likely to make a full recovery than those whose parents can work together. A process of gentle coaxing and encouragement to discuss options, to explore possibilities, and to reach compromises, is the most useful technique at this stage. It is important to support the parents in this venture and to point out when they are detouring or being distracted from their task. The value of having the children in the room at this stage is that the therapist helps the parents to see how the children may detour them from their task, or split them, or force cross-generational alliances.

When parents find the task difficult, it has proved useful to explore with them what is making it hard. This also applies when it becomes clear that there is an over-involved or over-protective parent-child relationship. Exploration of how or why the situation has arisen allows for the opening up of the possibility of change.

Michelle, 14 had a two-year history of anorexia nervosa, and had a very close relationship with her father. He believed she could do no wrong, and was a perfect child. Her mother, in contrast, was furious with her for not eating. It proved difficult to help the parents to adopt a more united approach to the problem. Further discussion of the father's attitude revealed that he couldn't bear to think of his daughter or indeed anyone else in the family, as anything but perfect, after his first marriage had broken up with much acrimony, and he had lost contact with his children.

Alternative explanations for parents being unable to work together and firmly encourage their child to eat include the possibility that one or both parents believe that taking a firm line with their child may make the problem worse, or that one parent seeks solace in a close relationship with a child to compensate for a lack of closeness in the marriage. Ultimately, however, the main task of enhancing the effectiveness of the parental sub-system must be achieved.

Once the parents have regained control, and crucial decisions have been made about hospitalisation and re-feeding, they can turn their attention to how much responsibility their child should have for other aspects of her life. Thus while the adults must remain in charge, parents can and should encourage as much age-appropriate autonomy as is safe and reasonable.

A commonly posed question is that of whether or not parental counselling of the nature described above should occur in the presence of the children. A major advantage of the children being present is that their involvement in the parental sub-system and any detouring of parental conflict via the children becomes obvious. Further, the therapist can help the parents to create a firm boundary between themselves and the children. For example:

Throughout the first two family meetings Margaret would interrupt her parents, either by contradicting them when they were in agreement, or taking sides with one against the other when they disagreed. This constant distraction served to detour them from their attempts to resolve their conflicts and to resolve how to help her eat. The therapist was able to point out when this happened and help the parents to find ways of blocking her interruptions, such as ignoring them. Had Margaret not been present at these sessions this process would neither had been noted nor resolved, and would probably have continued at home.

In general it would seem helpful to have the children present, unless matters that are exclusively those of the parents are being discussed.

The general techniques described in this section also apply to families in which the parents are separated or divorced. A substantial minority of children with eating disorders come from such families. The possibility of these children being caught in unresolved conflict and animosity is high. The parents still have to find a way of working together as parents, even if one or both have remarried. It is perfectly reasonable and indeed usually necessary to see separated parents together and to work on the parental tasks described above. Step-parents should also be incorporated in therapy if they have contact with the child.

The basic principle of the adults needing to be in charge applies to all families, including those with only one parent. Clearly some of the issues differ. For example, in theory a single parent has a harder task asserting parental authority, but ostensibly there is less chance of parental conflict. However, very frequently a single parent does have support either from friends and relatives, and similar problems tend to arise as with two-parent families. The principles of management and therapy are the same, and, providing the parent agrees, there is no reason why the other adults should not be involved in therapy.

COMMUNICATION

Another important theme in therapy is that of communication dysfunction. The various types include: (a) *excess communication* in which there is hardly any silence, with much interrupting and overlapping, allowing little chance to finish sentences or be fully heard; (b) *non-congruent communication* in which there is a lack of congruence between the content and the manner of delivery of a message. For example, a parent may say: "Now you really must eat this meal and if you don't there's going to be real trouble", but say it in a gentle tone of voice and with a smile, thus invalidating the message; (c) *deviant communication* in which other forms of dysfunctional communication occur, such as one person speaking on behalf of the whole family, or "mind-reading" in which one person repeatedly reports what another is supposedly thinking or feeling, or a general vagueness in which the point is never reached, or communications seem to lack any point or meaning; (d) *displaced communication* in which symptoms or behaviour replace words to communicate hurtful or painful feelings. This appears to be a particularly common phenomenon in children with anorexia nervosa; and (e) *inhibited communication* in which verbal communication is sparse and there are prolonged periods of silence.

There are a number of techniques for helping families to communicate in a more constructive way, and the choice will be determined by the type of dysfunction. For example, when communication is excessive and there are frequent interruptions, family members are encouraged to speak in turn, and interruptions are discouraged. Should there be a tendency for people to speak for unduly long periods, a time or word limit can be introduced. For example, the rule could be implemented that each person only speaks for 30 seconds, or says only 20 words. It is useful to appoint a referee from within the family, perhaps one of the children. Although this technique sounds artificial and perhaps constraining, it does introduce an element of fun, and is remarkably effective in helping families communicate more constructively. They find it difficult at first but after a few minutes are able to use it well, joke about it, and, perhaps most importantly, use it in other situations. The use of this technique can allow important points to be made, heard, acknowledged and responded to.

Non-congruent communication is best dealt with in a direct manner. For example, when the verbal and non-verbal components of a statement are contradictory, therapists can ask recipients of such messages what they thought the deliverer really meant, or therapists can gently point out that they are uncertain themselves what was really meant. This not only allows for some clarification, but may lead to discussion of ambivalence. For example, a parent may be uncertain regarding whether or not to take a firm approach to eating.

Deviant communication is also best dealt with directly. Again, it is possible to ask that each person speaks in turn, thus blocking one person from speaking for everyone else. It is also reasonable to place an embargo on people saying what others think or feel, suggesting that instead that person can be asked what *they* think or feel. Generally vague or unclear communications can be dealt with by saying something like: "Can you tell us in one sentence what is the most important thing you want your family to know?" or "What is the bottom line?"

Sarah, 12, had been eating poorly for two years and had lost 8 kgs. in weight. This had caused her mother considerable anxiety, which was in part expressed by a seemingly non-stop torrent of words. Although it was obvious she was very worried, it was not clear what she wanted to change. After some time the therapist asked her: "What is the bottom line of what you are saying?" She replied: "The bottom line? I'll tell you the bottom line. I want him [pointing to her husband] to help me and support me when I'm trying to get her to eat. He just hides behind his paper and then blames me!"

Displaced and inhibited communication patterns are much harder to tackle. Rather than using purely verbal techniques it is sometimes helpful to incorporate experiential methods such as sculpting (Byng-Hall, 1987), use of games (Schaefer & Reid, 1986), metaphor

(Bowen & Nimmo, 1986), role-reversal, and play-material. We find the latter two particularly helpful.

Role-reversal involves having family members exchange roles, so that, for example, the non-eating child plays the part of the persuading parent and vice-versa. This sometimes allows families to escape from their usual sequence of non-productive or sparse exchanges. For example:

> When Ruth aged 12 swapped roles with her mother, instead of pleading and cajoling she acknowledged "Ruth's" fears of eating but firmly insisted that she must eat or otherwise she would send her into hospital. She was showing her mother a way of handling her that she felt would be more helpful.

The use of toys or drawing materials can also help families to move forward. Many families can make constructive use of "sticklebricks" which consist of many different coloured, sizes and shapes of interlocking plastic pieces. They can be used to represent thoughts or feelings which have previously been unexpressed or unacknowledged. For example:

> The mother of Mia, a girl of 13 with anorexia nervosa, was quite unable to verbalise her anger and despair at the unhappiness of her family life. Mia was similar, and attempts to discuss this proved fruitless. The therapist introduced the "sticklebricks" and asked the family to select different colours to represent various feelings, and different sizes to demonstrate the strength of those feelings. The family were then asked to share out the feelings in whatever way seemed appropriate. To the amazement of the rest of the family Mia's mother immediately took all the bricks representing anger and sadness and hugged them to herself. Mia asked if she could have some of the sad bricks, and this led to a far more open discussion of each person's feelings.

FAMILY HISTORY

The family's past, its history and trans-generational influences (e.g. Lieberman, 1980) may all play an important part in the genesis and maintenance of the eating problem. Family myths and legends can serve a homeostatic function by governing family rules. For example, exploration through the use of family trees, photographs and documents can help to develop a new script which then allows the family to test out new rules and new experiences.

Ellen, 13, was born when her parents were in their forties. They had both come from families where conflict was frowned upon and avoided, on the basis that disagreement was unpleasant and could "make people ill". In consequence, although there was much that they disagreed on, their differences were never aired, and decisions were made on the basis of Ellen's wishes. When she developed anorexia nervosa, her parents believed that being firm with her and arguing about her intake could only aggravate the situation. It proved very difficult to dissuade them from this view, until exploration of their own families' backgrounds allowed for a more realistic view of the relationship between anger and illness.

CONCLUSIONS

Family therapy is a particularly useful treatment for early onset eating disorders. The main areas of consideration are enhancing the competence of the parental sub-system, improving communication, and linking relevant aspects of the family history to the current problem. It is important to gain the family's co-operation and to give them responsibility for finding more constructive modes of functioning, while supporting them in this quest.

REFERENCES

Bowen, B. & Nimmo, G. (1986). Going over the bridge—practical use of metaphor and analogy. *Journal of Family Therapy, 8,* 327–338.

Bryant-Waugh, R., Lask, B., Fosson, A., & D'Angelo, S. (In press). *Early-onset anorexia nervosa: A prospective follow-up study.* Paper presented at 6th International Conference on Eating Disorders, New York, 1992.

Byng-Hall, J. (1987). Family legends—their significance for the family therapist. In A. Bentovim, G. Gorell-Barnes, & A. Cooklin (Eds.), *Family Therapy: Complementary frameworks of theory and practice.* London and New York: Academic Press.

Lieberman, S. (1980). *Transgenerational family therapy.* London: Croom Helm.

Minuchin, S., Rosman, B., & Baker, L. (1978). *Psychosomatic Families.* Cambridge Mass.: Harvard University Press.

Palazzoli, M. (1978). *Self-starvation.* New York: Jason Aronson.

Russell, G., Szmukler, G., Dare, C., & Eisler, I. (1987). An evaluation of family therapy in anorexia nervosa and bulimia nervosa. *Archives of General Psychiatry, 44,* 1047–1056.

Schaefer, C. & Reid, S. (1986). *Game play.* New York: Wiley.

Stierlin, H. & Weber, S. (1989). *Unlocking the family door.* New York: Brunner/Mazel.

CHAPTER FIFTEEN

Group Therapy

Jo Trelfa and Clive Britten

INTRODUCTION

This chapter addresses some of the issues that we feel are important in attempting psychotherapeutic group work with children who are hospitalised for anorexia nervosa. Our experience has been derived from our work on the Mildred Creak Unit at the Hospital for Sick Children, Great Ormond Street, with children with eating disorders, as well as with children with a wide range of other psychiatric conditions.

A brief word about the severity of illness of some of the children on the Unit is necessary, to place our endeavour in context. Children admitted to the Unit with anorexia nervosa tend to be very severely ill indeed and may have lost up to half their body weight. Many of the children are fed naso-gastrically for at least part of their admission. Other children initially become ill with anorexia nervosa, which then evolves into a condition of pervasive refusal (Lask et al., 1991). Such children neither eat, talk, walk, nor care for themselves. Some anorectic children have auditory hallucinations, and others are frankly deluded at some point in their illness. Several, during their admission, begin to speak of events of a physically or sexually abusive nature. This chapter explores some of the ways in which groups can help children with these wide variety of problems.

We begin with some comments about group therapy with children and adolescents, before considering some of the work that has been done on groups for anorectics. We then discuss some of the key dynamics that we noticed in our own work. Subsequently we discuss how we work with these dynamics in the various groups we run, and end with some comments about the staff group.

SOME GENERAL CONSIDERATIONS

Behr (1988) has described the main differences between an adolescent group-analytic group and an adult group as follows: "Dynamic administration plays a much more prominent part in adolescent groups. Boundary activities (or boundary incidents) impinge more strongly on the group process, and the style and pace of communication reflect that of the adolescent membership: namely, rapidly changing themes, volatile moods, evanescent thinking and a tendency towards action." While at times these differences were evident in the groups we ran, the slightly younger age of the children on the Mildred Creak Unit, and the severity of their illness, meant that they were still dependent on their parents and were not yet ready to separate from them. For many, the adolescent process had not yet begun.

Roberts (1977) while discussing group therapy for "psychosomatic patients", suggested some modifications in therapeutic technique which we found were helpful in working with anorectic children. These include becoming more active and supportive in style, and modifying interpretations to avoid tacking denial too early or too directly.

Brown's (1985) paper "The psychosoma and the group" gives a clear account of various theories of alexithymia (a term used for the incapacity to find words for feelings), and uses case illustrations to develop the importance of the need "for patients to grow down as well as up".

The severely regressed state of many of the children on the Unit represents an enormous challenge to the therapist to find a constructive way to respond. This will be discussed further later in the chapter.

Polivy (1981) has made a theoretically reasoned case for group therapy to be a treatment of choice for anorexia nervosa, and cites group treatment as being especially helpful because it provides models for coping, consensual validation, peer feedback, and increased self-esteem, resulting from active participation. She goes on to describe both in-patient and out-patient treatment groups, and writes: "The group sessions are used to help the patients explore their feelings about relationships, themselves, love, sex, food, eating, starving, being fat, and being thin—central issues for anorectic patients." She mentions some helpful caveats about such groups. This is a useful paper clinically, although her patients are functioning much more autonomously than ours.

Lieb & Thompson (1984) have described a small in-patient group of four anorectic girls. Common themes are the psychological conflicts and defences in the patients' families, their concerns about becoming women, and the fact that food is seen as a way of controlling maturation. They all felt family pressure for high achievement, and also recognised their weight loss partially as an expression of frustration and anger with their families. The authors' cite the benefits of group therapy as helping to decrease the sense of aloneness and isolation, helping to develop a more cohesive sense of identity, and providing a sense of accomplishment from co-operating with others in the group. They write that the group seemed to be a major factor in decreasing the initial denial and resistance of these patients, that it facilitated learning to express feelings directly rather than through indirect or somatic channels, and the negative transferences in individual therapy can be helped by concurrent group therapy.

Strober and Yager (1989) have described a group-therapy approach which challenges perceptual distortions, and re-frames the anorectic's tendency to have a distorted self-image while viewing others realistically. They suggest that this is an example of increased sensitivity to external surroundings at the expense of self-understanding. Such re-framing allows an exploration of the anorectics' rather isolated, sham, social existence.

Hall (1984) has provided a comprehensive review of group treatment and states that, for anorectics, "The group needs to be experienced as safe, non-confrontative, and warm, allowing room for individual attention and support from the leader for each member, in order to facilitate self-expression with encouragement of gradual inter-personal interaction." She also deals with some of the issues involved in in-patient group work.

Edelstein and Moguilner (1986) have briefly discussed some of the issues arising from an in-patient group of late adolescent and young adult anorectic patients, and comment on the "egocentric tendency" and accusatory and punitive attitudes of the women. They also mention the difficulty those patients had in separating from their families.

In his paper on heterogeneous groups for children, Kennedy (1989) has discussed the relative advantages and disadvantages of homogeneous and heterogeneous groups. He mentions some of the qualities with respect to which sameness or difference can be judged. He quotes Yalom (1985), who concludes that for long-term intensive therapy, the rule is heterogeneity for conflict areas and homogeneity for ego strength.

OVERVIEW OF THE UNIT GROUPS

The groups on the Unit include formal therapeutic groups, the indefinable but ever-present ward milieu and a number of more informal group activities. The following description illustrates how these co-exist. After breakfast, the morning meeting is held. This deals with daily administrative matters. Although not a formal therapeutic meeting, it nonetheless gives children the opportunity to express their wishes and preferences, to voice complaints and to make suggestions, which for many of the anorectic children is a useful therapeutic exercise. After morning school, and before lunch, there is a daily group outing to a nearby park. Similarly, although this outing is primarily recreational, it gives the children an opportunity to face important issues like sharing, taking turns and working co-operatively. In the early afternoon of each day one of the activity groups is held, either the art group, the drama group or the social-skills group, all of which meet for one hour once a week. Later in the afternoon is the children's group, which meets three times a week for 45 minutes.

The groups on the Mildred Creak Unit are formed more as a result of pressure for admission than from consideration of group composition. Because of the preponderance of anorectic children on the unit, there is often a core of children with similar conflict areas. This can make it difficult for other group members, including the therapists, to challenge this core sub-group. It is often the case in the groups on the unit that slightly disinhibited conduct-disordered boys offer the most effective challenge to the anorectic patients.

SPECIFIC GROUPS

The Ward Milieu

The central group on the ward is one that exists all the time: that ever-changing group known as the ward milieu. The culture of the ward is contained and communicated via this group. It is here that the myriad interactions which set the tone and feel of the Unit occur. The philosophy of the Unit is communicated through this channel, whether it be strict or liberal, behavioural or analytic, nurturing or depriving. The atmosphere is largely created by the nursing staff, who have the most direct contact with the children.

The Children's Group

This group is run on group analytical lines, although the therapist's style is influenced by the ages and developmental stages of the children in the group. The predominant culture of the group is that of a children's group rather than an adolescent one. We find ourselves responding to the children's need for physical closeness. On many occasions gestalt techniques are used to help children express themselves and make sense of projections and identifications.

The children's group is the forum for exploration of any dynamic that is profoundly affecting the in-patient group as a whole. A psychotic or suicidal child has a major effect on the whole group, causing concern, consternation, fear and anger. The children's group is often the place where such feelings merge and can be acknowledged. Rarely, the group is used to explore the psychotic experiences themselves, and sometimes the feelings behind suicidal impulses emerge in the group.

The children's group is also the setting for the occasional group rebellion when the group does not form, and on the few occasions when this has happened the leaders of the revolt have been anorectic children who had passed from a passive, compliant stage one into the assertive stage two of their illness (see chapter 8). Under these circumstances, the group is held, and the behaviour addressed, to try to understand both individually and collectively what lies behind the revolt.

The Structured Groups

The structured groups are the social skills, art and drama groups. The facilitators construct a framework for the group, with a focus derived either from an issue which is alive in the group as a whole, or from one individual, if it has ramifications for the whole group. If it feels safe enough, the children are free to bring whatever they want to the group. Groups start with a warm-up, before a more work-orientated discussion, and then the task itself is undertaken. Flexibility and fluidity are essential, and, within limits, the group goes where the children take it.

The Social Skills Group.   This group offers a variety of ways to enable children to learn and develop their social skills. The group makes use of role-play, practical tasks, videos, games and outings (for which the children make the arrangements before and during the event). The key areas in which anorectic children need most help are those of assertiveness and self-confidence.

In one group, a carriage or tube-train was created, and the children took turns to play a number of different roles. One of these involved someone who had all their bags on the only vacant seat in a train, and the others had to deal with the situation as best they could. Denise, who normally found it impossible to confront others, played with great vigour a stubborn woman who was tired and didn't want to move her bags.

The Art Group and the Drama Group.   These groups are particularly useful for anorectic children. The non-verbal component, and the fact that issues can be explored at one remove, afford a setting in which children can begin to take the risk of participating.

Sometimes these groups are run in their pure form; at other times they borrow from each other. For example, in the drama group, paint is sometimes used to set the scene, to enable children to focus on something which is then expanded dramatically. In the art group, drama is sometimes used. In one group the children painted the contents of a magic shop, and this developed into a scene in which the children bartered with each other over the goods. Anita, a 15-year-old girl who was near the end of her admission for anorexia nervosa, wanted to exchange a locked birdcage for a pair of wings and a map.

Kalucy (1978) has referred to art therapy in the treatment of anorectic patients as having the stated aim of helping patients to communicate between the various aspects of their inner worlds. She cites helpful exercises of asking patients to depict their families drawing abstract concepts, such as anger and competition, drawing themselves "as they are" and "as they would like to be", and depicting themselves symbolically as animals.

KEY DYNAMICS
Regression

The single most striking feature of the children on the unit is the extent of their developmental regression. It is widely acknowledged that illness of any kind is often associated with a period of regression. The regression seen in the anorectic children on the Mildred Creak Unit is often profound, and in several children there is regression to a non-verbal stage of development. The most severely ill children—those with pervasive refusal—regress to a stage comparable to that of an infant.

There is often an initial period of group acceptance of a child's regression, and during this stage the group may explore the position of the newly admitted regressed child using various analogies. Frequently, images of animals emerge, and the metaphor of hibernation recurs, as does the image of a tortoise or a turtle withdrawing into their shell, or a hedgehog curling up into a ball. These images allow the group to explore the feelings that the animal might have in such circumstances. Fear is the most commonly supposed feeling.

An activity in a drama group session was devised in order to help the group make contact with Ria, who was silent all the time. The session consisted of two activities: The first involved everyone, including staff, sitting curled up. If tapped on the back by a staff member, the individual was asked to make a noise and the others had to guess who had been touched. The second involved getting into threes, in which one person was a quiet, frightened, curled-up animal, while the other two had to try to get to know the animal and comfort it, without speaking. Months later, Ria recalled in a brief written message that she had remembered the monkey noise that someone had made during a session.

On reflecting on the above session, it was clear that Ria had remembered it all, although at the time she had not responded.

Withdrawal

In our experience, a central dynamic of anorexia nervosa is that of withdrawal. This manifests itself in several ways and might include physical isolation, emotional withdrawal and restriction of communication. Pervasively refusing children withdraw most of their capabilities.

Children with anorexia nervosa are often initially withdrawn from the group, either because they are on bed-rest or because of their own difficulty in joining in. However, all are expected to attend the group therapies. They are included in the activity through their presence, hearing their feelings named, being thought about by the others, and hearing others talk of a similar stage in their illness. The extreme form of withdrawal is that of total silence:

Ruth developed anorexia nervosa which progressed to pervasive refusal, and she was totally mute for about one year. She then started talking in various settings, but never in her individual psychotherapy session. Judith did not speak spontaneously in any of the groups throughout the time the authors worked with her on the ward. Michelle started by being relatively communicative but once her pact with Judith started, she was mostly silent in groups. Judith and Michelle sat on the window-sill rather than on the chairs in the children's group. Whenever anyone spoke to or about them, they cringed. There were various attempts to include them. At one point Ruth sat on the window-sill in the hope of making them feel more a part of the group. This had no effect. Later Ruth lay on the sill, in an attempt to prevent Judith and Michelle sitting on it.

The children seemed caught between the feeling of exclusion on the one hand and that of invasion on the other. The group's attempts at including them was perceived by the girls as an invasion. We all struggled with this seemingly insurmountable problem: whether to leave the children in their hopeless isolation, or to try to approach them, in the knowledge that any gesture would be construed as an assault.

In a drama group in which children were asked to build a den, Michelle built an "empty hole" of pillows. She stayed in the middle of the hole and covered herself with another pillow, depicting herself as hollow and empty, and cut-off from the world. In the same session Ria sat curled up on the floor, and the group thought that she too was hiding in her den of silence and withdrawal. Ruth mirrored Ria, curling-up near her on the floor, trying to get a response from her, and when none came becoming very angry and eventually left the room.

The Constellation of Bad Parental Figures

Another major and recurrent theme common to many children with anorexia nervosa is a powerful constellation of bad parental figures, and a projection of this on to the group, the unit, and the hospital. This is expressed in a number of ways. In our experience, girls tend to be more verbal in their attacks, although, especially at first, the expression of anger is indirect.

A common feeling to arise in the group is that of parent figures failing to mediate the distance between parent and child. This is sometimes projected on to the therapists with: "You don't care, you're only doing this for the money." At other times it is: "Why can't you just leave us alone?" At times, this projection of the bad parental image is on to the therapists alone, sometimes on to the group itself. John said with anger and tears: "My only problem is this damned group."

At other times the projection is on to the Unit or hospital. These bad parental figures emerge in the drama group, and in one session the children took turns to be king or queen while the others were their subjects. In discussion afterwards, involving the whole group, the anorectic children talked with great feeling about the issues of controlling and being controlled.

Pairing

A phenomenon that occurs frequently on the unit is that of pairing between two anorectic children. This can have a benign and helpful aspect:

Ruth, who was improving after a prolonged illness, befriended Ria, newly admitted and severely ill. Ruth at the early stages was very helpful, patient and sympathetic towards Ria and often put into words how she thought Ria was feeling. Later on, Ruth became impatient, and later still there was a stage when she was punitive and bullying towards Ria.

Another more long-lasting, seemingly intractable and counter-therapeutic pairing was the previously mentioned relationship between Michelle and Judith. They excluded themselves from all groups and avoided eye contact. Any attempts to include them in group activities would be met with screams and shouts. This developed most strongly at a time when the possibility of sexual abuse was being explored with Judith. From notes that were written to each other, and to the staff, it seemed that the girls confided a secret to each other in a pact that swore them both to secrecy. The pairing between the children seemed to arise out their fear of, and as a defence against, the "bad parents".

Malignant Autonomy

This is a term coined by Story (1982), which he used in relation to symptoms. However, it seems a very apt description of the children's position in a wider sense. There is often a desperate, though ill-timed, attempt at individuation, based on a false faith in their own brittle strength, with a denial of their need for a relationship with others.

Sometimes the malignant autonomy is in relation to parental figures, and at other times to sibling figures.

Ellen gave a graphic example of this in an art group, when she painted an ice-cream cone as a memory of a holiday. When she was complimented on her picture by her peers, who also empathised with her for what she said about it, she immediately changed the image with black paint into a dagger. Shortly after this she entered an overtly suicidal stage.

Distortions

Phenomenologist's describe the key features in the psychopathology of anorexia nervosa as perceptual distortions, or illusions, for instance, of body size; cognitive distortions, for example the belief that one is overweight; somatic-sensory distortions, such as the failure to recognise hunger; and emotional distortions, for instance, the denial of affects. Experience and feelings are minimised or exaggerated. Thinking tends to become black and white. The shades become difficult to discern.

Yalom (1985) has explored Sullivan's notion of "parataxic distortion" where one relates to another on the basis of "personification existing chiefly in (a person's) fantasy". A group allows real feedback of how others see the individual. For a child with anorexia nervosa, Yalom's description is very pertinent. For example:

> At one stage Ruth perceived everyone as hating her and of thinking of her as a burden they'd be better off without. She would behave when with them according to this perception and set up a self-fulfilling prophecy in which the group became irritated with her. She realised that the group's irritation arose because of her behaviour and not because they felt she was a burden. She later spoke of her feeling of being a burden to her family.

OTHER SERIOUS PROBLEMS

Several children have psychotic experiences at some stage of their illness:

> When Diana was admitted she spoke of her belief that there were goddesses inside her stomach, who told her not to eat. It was several months after her admission that Judith first indicated she had been hearing the voice of a dead relative who told her not to eat and who threatened her with dreadful calamities if she did.

> Ellen became acutely psychotic during the course of her admission with delusions, hallucinations and violent behaviour.

Children are generally expected to attend group therapy during this phase, and the structure of the day is an important factor in maintaining reality. However, especially in drama therapy where the use of fantasy may be too disturbing, the children are offered some practical tasks that include them as part of the group. Sometimes an acutely psychotic episode can be worked with in the group; at other times the child may have to be taken out of the group and contained by other staff members. Whether it can be explored, or has to be contained, depends, among other things, on the state of the whole group, including the staff.

Many children with eating disorders have been the victims of abuse. The children's group may be used by the children as a safe place where this can be discussed and feelings begin to be expressed. While the details and the response may be worked on out of the group context, group therapy has a part to play in the process as a whole. Brown (1988) has discussed the relationship between safety, disclosure and evidence.

He describes a positive feedback loop whereby an increasing reality and feeling of safety allows increasingly more detailed disclosures to be made, which will contribute to the evidence necessary to take further steps to increase the child's safety.

For such children the different cultures of two groups can be used to explore a theme, with limits being enforced in one group, and the opportunity for safe exploration being afforded in another:

Ruth, while silent and curled up in exploratory interviews, was verbally abusive to her peers. In the children's group, steps were taken to contain this and protect the others, while in the drama group the issue was explored by using the fact that Ruth had taken to wearing a long black cloak from the dressing-up box when being abusive. "The Cloak" was actively explored. It had powerful magical qualities, and a drama gradually unfolded over the course of several weeks. All the children participated, and showed what it was like to have the cloak, or not to have it, how it felt with it on or off. Exploration of the feelings of anger, power, powerlessness and revenge were common. During this time Ruth explored what was happening to her, and the others talked of their relationship with her; some children alluded to abusive experiences in their past.

STAFF GROUP

We end with a brief word about the staff group. The dynamics of the ward groups are powerfully affected by the state of the staff group. Supervision and a staff support group are vital. A key factor determining the ability of the staff group as a whole to attend to the emotional communications of the children is the extent to which staff members have that experience themselves:

In the early stages of Ruth's admission, many of the nurses, in the process of bathing her, felt they were raping her. It wasn't until this was eventually shared in the staff group that several people realised that they felt similarly, and that it possibly held a clue to the trauma that this mute anorectic girl had suffered.

CONCLUSION

Our experience with these children has taught us that the work is slow and often painful. The inner worlds of many of these children are inhabited by angry and frightening figures. At times, there do not seem to be any inner helpful figures at all. Yet, from very small beginnings, change can continue. For instance:

Michelle had been totally withdrawn for several weeks. Someone tripped over in front of her, and she went to help.

This was the first sign of her emergence from withdrawal. Yalom (1985) has noted: "Altruistic acts often set healing forces in motion in group therapy."

REFERENCES

Behr, H. (1988). Group analysis with early adolescents: Some clinical issues. *Group Analysis, 21,* 119–133.

Brown, D.G. (1985). The psychosoma and the group. *Group Analysis, 18,* 93–101.

Brown, G.N. (1988). *Personal Communication.*

Edelstein, E. & Moguilner, R. (1986). Homogeneous groups as treatment modality for anorectics. *Psychotherapy and Psychosomatics, 46,* 205–208.

Hall, A. (1984). Group psychotherapy for anorexia nervosa. In D.M. Garner & P.E. Garfinkel (Eds.), *Handbook of treatment for anorexia nervosa and bulimia* (pp. 213–239). New York: Guilford Press.

Kalucy, R. (1978). An approach to the therapy of anorexia nervosa. *Journal of Adolescence, 1,* 197–228.

Kennedy, J. (1989). The heterogeneous group for chronically ill and physically healthy but emotionally disturbed children and adolescents. *International Journal of Group Psychotherapy, 39,* 105–125.

Lask, B., Britten, C., Kroll, L., Magagna, J., & Tranter, M. (1991). Children with pervasive refusal. *Archives of Disease in Childhood, 66,* 866–890.

Lieb, R. & Thompson, T. (1984). Group psychotherapy of four anorexia nervosa in-patients. *International Journal of Group Psychotherapy, 34*(4), 639–642.

Polivy, J. (1981). Group therapy as an adjunctive treatment for anorexia nervosa. *Journal of Psychiatric Treatment Evaluation, 3,* 279–283.

Roberts, J. (1977). The problems of group psychotherapy for psychosomatic patients. *Psychotherapy and Psychosomatics, 28,* 305–315.

Story, I. (1982). Anorexia nervosa and the psychotherapeutic hospital. *International Journal of Psychoanalysis and Psychotherapy, 9*(4), 267–302.

Strober, M. & Yager, J.A. (1989). A developmental perspective on the treatment of anorexia nervosa in adolescents. In D.M. Garner & P.E. Garfinkel (Eds.), *Handbook of treatment for anorexia nervosa and bulimia* (pp. 363–390). New York: Guilford Press.

Yalom, I. (1985). *The theory and practice of group psychotherapy.* New York: Basic Books.

CHAPTER SIXTEEN

Schooling

Anna Tate

INTRODUCTION

School is part of everyday life for all children. It stimulates healthy intellectual and creative functioning, enhances self-esteem and a sense of achievement, and provides an opportunity for children to relate to peers and adults outside the family.

Although there is a valid role for education in the treatment of anorexia nervosa and related eating disorders, the measures of success (described below) may be in stark contrast to those commonly associated with mainstream schooling.

In this chapter, I describe the way in which children suffering from eating disorders function in mainstream schooling, identify the features of eating disorders that impinge on healthy intellectual and social functioning at school, and, finally, describe how education within a multi-disciplinary child psychiatry team can contribute to the treatment of eating disorders. All the examples are of children aged between 10 and 14, admitted to our in-patient child psychiatry facility.

MAINSTREAM SCHOOLING

Success at school, particularly at secondary level, is generally associated with good behaviour and academic attainment, regular attendance, punctuality, compliance, good manners and diligence, and is usually aided by parental support for the pupil. By such measures, the majority of children suffering from eating disorders are not reported as presenting problems at school. Invariably their school attendance is excellent. They are perceived by their teachers as achieving well for their ability. Indeed, some are high achievers and, on the whole, their parents are supportive of the school.

However, on closer inspection, or possibly by different measures of success, teachers are aware of and do report the difficulties these children are experiencing at school. For example, teachers frequently report these pupils as solitary children who are not much liked by their peers and who frequently appear tearful, miserable or unhappy.

Moreover there appears to be a tendency on the part of teachers to excuse and even reinforce this behaviour:

> During an interview carried out by a nurse at Ellen's school, her teacher said that she had nothing but praise for Ellen's academic work and that neither she nor any of the other staff had ever noticed that there was anything wrong. With reference to Ellen's social isolation the same teacher said that it was easy for Ellen to be aloof and separate from her peers, as the latter were often silly, childish and unintelligent. Ellen's teacher thought that one solution to Ellen's isolation was to place her in a group of "high-achievers", thereby addressing her social needs by reinforcing her academic success.
>
> Similarly, Bridie's teacher described her as "the perfect pupil though unforthcoming with oral work", while Anita's teacher believed her to be "a very private child".

It is interesting to speculate why teachers do not recognise isolation as a problem for the school child. One possible explanation is that these pupils are well-liked by teachers because they conform to expectations and achieve well, and therefore the teacher cannot see any weakness. Another explanation might be that these children evoke in their teachers the desire to be protective and thereby deny any problem. They can arouse powerful emotions in those working with them. Such emotions may distort the professional's view of their functioning, especially when the profession concerned is not experienced in working with children suffering from eating disorders, as is the case with the mainstream teacher.

Sometimes this can result in the teacher forming a quite inappropriate relationship with the child.

> One of Tracey's teachers formed a particularly close and affectionate relationship with her, and went to great lengths to look after her once

she had been hospitalised. The teacher visited her frequently, wrote letters and managed to attend professionals' meetings, without the permission of the head teacher, by intercepting her letters. Eventually, when Tracey was made a Ward of Court, the teacher was denied access and it was reported that at this point she applied to the local council to become a foster parent to her.

Although the above is an extreme example, many teachers maintain contact with pupils once they are hospitalised.

Judith, aged 12, was visited each weekend by a teacher who said that she did not have a particularly close relationship with her, but felt it was important to visit in case she wanted to confide in something outside her immediate family. The teacher admitted that she had not realised that Judith had plenty of access to non-family members within the in-patient child psychiatry unit and agreed to reduce her visits with the intention of eventually curtailing them altogether.

Other teachers maintain contact with hospitalised children in order to provide school work for them.

Ruth's teacher, on hearing that she had been hospitalised for anorexia nervosa and had subsequently stopped speaking, visited to take in work. He reports: "Ruth sat throughout with her head bowed and gave no indication that she was comprehending what was said." However, the school work was left and more was provided at a later date.

Although some teachers express concern about the obvious physical and emotional effects of an eating disorder, they may have no concern about the pupil's school work.

One of Anita's teachers commented: "I have not noticed any change in her work. She is still as conscientious and hard-working as ever, but I am extremely concerned about her health, mind and general well-being."

It may be that such an attitude represents the teacher's attempt to focus on a still healthy part of the child's functioning, but it is unhelpful to assume the child's attitude towards school work can be separated from the eating disorder, the features of which inevitably interfere with all aspects of functioning.

During a four-year period, Jane was admitted three times to the same child psychiatry unit and each admission was interspersed with several admissions to the local paediatric hospital. Finally she was admitted at 71% weight for height suffering from anorexia nervosa with intractable vomiting and oesophageal bleeding. She had arranged for school work to be set for her and her teacher reported her to be: "fastidious, conscientious, meticulous and hard-working. If the school project requires ten pages, Jane would do twenty pages. She displays an extreme compulsion to work which appears to be the result of family pressure."

Similarly, Ruth's teacher reported that once hospitalised she became fastidious about her work, showing signs of obsession over its content and presentation. Ruth's handwriting looked like a typed script, it was so even and perfect. As her illness increased in severity, her writing, still perfect, decreased in size so that it was practically illegible.

HOW EATING DISORDERS IMPINGE ON SCHOOLING

While patients with an eating disorder may have no specific learning difficulty, they do have special educational needs. These include learning to acknowledge and cope with the features of their illness that affect their school performance; their denial that they are physically ill and may be too weak to continue with the demands of a normal school day; their pursuit of perfectionism which causes them to drive themselves to achieve while remaining dissatisfied with the results; their obsessional traits which result in compulsive work habits; and their difficulties in personal relationships which can interfere with appropriate peer and teacher interaction.

It is important to consider how much pleasure and satisfaction a child derives from hard work and to ask whether the compulsion to work represents a desire to succeed or a desire to please others; a wish to be seen as acceptable or good by parents and teachers; or another way of inflicting self-punishment such as the gruelling programme of physical exercise such children put themselves through. Is it a clear indication that it is home, not school, which induces stress and unhappiness or is it a means of denying emotional difficulties by saying: "Things can't be so bad, I'm doing well in school"? Whichever answer or combination of answers may be true for any one individual, the fact remains that for many children suffering from eating disorders, school work is clung to as practically the last vestige of normal life.

Parents, too, are reluctant for their children to abandon school work, however ill they may be, possibly for fear that they blemish an otherwise impeccable school career.

Nadia was admitted to hospital suffering from anorexia nervosa at 64% weight for height, yet carried an enormous school bag full of text books, while her mother expressed concern that Nadia did not fall behind her classmates while in hospital.

Possibly parents of eating-disordered children look to the school for some reinforcement of their fragile self-esteem. Teachers consistently report that such parents are supportive of the school, indicating that for parents, as well as pupils, school can be a place to be accepted as competent, successful and well-functioning. Once children are hospitalised, teachers frequently report the same parents as having unrealistic expectations of their children or to be exerting unnecessary pressure on them to achieve.

This observation is confirmed by Graham's statement (1991) that anorexia nervosa occurs "more commonly in middle-class families, and often in those with an apparently particularly high moral standard of behaviour, strongly influenced by their 'work ethic'". Certainly it seems to be the case that the higher the parental social status, the higher the parental expectation of the child.

The combination of parental pressure to succeed and the compulsive work habits of children suffering from eating disorders may camouflage the true picture of how these children experience school. To what extent may obsessional tendencies drive children to achieve beyond their intellectual capacity, causing stress and anxiety? Indeed, many children suffering from anorexia nervosa who are achieving well at school report that they find the work difficult. The desire to produce perfect work or the best piece of work could create covert rivalry with peers and interfere with the development of friendships. Parental pressure to succeed academically might reinforce poor self-esteem by devaluing other aspects of personal development.

While most children with anorexia nervosa work compulsively, children with other eating disorders may do the opposite. For example, school work is one of many aspects of everyday functioning that children with pervasive refusal syndrome forego (Lask et al., 1991; see also Chapter 2). Similarly children with food-avoidant emotional disorder (Higgs, Goodyer, & Birch, 1989; see also Chapter 2) may manifest school-phobic features. These children are usually not reported as having displayed any school problems before the onset of the illness and are usually described as intelligent and hard-working.

A small number of children who develop eating disorders under-achieve at school.

John, aged 11, with an IQ of 130, had been referred with anorexia nervosa. He attended a boys' prep school where he was considered average in the lowest of three streams, having been moved down from a higher form because his work had deteriorated. His parents' expectation was that he would follow in the family tradition of attending a famous British public school. The onset of anorexia nervosa coincided with preparation for the entrance examination and John began to express anxiety about his performance at school. Consequently his parents had to consider whether some other form of education would be more appropriate.

John's school problem illustrates the point that within a family where communication is poor and emotions are not openly expressed, parental pressure to succeed can be counterproductive, despite superior intelligence, and may contribute to the genesis of an eating disorder.

Teachers and parents cannot be expected to identify or diagnose psychiatric illness in children but can be expected to recognise and acknowledge the clear indications that a child is experiencing emotional difficulties. The following examples illustrate some of the ways teachers have excused worrying behaviour before the diagnosis of a serious eating disorder.

Judith did not speak to staff and peers and avoided all eye contact. She presented no behavioural problems and her teachers estimated her to be above average in intelligence, (although her IQ was actually 89). Her acute social withdrawal was thought to be due to shyness.

Ellen was the daughter of a school inspector and a deputy head-teacher. She was the object of considerable parental pressure to succeed, especially as her elder brother had not done well at school. She was in an "A" stream and consistently achieved high marks in course-work and examinations but she could not accept praise and was always dissatisfied with her work, feeling that she could have done better. Her perfectionism was understood by her teachers to be modesty.

Denise was a bright pupil who was always top of her class but her father described her as "having to get it right". She had developed headaches and loss of appetite before the onset of anorexia nervosa. Her obsessiveness was manifested by physical symptoms which remitted once the anxiety had passed.

A child who is socially withdrawn and unsatisfied by diligence and attainment, who valiantly strives to continue with education while gradually starving, should not be regarded as stoical by teachers, parents and those in caring roles, but should be seen as a child suffering from an illness with strong compulsive and obsessional features.

There must be good liaison so that a teacher who suspects that a pupil has an eating problem has the opportunity to discuss this with a colleague, whether it be another teacher, an educational psychologist, the school nurse or a counsellor. This sort of discussion may help the teacher to be objective about the child's needs and to consider how to discuss these with the parents. In the same way that it is vital for parents to work together in managing eating at home, it is crucial that the school works with the parents to help the child. If the child is receiving medical treatment, the teacher may wish to seek advice about how to help the child at school after obtaining permission from the parents. The more professionals share information and agree roles, the more beneficial this is likely to be to the child. Moreover, it is inadvisable for any teacher who knows of a child with an eating problem, to try to help her without having discussed the matter with other professionals or the parents. Any help offered at school must always be within the realm of professional boundaries and appropriate to the school environment.

Activities at school can provide creative outlets for the child, help raise self-esteem and facilitate social interaction. Teachers can encourage particular friendships and enable a child to feel that they have something to offer the peer group, rather than focusing simply on academic attainment. Some schools are able to adjust a pupil's timetable to meet her personal needs and may arrange a restricted involvement in PE and games while the pupil's weight remains of concern. Leisure or creative pursuits could be offered during games times and possibly during lesson breaks to avoid excessive exercising. Some teachers are able to give support at lunchtime or to see a child, individually, once a week to talk about any school matter. However, not all schools can be this flexible and it is important for parents and teachers to assess whether a school is suitable to meet the emotional and psychological needs of a child with an eating disorder. If it cannot, it may be necessary to consider a change of school.

It may not be helpful to provide school work for children once they are too ill to attend school, except on the advice of those professionals treating them. Furthermore it is more helpful for professionals to liaise directly regarding school work, rather than through parents or the patient, thereby ensuring that they are working together in the best interests of the child. Encouraging and providing creative pursuits for these children provides a good balance to the self-destructiveness of their illness and allows them to display a healthier, more appropriate part of themselves. It also releases children from the burdens and responsibilities of pursuing a normal school syllabus. This is especially difficult when the child is separated from the school and is working in isolation from fellow pupils and the teachers who set the work.

AN IN-PATIENT SCHOOL PROGRAMME

On admission to our child psychiatry unit all patients attend school for two hours in the morning irrespective of their weight. Patients under 75% weight for height are on bed-rest in the afternoons and those between 75% and 80% are allowed to attend school for two afternoons in addition to the five mornings. Patients above 80% weight for height attend school full-time. This programme is part of the ward management and as such is the responsibility of the nursing team (see chapter 9). A clear boundary of responsibility exists which frees the teacher from becoming involved with issues of weight gain.

The programme itself has several advantages. All new patients are included in the classroom group, which inevitably involves a good deal of social interaction, and this is especially important for the more solitary children. It gives the children goals to work for, other than gaining weight. For some children this can be a face-saver: "I put on weight because I want to be in school." However, perhaps most importantly, it allows the patient to participate in constructive and creative activities with peers, without measuring attainment. No child is allowed formal school work until they are attending school full-time (i.e. their weight for height exceeds 80%). A clear message is given to the parents and children by both the nurses and the teacher that until the child is able to attend school full-time, they are too ill to participate in academic work.

For many children and parents this is difficult to accept, but it is important to recognise that at this stage of the illness, a parent's worries about the child at school could be a diversion from fully acknowledging the illness or factors contributing to the illness, such as family issues. A clear statement that there will be no formal school work until the patient is attending school full-time disallows this diversion. The parents are also expected to reassure their child that the main concern is working together to effect a healthy recovery, thereby removing pressure and worries connected with achievement. Children with eating disorders require opportunities to learn how to take control in a responsible way which does not cause them harm. The withdrawal of academic work gives the patient freedom from a set school curriculum and some control or choice over how to be occupied in the classroom. This is complementary to the eating management which avoids battles over food. On our Unit, conflicts about autonomy and control are not discussed at the table, but recognised as important issues in personal development. Consequently they are tackled in the context of a non-life-threatening, stimulating and pleasurable experience—that of school—as a means of learning how to cope with these phenomena in a responsible and age-appropriate way.

In school, pupils follow a set curriculum. Children with eating disorders appear to rely heavily on this work to keep them occupied, even though they gain little intrinsic satisfaction from their efforts. The work seems to be carried out mechanically, but with such concentration and single-mindedness that it appears to have the function of preventing any personal thoughts or feelings, particularly painful or frightening ones.

Mark, 13 years, was trying to prepare for common entrance examinations while in hospital suffering from anorexia nervosa. He was working compulsively both in and out of school hours. However, when asked about his work he said that he derived no pleasure from and had little interest in it.

Once the prop of set work is removed, most children find it difficult to organise and use their time. Many say that they are not good at anything but it usually takes no longer than a week for them to decide on something they could try. Initially some children resist all offers of help from the teacher and politely dismiss suggestions for work.

Tracey felt that the Unit teacher was not her "proper teacher" and this was understood in the context of her struggle for control over who was allowed to help her.

Bridie felt that the Unit school was not a "proper school" and gave the impression of passing her time until she could return to the "real thing". This was understood in the context of a denial regarding the severity of her condition and the way it had interrupted her progress through life.

The continuity of attending school daily is important whether or not the work involved is academic. The classroom can provide an enabling and therapeutic milieu, which is compatible with that of the child psychiatry unit, while remaining separate from all the issues connected with food, eating and the family.

The classroom structure and content are child-centred. Rules are kept to a minimum and personal boundaries are added for individual children as required. In general the rules are: (a) to share all equipment and resources in the classroom; (b) not to interfere with others when they are working; and (c) not to damage property or work other than one's own.

In stage two (Chapter 8) of eating disorders, when children are learning to express their anger, it is important to offer the option of destroying their own work (never other children's) as a means of expressing anger. Once a child has done this there is an opportunity to discuss with them other more appropriate ways of expressing anger.

The expectation of the teacher is that every child is occupied in a constructive or creative way, and that they work towards participating in a wide range of activities during the course of a week. These would include project work on such non-emotive topics as the weather, magnetism, science experiments, the seasons, etc.; creative work such as textiles, making books, painting, printing; reading books and stories; and using the computer. In a classroom where there are children of mixed ages and abilities it is necessary to provide a wide range of books and educational materials. This further removes the educational boundaries that children may have experienced in their school of origin. The syllabus and expectations of age and ability are removed, leaving children free to explore classroom activities and literature which have not been readily available to them. Some children enjoy reading books that were their favourites earlier in their lives and this may help them recall memories from a period before the onset of illness.

> Bridie discovered that she enjoyed sewing. She thought she was bad at it and made many mistakes but began to experiment with making her own clothes.

Removing barriers of age, ability and subject-matter can enable children to begin relating to each other in new ways and to start asking for and offering each other help and encouragement.

In general, children with eating disorders do not have problems with concentration and motivation. The actual content of the classroom work is less important than 1) the ideal of working for personal pleasure and satisfaction; and 2) the relationships between the child, her teacher and her peers. Although it is helpful to engender the spirit of co-operation and of peers helping one another, it is equally important to encourage assertiveness when appropriate and for the teacher to challenge behaviour such as teasing or bullying.

> Ruth, when preparing for her discharge, was receiving home tuition one day a week. Inevitably she had many mixed feelings about discharge and often, on her return to the Unit, would bully children in school. In particular she picked on two children, who both exhibited very similar symptoms to those Ruth had shown. They were silent, undemonstrative and unassertive. One, Judith, always sat in the same seat, and Ruth would make sure she got there first, virtually reducing Judith to tears. Sharon was another victim. She was dependent upon what she called a "dotty" for moving round the Unit. This was a long, stuffed toy, rather

like a draught excluder for a door, which had been made by a nurse from a spotted fabric. Its purpose was to help her walk without being held by a member of staff. To use it Sharon held one end and a nurse the other, thus providing an intermediate stage between walking together holding hands, and walking together without physical contact. Ruth loved to hide Sharon's "dotty" thus denying her the means to leave the classroom.

The part of Ruth which was still closely identified with Judith and Sharon caused her to enact her ambivalence about leaving by bullying them. In this situation it was the role of the teacher to help Judith and Sharon stand up to Ruth and express their feelings to her. At the same time Ruth was helped to express her own feelings about leaving the Unit and face a return to the outside world and a new school. Furthermore the teacher helped Ruth to differentiate between these problems that could be worked on in the classroom, i.e. those pertaining to school, and those which belonged in other therapeutic settings such as the children's group (see chapter 15).

Many themes for topic and creative work that are used with great success in mainstream schooling are completely avoided in our classroom. These would include food, any aspects of body functions and size, the family, the home and autobiography. Such subjects can lead to the blurring of boundaries between the personal problems dealt with outside school in other therapies, and school-work itself. While the teacher has the authority to deal with the behaviour and feelings demonstrated in the classroom, it is imperative that she remains neutral and uninvolved in family and personal issues. Inevitably, as a member of the multi-disciplinary team, the teacher is aware of all the information available about a child and, if asked, can reassure the child about this. This prevents a child being able to have secrets with a particular team member, and create splits among the team. However, the teacher should not refer to such information in the classroom. Instead the teacher should link events in the classroom to those on the Unit by involving appropriate members of the team.

Michael, an intelligent 14-year-old boy, suffered from ulcerative colitis and anorexia nervosa. He resisted all offers of help from the teacher and repeatedly set himself unrealistic, impossible goals which inevitably led to failure and abandonment of the project. For example, one task he set himself was an investigation into the tessellation of polygons. The case formulation included the possibility that Michael's hospitalisation allowed him to escape from a very unhappy family situation. However, in order to maintain this position he had to remain ill. It seemed important for the teacher in the presence of a nurse to discuss with

Michael the issue of unsuccessful problem-solving so that this could be taken up by the nurse in relation to his home circumstances. When professionals work together in this way it provides a positive model of problem-solving for the patient.

The teacher can employ a variety of techniques to help eating-disordered children to control their obsessional tendencies. One of the simplest ways is the acknowledgement of the child's feelings. To be effective, it is necessary to observe the child in the classroom and understand the relationship between their feelings and obsessional behaviour.

Frequently Denise would suddenly stop working as if struck by a vivid memory, sigh and say: "I'm going to water the plants." This happened several times each day, and it seemed as if she had been overcome by sudden anxiety. By beginning with an acknowledgement of what Denise's feelings appeared to be, the teacher moved to sit with her when she sighed in that way, remarking initially: "You seem upset," and subsequently: "Have you got that feeling again?". Gradually this led to an open acceptance that from time to time the same feeling would recur and the teacher began to suggest outlets for her such as: "Shall we tell your worker?" Denise continued to water the plants daily (in fact she was suspected of drinking secretly while doing so) but the plants were saved from the danger of over-zealous watering.

Anita was obsessionally slow with her work. She had decided to colour a photostat copy of a Roman mosaic tile and had to choose one from about twenty possible designs. She had narrowed down the choice to three or four but just could not make up her mind which to choose. When the teacher sat beside her to point out how long this exercise was taking (approximately four hours of school time) it emerged that each tile contained something that Anita liked and she was "paralysed" by the fear of making the wrong choice. Anita agreed to have a time-limit set by the teacher and accepted reassurance that she could always choose another design at a later date, or even change her mind once she had started. At that particular moment the teacher's priority was in helping Anita to make a choice. With continued acknowledgement of her feelings and gentle pressure to delay less, Anita used the teacher's help to work more quickly and gain some confidence about making choices.

It is common for the competitiveness that children had previously focused on their work to emerge in the Unit school in the form of rivalry among peers.

For Michael this took the form of challenging the limits. He was determined to be different from the other patients; his refusal to ask for help or direction from the teacher has already been described. Moreover he refused to sit in the classroom, demanding to work in an adjacent area during school time. In the context of the in-patient group, in which two girls had formed a powerful and influential alliance, Michael's behaviour was understood to be a way of competing for power and attention. The teacher handed the problem over to his worker, who suggested a compromise. Michael could sit outside the classroom for some of school time providing he was working on subject-matter approved by the teacher. He had to make himself a timetable showing exactly when he would be sitting outside the classroom (this had to be for less than half the school week) which was to be agreed by his worker and teacher. The compromise addressed both areas of conflict and was accepted by all.

Frequently children will arrive at the classroom in distress, for example having just returned from psychotherapy or an assessment interview. While the teacher should be sympathetic towards feelings arising from events outside the classroom, essentially the classroom should provide a break or refuge from all the burdens and responsibilities of illness. By encouraging children to leave these feelings outside the classroom, the teacher is helping the child to express their feelings in a more appropriate manner and place. If the child's distress is such that it cannot be contained, it is not the teacher's responsibility to deal with it, but to hand the situation over to a member of the nursing staff.

Denise, a 12-year-old girl with pervasive refusal syndrome (Lask et al., 1991), had been sexually abused and, on admission to hospital, was totally non-compliant. She screamed, kicked, bit and punched, and resisted any attempt by nurses to care for her. On arrival at school she insulted the teacher and denigrated herself and the other children. She felt she could not stay in the classroom. An agreement was reached that she should stay in the classroom and behave in an acceptable manner for a very short period of time, initially five minutes, followed by a period sitting outside the classroom in which she could write in her "worry book", which was later read by her worker. Gradually the amount of time in the classroom was increased until Denise felt comfortable enough to attend school full-time. She no longer needed to use her worry book during school, allowing the teacher to acknowledge her feelings and reassure her that the staff were taking them seriously.

It is common for children to first show changed behaviour in the classroom. Sharon, for example, made her very first communications when she began to mouth words to her teacher. Perhaps children feel safer in a neutral setting, or peer-group interaction in a school setting may enable children to move out of the sick role, even if they slip back into it outside school. Getting better involves many anxieties, particularly that of discharge from hospital, and some children need reassurance that their worries will still be acknowledged by the teacher and other staff members.

> Denise wanted to do maths, but was worried that if she did so the doctors and nurses would assume that she was better and discharge her. This concern was dealt with by giving her very simple tasks initially, and only slowly increasing their complexity.

Other children are very keen to re-start school subjects. Usually the teacher allows two subjects to begin with, selected from English, Maths, a language or a favourite subject, and ensures only one subject is studied on any one day and only for a short period of time—between thirty minutes and one hour. For the remainder of school the child continues as before. At this stage it may be helpful to have work set by teachers from the child's original school.

Planning for a child's discharge involves the whole team and considerable thought is given to education. If the child is to return to her original school, a graded re-introduction may be organised. In this five-day Unit, the child spends weekends at home, so it is usually easy to arrange one day at school at the beginning of each week, later increasing to two. This provides an excellent stepping-stone from in-patient to out-patient status. As well as allowing the child to spend more time in the family home, it provides her with the necessary support to make a successful transition to normal daily life. At school, as well as coping with the work, the child must cope with facing teachers and peers, and deal with questions about her long absence. Friendship groups may have re-formed with the result that the child feels excluded. Moreover it provides the opportunity for children to be set work at school which they can bring to the Unit, thus facilitating their ability to cope with the expectations of school course-work.

A professionals' meeting is usually organised to make such arrangements. The parents are invited to attend, together with members of our team, the school teachers and other professionals from the community, such as the educational psychologist. This meeting is an invaluable opportunity to share thinking about the child's needs and to explore the extent to which the school can be flexible in meeting them, or, indeed, feels confident in dealing with them. Inevitably the child will have missed a great deal of course-work and, depending on their age, the extent to which they need to "catch up" has to be addressed. Unless it is important for examination work, "catching up" should be discouraged, preventing compulsive work habits re-emerging at school. At examination level it may be possible for the child to study fewer subjects, allowing more time to spend on each, or to recommence a school year, in order to catch up with work that has been missed. It is not advisable for a child who is discharged from hospital to be entered for examinations during the term in which they return to school. This would only create unnecessary pressure and anxiety when the focus should be to rehabitate them into their family and school and to consolidate their recovery from the eating disorder.

Many children cannot return to their school of origin for a variety of reasons. For some, their emotional and physical needs require long-term professional support and cannot be met living at home. Another group is those children for whom relationships in the family have broken down, including some who have been sexually abused. In such cases the team must consider the most appropriate placement for the child. Among the wide range of residential schools can be found some offering a broad curriculum with plenty of creative work, a sense of community, with consistency between teaching and care staff, and a high teacher-pupil ratio. Other possible considerations are long-stay psychiatric settings, small-group homes and therapeutic communities. Once residential provision is indicated the question of finance has to be considered. Funding is a matter for community authorities and hospital staff have no power other than to make recommendations. Some local education authorities are reluctant to fund special education for children who display no specific learning difficulties, and in these circumstances it may be necessary to arrange joint funding by the education authority, the local area health authority and/or the social services department.

Michael's relationship with his parents had broken down. Before the onset of anorexia nervosa his parents had locked him out one night and he had slept in the garden shed. From that time he had refused to live at home and would not contemplate doing so. He suffered from ulcerative colitis and had medical needs as well as psychological problems which required on-going help. A therapeutic community was the ideal setting for him and he was offered a place in a very good one. Unfortunately it was extremely expensive and his local education authority refused to fund it on the grounds that he had no specific learning difficulties. Eventually, joint funding was arranged but only after Michael had spent several months in foster care.

All discharge arrangements require close liaison and good communication between hospital staff and professionals in the community. The Unit teacher makes it clear to the child's school that she is available to offer advice and support, once the child is discharged.

CONCLUSION

By working compatibly with other disciplines, teachers can make a significant contribution to the management of anorexia nervosa and related eating disorders. The teacher needs to respect professional boundaries and limitations while being sympathetic and observant in the classroom. In dealing with behaviour as it arises, the teacher will bear in mind the wider context of that behaviour, pass on relevant information to colleagues, and consult with them regarding possible solutions. The teacher can help children to express themselves through creative pursuits and can engender feelings of achievement which are not linked to academic success, thus enhancing self-esteem. Moreover the teacher can help children express the bad as well as the good feelings they may have experienced working as part of a group. Finally the teacher can help children feel satisfied with their effort, even if the results are not perfect, and help them to surprise themselves by accomplishing something they had previously felt they were unable to achieve.

REFERENCES

Graham, P. (1991). *Child psychiatry: A developmental approach.* Oxford: Oxford Medical Publications.

Higgs, J.F., Goodyer, I.M., & Birch, J. (1989). Anorexia nervosa and food avoidance emotional disorder. *Archives of Disease in Childhood, 64,* 346–351.

Lask, B., Britten, C., Kroll, L., Tranter, M., & Magagna, J. (1991). Children with pervasive refusal. *Archives of Disease in Childhood, 66,* 866–869.

Epilogue

The complexity and severity of childhood onset anorexia nervosa and related eating disorders present a major challenge to the child's health, her carers, clinicians and researchers. Much remains to be learned and understood, including the nature and interactions of predisposing, precipitating and perpetuating factors, and what constitutes the most effective of treatments.

Little is known about the prevention of childhood onset eating disorders. Theoretically it might be possible to reduce the incidence by discouraging children, other than the very overweight, from embarking on rigorous dieting. A programme of nutritional counselling, focusing on the growing child's needs, with parental involvement, might be a suitable way forward. Media pressure to participate in current preoccupations with slimness and fitness represents a powerful influence. This is compounded by the increasing exposure of young children to sex in magazines and newspapers, and on television and video tapes. It is possible that some children find the intensity and explicitness sufficiently worrying for a subconscious avoidance mechanism to commence. It is perhaps a little optimistic to expect messages to be portrayed on screen and in the popular press in a more balanced way, and we may have to wait for current trends to be replaced by healthier ones. Parents might be able to help by at least discussing with their children the values that are so vigorously promoted in the media, and helping their children to become more discerning.

Early detection of eating problems may help to reduce morbidity. Recent studies have shown that the majority of paediatricians and general practitioners are likely to overlook the diagnosis of childhood onset anorexia nervosa (Bryant-Waugh, Lask, Shafron, & Fosson, 1992) and that there is a considerable delay from the point of onset to the time that the correct diagnosis is made (Fosson, Knibbs, Bryant-Waugh, & Lask, 1987).

One promising area is future biomedical research. More sophisticated techniques are becoming available for investigating physiological and biochemical processes such as appetite regulation and gastric emptying. These include the use of the electrogastrogram and the measurement of gastrointestinal hormones. The latter are of particular interest in that both cholecystokinin (CCK) and vasoactive intestinal polypeptide (VIP) have receptor sites in both the gut and the brain (see Chapter 3). The possibility of physiological links between disordered eating and the abnormal thoughts and feelings that accompany it has been raised by research in this field (Alderdice, Dinsmore, Buchanan, & Adams, 1985). A breakthrough in our understanding at this level could have major implications for treatment.

Finally we must remain aware of the continuing need to review and improve our treatment skills. The prognosis of eating disorders remains poor, with a high relapse rate and prolonged morbidity. We need more studies along the lines of that by Russell, Szmuckler, Dare, and Eisler, (1987) which attempt to evaluate the effectiveness of specific treatments for particular populations. However, it is likely that the most effective approach for the treatment of children with eating disorders will prove to involve a combination of treatments.

Bryan Lask and
Rachel Bryant-Waugh

REFERENCES

Alderdice, J., Dinsmore, W., Buchanan, K., & Adams, C. (1985). Gastrointestinal hormones in anorexia nervosa. *Journal of Psychiatric Research, 19,* 207–213.

Bryant-Waugh, R., Lask, B., Shafron, R., & Fosson, A. (1992). Do doctors recognise eating disorders in children? *Archives of Disease in Childhood, 67,* 103–105.

Fosson, A., Knibbs, J., Bryant-Waugh, R., & Lask, B. (1987). Early onset anorexia nervosa. *Archives of Disease in Childhood, 62,* 114–118.

Russell, G., Szmuckler, G., Dare, C., & Eisler, I. (1987). An evaluation of family therapy in anorexia nervosa and bulimia nervosa. *Archives of General Psychiatry, 44,* 1047–1056.

Author Index

Subject Index